VIETNAM AT WAR

Mark Philip Bradley is Bernadotte E. Schmitt Professor of International History at The University of Chicago. He is the author of *Imagining Vietnam and America: The Making of Postcolonial Vietnam, 1919-1950*, which won the Association for Asian Studies Harry Benda Prize, and the co-editor of *Making Sense of the Vietnam Wars* (also published by Oxford University Press). He is currently completing a book that explores the place of the United States in the twentieth century global human rights imagination.

Praise for *Vietnam at War*

'[T]his book will further solidify Bradley's well-deserved reputation as the historian leading the way toward understanding the Vietnamese war experience from a perspective that is simultaneously global and local.'
Journal of Vietnamese Studies

'If [readers] open their minds and imaginations to a presentation that presents the Vietnamese at the centre of the Vietnam War, this is the book they must read.'
David Hunt, *Cold War History*

'Consciously written to render the Vietnamese visible in ways too few American histories of the war do, Mark Philip Bradley's important history *Vietnam at War* mines Vietnamese novels, poetry and films, as well as a plethora of overlooked works of scholarship, to paint a more complete picture of the lived experience of the war for the people of Vietnam.'
The Nation

'In this corrective study, Bradley ... draw[s] on the war diary of a conflicted provincial physician, a novel about a paratrooper who is afraid to jump, irreverent peasant verse, playful proverbs ("The moon in China is much rounder than in the USA"), and the nineteen-sixties antiwar songs of the draft-dodging Trịnh Công Sơn.'
The New Yorker

'What this book makes dramatically clear is that although the outside powers-the United States included—influenced events, sometimes quite significantly, the war remained in essence a struggle among Vietnamese, and indigenous forces ultimately determined the outcome.'
George C. Herring, *Journal of Cold War Studies*

'Perhaps the greatest success of Bradley's books is the sophisticated synthesis it provides of the ideas, identities and engagements of the Vietnamese with the wars for Vietnam and then, afterwards, with the struggle to define Vietnam in the context of its history.'
Journal of American Studies

'Mark Bradley's keen observations on the past and present in Vietnam make this a book that deserves to be ... the focus of many class discussions inside the academy, but also among those interested in the war and its contested outcome. It is the right book, at the right time.' Lloyd Gardner, author of *Approaching Vietnam* (in H-Diplo roundtable)

VIETNAM AT WAR

MARK PHILIP BRADLEY

OXFORD

UNIVERSITY PRESS

OXFORD

UNIVERSITY PRESS

Great Clarendon Street, Oxford, OX2 6DP,
United Kingdom

Oxford University Press is a department of the University of Oxford.
It furthers the University's objective of excellence in research, scholarship,
and education by publishing worldwide. Oxford is a registered trade mark of
Oxford University Press in the UK and in certain other countries

First published in 2009
First published in paperback 2012

Impression: 2 4 6 8 10 9 7 5 3 1

British Library Cataloguing in Publication Data

Data available

Library of Congress Cataloging in Publication Data

Data available

ISBN 978–0–19–280349–8 (Hbk.)
ISBN 978–0–19–965798–8 (Pbk.)

Printed in Great Britain by
Clays Ltd, St. Ives plc

For Anne

ACKNOWLEDGEMENTS

This book emerges from almost twenty years of teaching and writing about the history of the Vietnam wars. It could never have been written without my experiences in the classroom teaching super-smart undergraduates at the University of Chicago, North-western University, the University of Wisconsin-Milwaukee, and Harvard University. Their probing questions and deep engagement in the history of the wars for Vietnam not only sharpened my own approaches to them but helped me appreciate how eager a younger generation has been to understand the wars in their Vietnamese and global contexts. I was especially fortunate to team-teach a course on the wars at Northwestern with Mike Sherry, who has an amazing ability to convey engagement and erudition in the classroom effort-lessly and whose close reading of this volume in manuscript made it a far better book.

Over this same time, I have been fortunate to come to know a marvellous group of scholars in Vietnamese studies and the history of the Vietnam wars in the United States, Europe, and Vietnam whose work has deeply influenced my approach here. They include such senior scholars as William Duiker, David Elliott, Lloyd Gardner, George Herring, David Hunt, Ben Kerkvliet, Ben Kiernan, Greg Lockhardt, Bob McMahon, David Marr, Ngo Vinh Long, Keith Taylor, Jayne Werner, and Alexander Woodside. The last decade has prompted an explosion of exciting new scholarship on Vietnam, and I have learned incalculable amounts from the work of and con-versations with Michael Allen, Bob Brigham, Cam Nguyen, George Dutton, Christoph Giebels, Chris Goscha, Hang Nguyen, Judy Henchy, Seth Jacobs, Heonik Kwon, Mark Lawrence, Anne Marie Leshkowich, Fred Logevall, Shawn McHale, Shaun Malarney, Ed Miller, Kim Ninh, Sophie Quinn-Judge, Nora Taylor, Philip Taylor, Arne Westad, and Peter Zinoman. In Vietnam I am especially grateful to Luu Doan Huynh, Luu Van Loi, Phan Huy Le, Tran Huu Dinh, and Vo Van Sen for their warm intellectual fellowship, and to the Institute of International Relations, the Institute of History, and the University of Hanoi for their assistance in my research.

Two scholars, Hue-Tam Ho Tai and Marilyn Young, have been critical in my efforts to undertake this project and I will never be able to repay my debts to them. Although neither of them will agree with all that I write here, I could never have written this book without what I have come to know about Vietnam from Marilyn and Tam Tai. For me they will always be the model scholars and teachers that I hope one day to become. I am also in Marilyn's debt for her supportively critical reading of this volume in manuscript.

It has been a pleasure to work with Oxford University Press on this project, especially Christopher Wheeler, Matthew Cotton, and David Reynolds. They have been enormously patient in its long gestation period. I am also grateful to an anonymous reader for comments on the manuscript and to the Press's ever-helpful editing and production staff. I am especially indebted to Laurien Berkeley for her careful copy-editing.

In the end, my family—my wife, Anne Hansen, and my children, Ilsa and Peter Bradley—made it possible to complete this project. I know Ilsa and Peter would prefer the book be dedicated to them (next time, guys) but this one is for Anne . . . with love and gratitude.

M.P.B.

CONTENTS

LIST OF ILLUSTRATIONS

LIST OF PLATES

ABBREVIATIONS

ARVN	Army of the Republic of Vietnam
CIA	Central Intelligence Agency
CIP	Commercial Import Program
COSVN	Central Office for Southern Vietnam
DRV	Democratic Republic of Vietnam
NLF	National Liberation Front of South Vietnam (Mat Ran Dan Toc Giai Phong Mein Nam Viet Nam)
OSS	(US) Office of Strategic Services
PAVN	People's Army of Vietnam
PLAF	People's Liberation Armed Forces (Quan Do Nhan Dan Giai Phong) (of the NLF)
PRG	Provisional Revolutionary Government (of the NLF)
VNQDD	Viet Nam Quoc Dan Dang (Vietnamese Nationalist Party)

Vietnam at war, 1954–1975

An-My Lê, *Untitled*, Ho Chi Minh City, 1995

PRELUDE

In the early 1990s a short story by a young author, Tran Huy Quang, entitled 'The Prophecy' ('Linh Nghiem'), appeared to great interest in Hanoi. It told the tale of a young man named Hinh, the son of a mandarin, who longed to acquire the magical powers that would one day enable him to lead his countrymen to their destiny. The destiny itself does not particularly concern Hinh, but he is intent upon leading the Vietnamese people to it. In a dream one evening, Hinh meets a messenger from the gods, who tells him to seek out a small flower garden. Once he reaches the garden, Hinh is told, he should walk slowly with his eyes fastened on the ground to 'look for this'. It will only take a moment, the messenger tells Hinh, and as a result he will 'possess the world'.

When he awakens, Hinh finds the flower garden and begins to pace, looking downward. Slowly a crowd gathers, first children, then the disadvantaged of Vietnamese society: unemployed workers, farmers who had left their poor rural villages to find work in the city, cyclo drivers, prostitutes, beggars, and orphans. Watching Hinh, they ask in turn, 'What are you looking for?' He replies, 'I am looking for this.' Hopeful of turning up a bit of good luck, they join him, and soon multitudes of people are crawling around in the garden. Hinh looks around at the crowd searching with him and believes the prophecy has been fulfilled: he possesses the world. With that realization Hinh goes home.[1]

To Vietnamese readers the story was immediately recognized as a parable, with Hinh representing Ho Chi Minh, the pre-eminent leader of twentieth-century Vietnam. The prophecy was seen as coming from a secular god, Karl Marx. 'This' was the promise of a socialist future, which the author of 'The Prophecy' and many of his readers in Hanoi increasingly believed to be a hollow one. For them, socialist ideals did enable Vietnamese revolutionaries to develop a mass following and establish an independent state, throwing off a century of French colonial rule. But in the aftermath of some thirty years of war against the French and the Americans, their hopes for a more egalitarian and just society appeared to remain unfulfilled.

'The Prophecy' and the meanings its readers gave to it in the early 1990s may seem like an odd place to begin a history of the wars that engulfed Vietnam from 1945 to 1975. But that choice makes good sense if you want, as I do in this book, to tell the story of Vietnam at war from the perspective of Vietnamese history. In truth, there were many Vietnam wars, among them an anti-colonial war with France, a cold war turned hot with the United States, a civil war between North and South Vietnam and among southern Vietnamese, and a revolutionary war of ideas over the vision that should guide Vietnamese society into the post-colonial future. The contest of ideas began long before 1945 and persists to the present day in yet another war, this one of memory over the legacies of the Vietnam wars and the stakes of remembering and forgetting them.

For most Vietnamese, the coming of French colonialism in the late nineteenth century raised profound questions about their very survival as a people and pointed to the need to rethink fundamentally the neo-Confucian political and social order upon which Vietnamese society had rested. As one young Vietnamese asked in a 1907 poem:

> Why is the roof over the Western universe the broad lands and skies,
> While we cower and confine ourselves to a cranny in our house?
> Why can they run straight, leap far,
> While we shrink back and cling to each other?
> Why do they rule the world,
> While we bow our heads as slaves?[2]

Throughout the twentieth century, in both war and at peace, and into the twenty-first century, the Vietnamese have searched for answers to the predicaments posed by colonialism and the struggle for independence. As they have done so, a variety of Vietnamese actors have appropriated and transformed a fluid repertoire of new modes of thinking about the future—social Darwinism, Marxist-Leninism, social progressivism, Buddhist modernism, constitutional monarchy, democratic republics, illiberal democracies, and market capitalism to name just a few—to articulate and enact visions for the post-colonial transformation of urban and rural Vietnamese society. But the end of the Vietnam wars did not bring a final resolution to these competing visions. When North Vietnamese tanks entered Saigon on 30 April 1975 to take the surrender of the American-backed South Vietnamese government, Vietnam was reunified as a socialist state. The long war for independence was over. Yet even today, as the searchers in 'The Prophecy' suggest, the meanings accorded to 'running straight and leaping far' remain deeply con-tested. In one of many present-day paradoxes, the Vietnamese state seeks to develop a market economy as it maintains its commitment to socialism, while an increasingly heterodox Vietnamese civil society simultaneously embraces the global economy, yearns for the unfulfilled promises of socialist egalitarianism, and reinvents many of the spiritual and familial practices the socialist state spent the war years trying to stamp out. Indeed, a walk today through a typical city block at the centre of Hanoi or Saigon, a block in which a refurbished Buddhist temple might be flanked by a Seven–Eleven store on one side and the local communist party headquarters on the other, quickly reveals these everyday contradictions and tensions.

This book approaches the history of the Vietnam wars against that wider canvas. In doing so it marks a sharp departure from prevailing narratives in the West, which have until recently ren-dered the Vietnamese almost invisible in the making of their own history. Literally thousands of scholarly books, along with popular recountings in memoirs, novels, and films, and on television, have explored the wars for Vietnam. But their focus has largely been on American and, to a lesser extent, French actors. During the American war itself, the nature of the United States' 'enemies' and 'allies' in Vietnam were viewed in monochromatic tones and set against the larger cold war rivalries between the US and the Soviet Union. For American decision-makers from presidents

Truman to Nixon, the leadership of North Vietnam was seen as surrogates of Moscow and Beijing, and the National Liberation Front (NLF) in turn as a puppet of the North. South Vietnam's political and military leaders were either lionized as anti-communist saviours or dismissed as hopelessly corrupt incompetents (though, at least for public consumption, a new saviour was usually in the making—or waiting in the wings). Many opponents of the war saw the key Vietnamese players in almost diametrically opposed terms: they were severely critical of the South Vietnamese state and strongly supportive of what they saw as the struggle for national liberation by North Vietnam and the NLF. If their understanding of Vietnamese actors marked a welcome departure from official invocations of international communist conspiracies, they nonetheless advanced a unitary and almost timeless rendering of the Vietnamese past. The nature and tenacity of the North and the NLF were mapped onto a singular Vietnamese identity shaped by traditions of fierce resistance to foreign invaders, which began with the Vietnamese struggle against China as early as the first century BC. The very few popular works giving some attention to Vietnamese history that appeared during the war itself, such as Frances Fitzgerald's Pulitzer Prize-winning *Fire in the Lake*, tended to see Vietnam as a smaller China whose politics and culture remained rooted in the shared Sino-Vietnamese Confucian sensibilities of the past. In Fitzgerald's traditionally minded telling, the indigenous legitimacy of Ho Chi Minh and the North Vietnamese state rested on these enduring purported commonalities. Like the emperors who ruled Vietnam in previous centuries, Fitzgerald argued, Ho enjoyed the mandate of heaven.[3]

In the aftermath of the war, the field of Vietnamese studies in the West slowly began to grow. Scholarship which drew on deep engagement with Vietnamese-, French-, and Chinese-language sources initially focused on pre-colonial and colonial Vietnamese history, and in the late 1970s and early 1980s some of the most sophisticated and important work in Asian history came from historians studying Vietnam.[4] But the main interpretative lines did not fully break out of what several scholars have recently termed the 'grand narrative of national struggle against China, France and America'.[5] Cracks, however, were starting to emerge. As David Marr argued in his magisterial *Vietnamese Tradition on Trial* (1981), the 'cumulative effect of the stress on traditional strengths', including 'relative ethnic and linguistic homogeneity, ancient civilization, and a proud record of struggle against northern invaders', served to 'downgrade the historical significance of major transformations occurring during the colonial period in Vietnam'.[6] And yet, as his title suggested, Marr too continued to perceive a tradition against which a variety of elite Vietnamese anti-colonial discourses took shape. The nationalist scaffolding of Vietnamese history began to collapse more fully in the 1990s as both senior and younger scholars questioned the basic premises of more traditional narratives. They pushed against the nation as the appropriate frame for Vietnamese history and opened up the local, multi-ethnic, regional, and global complexities and contestations of the Vietnamese past. Their analytical inclinations were reinforced by a changing research climate in Vietnam, with the ebbing of cold war era tensions. In the wake of the *doi moi* reforms of the late 1980s, which brought the market economy to Vietnam, Western scholars were for the first time since the war able to work in Vietnamese archives and libraries and to undertake oral history and ethnographic research. This new work, of which my own research has been a part, drives the analysis offered in this book.

The narrative of Vietnam at war presented here does not ignore the role of American and French actors in the wars for Vietnam and the ways in which the cold war shaped dimensions of the conflict. It considers their impact, along with those of global actors in the Soviet Union, France, Great Britain, eastern Europe, China, South Korea, and newly decolonizing states in South and South-East Asia. But it does so with an appreciation for the agency of the Vietnamese in these encounters, attentive especially to the stresses and strains of wartime alliance politics in policy-making by the North and South Vietnamese governments. My overarching focus, however, remains on the Vietnamese themselves and their own multiple perspectives on the war. This book examines the thought and actions of high policy makers in Hanoi and Saigon while exploring how northerners and southerners, men and women, soldiers and civilians, urban elites and rural peasants, and radicals and conservatives came to understand the thirty years of war that unfolded around them and made sense of its aftermath. It begins with the prophecies of the future that first emerged at the dawn of the twentieth century in the Vietnamese encounter with French colonialism.

Vo Nguyen Giap and Ho Chi Minh, *c.* Second World War

1

VISIONS OF THE FUTURE

On 2 September 1945 Ho Chi Minh mounted a raised wooden podium in Hanoi's central Ba Dinh Square. Before an enthusiastic crowd of more than 400,000, he proclaimed Vietnam free of French colonial rule. The speech marked the culmination of the August Revolution, which brought to power the first post-colonial independent Vietnamese state, the Democratic Republic of Vietnam (DRV). Ho began his speech this way: 'All men are created equal. They are endowed by their Creator with certain inalienable rights; among these are life, liberty and the pursuit of happiness.' Drawing on the American Declaration of Independence and the French Declaration of the Rights of Man and the Citizen, he contrasted the universal ideals of liberty with the lived realities of more than eighty years of French colonial repression. 'Vietnam', Ho concluded, 'has the right to enjoy freedom and independence, and in fact has become a free and independent country.'[1]

If decades of French colonialism symbolically fell away to the cheering crowd at that moment, no one standing in Ba Dinh Square, including Ho Chi Minh, could have known what would come next, or the subsequent ironies of employing these canonical American and French texts to frame Vietnam's own Declaration of Independence: war against France, the cold war, the division of Vietnam north and south, the American war. It would be thirty years until the promises Ho made on that hot Sunday afternoon were fully a reality on the ground. All this was yet to come. But even if events had unfolded somewhat differently, the vision that would guide Vietnam into the era of freedom and independence was not fully clear nor free of contest in September 1945.

For much of the first half of the twentieth century, French colonialism posed both a political and an existential crisis for many Vietnamese as they experienced the collapse of the pre-colonial imperial order and the searing material, intellectual, and spiritual dislocations of French rule. As they looked to the future, what it meant to be Vietnamese was as much the issue as how to bring French rule to an end. Vietnamese reformers and radicals, Confucian traditionalists, Catholics and Buddhists, elders and students, men and women, and villagers and urbanites perceived the meanings of colonialism through a variety of lenses and offered sometimes competing visions of the past, present, and future. From the interior and intimate spaces of the family to the imaginings of anti-colonial mass movements, new articulations of the potentialities of national independence to build a more just and humane society emerged throughout Vietnam.

The crises faced by the Vietnamese, and their responses, were rooted in local conditions but also deeply affected by global processes. Like Vietnam, most of Asia, Africa, the Caribbean, and the Middle East in 1900 were ruled directly or indirectly by the Western colonial powers. As late as the outbreak of the Second World War almost a billion of the world's people lived under direct colonial control. In the global rupture of decolonization that burst forth in the two decades after 1945, of which Ho Chi Minh's assertion of Vietnamese independence was a part, this imperial order collapsed. At times it did so peacefully, but more often after protracted warfare and violence. The French and the American wars in Vietnam were a part of these struggles. But for the Vietnamese, like many colonized peoples, decolonization was just as much about the working out of contending conceptions of the self, society, and the state that first emerged under colonial rule as it was about realizing post-colonial independence.

The Coming of French Colonial Rule

French imperial rule came to Vietnam from the mid- to late nineteenth century. In this era of high imperialism, when much of the world was carved up by the Euro-American powers, the French saw Vietnam both as a strategic buffer against British and Dutch colonial power in South-East Asia and as a base for future expansion into southern China. They were also attracted by the potential economic wealth of Vietnam's southern Mekong delta. Three southern provinces of Vietnam around present-day Ho Chi Minh City were seized by the French navy in campaigns beginning in 1861, and formally ceded to France by the Vietnamese emperor Tu Duc in 1863. The French took three additional southern provinces in 1867. Preoccupied by defeat in the Franco-Prussian War and the Paris Commune in the early 1870s, the French state began to seek control of northern and central Vietnam in 1874. Initially repulsed by Vietnamese military forces, supplemented by troops who had come from China at the request of the Vietnamese emperor, a renewed French military effort in the early 1880s brought all of Vietnam under French imperial rule by 1883.

As the French came to Vietnam, they encountered a state and society that traced its origins to as early as 2500 BC in the Red River delta of northern Vietnam, where indigenous lords and kings governed a peasant population largely engaged in wet rice agriculture. For some one thousand years from 111 BC to AD 939 Vietnam was a Chinese protectorate, initiating a complex relationship between the two peoples. On the one hand, the Vietnamese aggressively fought against Chinese rule. After throwing off Chinese control in AD 939, the Vietnamese put up successful resistance to repeated Chinese efforts to reclaim Vietnam between the tenth and eighteenth centuries. These efforts to retain independence produced a powerful indigenous tradition in folk tales of the Vietnamese as indomitable resistance heroes. Among them were Ba Trieu, who in AD 248, legend has it, led her troops against the Chinese riding on an elephant; naked from the waist up, she used her 2-metre-long breasts as weapons against the enemy. Le Loi, too, successfully brought an end to a twenty-year Chinese occupation of Vietnam in the early fifteenth century by drawing on tactics of surprise and guerrilla warfare.[2]

But as Vietnamese elites fought the Chinese, they also consciously borrowed Chinese patterns of governance and Confucian
social norms, and Chinese forms and practices increasingly came to
structure state and society. The three Confucian bonds—emperor to
subject, father to son, and husband to wife—along with venerating
ancestors and familial lineages through filial piety (*hieu*), shaped the
Vietnamese political and social order. So too did Chinese practices
of training and selecting Confucian superior men (*quan tu*) as the
scholar-officials, or mandarins, who would serve the emperor in
governing the state. They were chosen through a system of written
examination borrowed from China that tested knowledge of Confucian classical texts. Vietnamese emperors, who had to contend
with powerful regional landed families, found Chinese models and
their emphasis on a meritocratic rather than inherited elite an effective way of building centralized state power. The exams became so
important to elite families that passing them became known colloquially as the 'big graduation'; by contrast marriage was merely
known as the 'small graduation'.

The Confucian order in Vietnam reached its apogee in the
nineteenth-century Nguyen dynasty. Use of the imperial examination
system intensified, and detailed written codes for justice, taxes, and the
military were drawn from Chinese models. Local government was
reorganized along Chinese lines, with divisions for provinces, prefec-
tures, districts, and villages. In fact, under the Nguyen, the presence
of the Vietnamese state in local affairs was more pervasive than in
China: Vietnam was about the size of one medium Chinese province,
making the local divisions and administration of government in Vietnam far more numerous and complex than in China. One physical
manifestation of the powerful Chinese influence on the Nguyen state
was the layout and style of the new imperial capital established in Hue.
The emperor's palace was a miniaturized but faithful replica of the
Forbidden City in Beijing, the home of the Chinese emperor.[3]

If Confucianism made deep inroads into Vietnamese state
and society, so too did Mahayana Buddhism. The highpoint of
Buddhist influence on the state was during the Ly and Tran dynas-
ties (1009–1400), but its popular sway never waned. Vietnamese

Buddhism freely intermingled two strains of Mahayana thought, the more devotional Pure Land and the meditative and textual Zen schools. Local beliefs in spirits, divination, magic, astrology, fertility cults, and tutelary deities also shaped the syncretic practices of Vietnamese Buddhists. Women were especially important in Vietnamese Buddhism as men largely dominated the discourses and practices of the Confucian state. These divisions were most evident in two institutions common at the village level: the communal house (*dinh*), where the political affairs of the village were debated, was restricted to men, while the support and maintenance of the Buddhist temple (*chua*) and its clergy, who were sometimes nuns rather than monks, was usually undertaken by women.

Catholicism was introduced into Vietnam in the seventeenth century by Portuguese and other European missionaries and attracted a large number of converts in northern Vietnam until it was proscribed by the Vietnamese imperial state in the 1680s. Campaigns against missionaries and converts ebbed and flowed, though they were particularly fierce in the early nineteenth century under the Nguyen emperor Minh Mang and served as a pretext for French military intervention and the establishment of colonial rule. By 1939 as much as 10 per cent of the northern Vietnamese population were Roman Catholics, who often lived in separate villages in some tension with their non-Catholic neighbours.

Southern Vietnam's development was somewhat different, and its historical, geographic, and cultural heterodoxies contrasted with the more homogenous and orthodox North. Only in the fifteenth century did the Vietnamese begin what is known as the 'march southward' (*nam tien*), conquering and colonizing the Muslim Cham and ethnic Khmer, who inhabited what is now central and southern Vietnam. Overseas Chinese, who came to southern Vietnam after the fall of the Ming dynasty in China in 1644 and were later followed by diasporic merchant families that made up the broader trading networks linking China and South-East Asia, controlled much of the emergent economy in the South. Parts of the Mekong delta were only settled as late as the early twentieth century. Among the ethnic Vietnamese, the impact of Confucian models was less intense in the South, particularly in rural areas, and the influence of Buddhism stronger, including its Theravadan forms, prevalent in neighbouring Cambodia and Laos. For much of the seventeenth and eighteenth centuries, when Vietnam was divided between two warring families, a militarized state dependent on powerful regional families controlled central and southern Vietnam while a more Confucian regime ruled in northern Vietnam.[4]

Geographies reinforced regional differences. Dry weather, over-population, and periodic flooding of the Red River posed difficulties for agricultural production in the North and prompted a tightly knit communal village structure, in part to maintain the dikes necessary to prevent the dangers of flooding. By contrast, the sparser settlement and fertile character of the Mekong delta in the South produced a looser village social structure, with southern peasants typically more individualistic and entrepreneurial in their outlook than their northern counterparts. Central Vietnam, with limited arable land and a treacherous coastline plagued by typhoons, was considerably poorer than northern or southern Vietnam and the frequent site of elite and peasant unrest both before and after the coming of French rule.

Whatever these regional differences, the bulk of Vietnam's pre-colonial population lived in rural villages. While hardly egalitarian utopias, they were organized in ways that worked to limit severe gaps between rich and poor. Communal lands (*cong dien*), often 25 per cent of village land, were periodically redistributed to support poor and landless peasants. Social convention in the form of patron–client ties between large landowners and village notables and small-holders, tenants, and the landless forced wealthy villagers to consider the interests of poorer residents. Patron–client ties were hierarchical and unequal, but they promoted reciprocity. In times of poor agricultural harvests, for instance, patrons and agents of the Viet-namese state at the local level often reduced the tax and other burdens on middle and poor peasants. These ties were also highly personal as both patron and client usually lived in the same village. If a patron became too exploitative, oppressed clients could resort to subtle social pressures (ostracism, ridicule, or insult), shift patrons, flee the village, or, in extreme cases, resort to murder and open rebellion. Far from conflict-free, pre-colonial rural society none-theless operated through these universal social norms to produce relatively stable levels of familial and individual well-being.[5]

French conquest of Vietnam brought profound disruptions to the political and social organization of Vietnamese society and to the lives of indigenous elites and peasants. At the political level, the Confucian-based imperial system of governance was replaced by French control. Colonial Vietnam in the South, in what was called Cochinchina, was ruled directly by French officials under French law. The emperor was preserved as a figurehead in central and northern Vietnam, which the French termed the protectorates of Annam and Tonkin, but real power rested with colonial officials. In the economic sphere, the French created a huge rice industry in the Mekong delta. By 1930 colonial Vietnam was the third largest exporter of rice in the world. The French also built large rubber and coffee plantations in the South and expansive mining oper-ations for coal and minerals in the North. Beyond the need for indigenous labour to service the colonial extractive economy and lower-level positions in the colonial bureaucracy, there was little place for the Vietnamese in the new imperial order.

The introduction of the modern capitalist economy into the Vietnamese countryside destroyed many of the protective conven-tions that had shaped pre-colonial rural society. Increased bureau-cratic intervention by the French colonial state strengthened the authority of local landowners and made it easier for them to ignore local opinion. It also prompted the seizure of communal lands, increasing rural stratification. Commercialization of the economy forced the use of cash rather than barter in the terms of trade. It placed many smallholders into a dependent tenancy and landless peasants into staggering debt. One Vietnamese villager from central Vietnam recalled the differences these transformations made in the lives of his family in this way: 'There was a rich family protecting my family for many years. Even before I was born they rented us land very cheaply. . . . But during the French time they raised the rent so high it was ridiculous.'[6]

Rapid demographic growth—the Vietnamese population increased from 9 million in 1890 to 37 million in 1930—put serious pressure on cultivatable land and caused the terms of agricultural tenancy to decline further. Those whose circumstances forced them to become wage labourers in colonial plantations and mines faced horrible working conditions, low pay, and maltreatment.[7] Increases in the rural tax burden of as much as 500 per cent under French rule added to peasant woes. The French used the head and land tax to finance the cost of its colonial project in Vietnam, policies that greatly intensified rural indebtedness. So too did new colonial era taxes and monopolies on salt, alcohol, and opium. Despite self-serving French claims to be carrying out a *mission civilisatrice* in Vietnam, colonial policies affected the lives of Vietnamese peasants in devastating ways and significantly increased the potential for class tension and disorder in the countryside.[8]

Reformers

Resistance to French rule emerged almost immediately among Vietnamese elites. Patriotic court officials and provincial elites launched the Save the King (Can Vuong) movement in the face of French conquest of northern Vietnam in the 1880s. Seeking to restore the emperor and preserve traditional society, the movement was ultimately ineffective against superior French fire power. Out of these failed efforts, a second generation of anti-colonial reformers emerged in the first decade of the twentieth century. They began to look beyond Vietnamese traditions to understand Vietnam's humiliating defeat by the French and to recast the meanings of state and society. For the first time, European and American historical experiences became a major part of Vietnamese political discourse.[9]

The elites who led this movement for reform were born in the 1860s and early 1870s into scholar-gentry families from north and north-central Vietnam. Like their fathers and grandfathers before them, they had studied classical Chinese texts to prepare for the imperial examinations. Members of the reform generation, who came of age in the 1880s at the time of French conquest of northern

Vietnam, watched as the slow French enervation of Vietnamese political, economic, and social life undermined the Confucian premises that had shaped their view of the world. For these young men, the failure of the Save the King movement, in which many of their fathers had played a leading role, demonstrated that Confucian principles alone provided an inadequate response to French rule and heightened the urgency of reversing what they increasingly termed 'the loss of country' (*mat nuoc*) or 'national extinction' (*vong quoc*).

To explain Vietnam's predicament and formulate a new vision for the transformation of Vietnamese society, the reform generation for the first time reached outside their own traditions. Reformers were captivated by the philosophical writings of Rousseau and Montesquieu; the nation-building efforts of Peter the Great, Garibaldi, and Bismarck; and the inventiveness of James Watt. Americans, including figures such as George Washington, Patrick Henry, and Thomas Edison, were also widely celebrated as deserving emulation by the Vietnamese. Among the most compelling Western thinkers for the Reform movement was Herbert Spencer. To Vietnamese reformers Spencerian conceptions of social Darwinism offered a powerful explanation for the weaknesses in traditional society that had led to Vietnam's domination by the French. It also pointed to the strengths of the West that offered a potential path for Vietnam's future development.

Significantly, social Darwinism entered Vietnam indirectly. Unable to read European or American texts themselves, Vietnamese reformers encountered the West in the writings of Liang Qichao and Kang Yuwei, the leading advocates of political and cultural reform in China, and through what they came to know about the reform of Japanese society under the Meiji restoration. An Eastern Study (Dong Du) movement brought Vietnamese students to Japan, where they came in closer contact not only with the works of Chinese reformers such as Liang Qichao, who was living in Yokohama, but also with the ideas of Japanese thinkers who had guided the country's rapid economic modernization and bid for Great Power status under the Meiji.

The Reform movement in Vietnam was launched in 1904 with the publication of an anonymous tract entitled *The Civilization of New Learning* (*Van Minh Tan Hoc Sach*).[10] Infused with the social Darwinian themes that had characterized the writings of Chinese and Japanese reformers, the manifesto offered a wide-ranging critique of Vietnamese society and a prescription for the future. It argued that Vietnamese society was 'static' (*tinh*) and Western civilization was 'dynamic' (*dong*). Using Spencerian rhetoric, the manifesto suggested that ceaseless change produced a strong civil society: 'the more ideas, the more competition; the more competition, the more ideas'. Appreciation for the importance of Darwinian intellectual competition in Europe and America, it continued, produced innovations in political thought, education, commerce, and industry. In Vietnam, by contrast, rigid adherence to classical Chinese learning and suspicion of foreign ideas had foreclosed dynamic change.

Despite this grim Spencerian critique of traditional society, Vietnamese reformers were not without hope for the future. Because East Asian interpretations of Spencer's thought often downplayed its relentless determinism in favour of a more optimistic voluntarism, social Darwinism as the Vietnamese received it also presented a path to national revival. For Chinese and Japanese reformers who first encountered European and American thought in the late nineteenth century, willpower took on a Western-inspired emphasis of an enterprising and adventurist spirit relentlessly working to master the world. This recasting of the transcendent power of the human will allowed East Asian reformers and, later, their Vietnamese counterparts to look past the deterministic and impersonal socio-historical forces fundamental to Western conceptions of social Darwinism and formulate a voluntarist Darwinian prescription for social evolution.[11]

The mixture of a sharp critique of Vietnamese society and optimism for future reform shaped the sensibility of *The Civilization of New Learning* and much of the Reform movement's activities. Chastising the traditional elite for 'following old ways' and blocking the development of modern industry in Vietnam, *The Civilization of*

New Learning asked, 'Has anyone shown the skill or the talent . . . of a Watt or an Edison?' The 'talents of men like these', it argued, 'truly merit awe'.[12] Reformers worked to establish indigenous commercial enterprises and agricultural societies to reverse traditional scholar-gentry disdain for commerce and to emulate the perceived sources of Western wealth and power.

They also organized the Dong Kinh Free School (Dong Kinh Nghia Thuc) and the publication of a newspaper, *Old Lantern Miscellany* (*Dang Co Tung Bao*), which served as critical forums for the introduction of new currents of thought. Reflecting the centrality of European and American models to the Reform movement's writings, a poem written for the Dong Kinh Free School sharply delineated the Vietnamese and Western experiences and warned of the need to shift Vietnamese sensibilities:

> Our country from a very old time
> Always diligently and uninterruptedly followed Chinese learning.
> Aping old-fashioned and narrow-minded skills,
> We are paralysed in a state of near-exhaustion.
> What do we know from the outside? From America? From Europe?[13]

By emulating the achievements of the West, the leaders of the Reform movement believed they could transcend French colonialism and regain their rightful place as the leaders of a newly strengthened Vietnam. But while reformers in Vietnam were remarkably open to European and American ideas, they continued to see themselves as Confucian superior men and rendered concepts of personhood and the obligations of the individual to society through Confucian norms and values. Viewed within the interpretative veil of Chinese and Japanese informants, the revolutionary currents of Western thought that animated the discourse of reform in early twentieth-century Vietnam continued to be refracted through the conservative neo-Confucian outlook of the East Asian classical world. *The Civilization of New Learning* insisted reform was to be led by and directed to Vietnamese elites, arguing one could not 'open up' the intellects of the masses until elite attitudes had changed.[14]

Perhaps the most sustained and revealing example of the persistence of Confucian sensibilities in shaping reformist ideas is Phan
Chu Trinh's *Rare Encounters with Beautiful Personages* (*Giai Nhan Ky
Ngo*). Phan Chu Trinh, one of the leaders of the Vietnamese reform
movement, intended this poetic adaptation of a Japanese novel from
the 1880s to introduce Vietnamese readers to the revolutionary
histories of Europe, the United States, and Japan. His narrative of
the American revolution, for instance, begins not with impersonal
Darwinian forces but through the appearance of properly cultivated
individual heroes such as George Washington. Like Washington, in
whose teeth he places a mandarin's badge of office for the commander's fateful trip across the Delaware River, the revolutionary
leaders in Phan's poem display all of the virtues that Vietnamese
elites commonly ascribed to Confucian superior men: righteous-
ness, self-sacrifice, courage, and devotion to country. His emphasis
on the role of individual heroes in the revolutionary struggle
reflected the broader reformist sentiment that politics and social
change remained an elite domain. Phan Chu Trinh's idealized
portrait of American patriots as virtuous Confucian and voluntarist
social Darwinian heroes offered a model for what a reformed and
revitalized elite could accomplish in Vietnam.

If Phan Chu Trinh saw reform and independence as a long
process of social and cultural transformation, the other leading
reform era figure, Phan Boi Chau, advocated a much quicker
transition to the post-colonial future. Phan Boi Chau exemplified
and shaped the broader sensibilities of the reform generation: he was
intensely critical of French rule, embraced Western learning as a
model for the Vietnamese, and believed in the need for elite leadership. He organized the Eastern Study movement, and his writings
formed the basis of the curriculum at the Dong Kinh Free School.
But Phan Boi Chau's reform efforts were increasingly directed less to
the sociocultural realm than to political organization aimed at bringing a quick end to French colonialism. His Reformation Society
(Duy Tan Hoi), active in the first decade of the twentieth century,
called for an independent Vietnam under a constitutional monarchy;
later, inspired by the Chinese revolution of 1911, he founded the

League for the Restoration of Vietnam (Viet Nam Quang Phuc Hoc), which sought to put in place a democratic republic. Little came of these ambitious efforts, but both groups reflected his willingness to use violence for anti-colonial ends. The Reformation Society was instrumental in a wave of anti-French demonstrations in 1908, including tax protests in central Vietnam and a plot to poison the food of the French colonial garrison in Hanoi. The League was involved in a series of terrorist incidents that ultimately led to Phan Boi Chau's imprisonment. Although Phan Chu Trinh's vision of reform was more measured, and he was a vocal opponent of anti-colonial violence, the French accurately sensed that his reformist visions undermined imperial control. They sentenced him to life imprisonment, later commuted to exile in Paris.

Radicals

A series of political and intellectual upheavals in colonial Vietnam of the 1920s ushered in a new generation of radical political thinkers and activists. Student demonstrations in Hanoi to protest the French decision in 1925 to sentence Phan Boi Chau to life imprisonment for his anti-colonial activities, and the public funerals organized by students throughout Vietnam to commemorate the death of Phan Chu Trinh in 1926, marked the beginnings of a transformation in Vietnamese anti-colonial thought and practice. Despite the homage these young radicals paid to the two leaders of the reform generation, they were dissatisfied and impatient with the scope and pace of the Reform movement's prescriptions for Vietnamese society. They struggled to voice a more far-reaching redefinition of the relationship between individuals and society and to imagine a new revolutionary post-colonial Vietnam.

The radicalized 'new intelligentsia' (*gioi tri thuc*) of the 1920s—secondary and university students along with clerks, interpreters, teachers, and journalists recently graduated from school or expelled by the French for their political activities—were the products of the French-controlled education system that began to supersede the traditional academies that had taught the Chinese classics and

Confucian morality. For their secondary education, many attended French lycées in urban centres, with some going on to university study in Hanoi or in France. The French and French-trained indigenous teachers at the secondary and university levels offered students a Western-oriented curriculum, one differing sharply from the Confucian examination system that had shaped the world-views of their fathers and grandfathers. The experience of French education, particularly its veneration of Western ideas and values, had a corrosive effect on the relationship between student radicals (usually men) and their families as it accelerated the fraying of Confucian familial and social bonds under French colonialism.[15]

Reflecting these profound differences in generational sensibilities, student activists aimed to address the dilemmas of youthful alienation with calls for the re-creation rather than reform of the moral and social order in Vietnam. Indeed, the young radicals were initially driven by individual and family concerns as many students came to perceive disturbing links between what they saw as the confining boundaries of traditional family life and the burdens of colonialism. Young radicals sought to break with the Confucian past and the colonial present by investigating and appropriating alternative civilizational discourses in ways that would force a reconsideration of individual behaviour and obligations towards society.

They took full advantage of a modest French loosening on restrictions governing freedom of expression in 1925 to participate in the indigenous publishing boom of the late 1920s. In an outpouring of books, pamphlets, and periodicals, young radicals introduced a far-reaching and sometimes subversive range of Western thinkers: philosophers such as Kant, Hegel, Spinoza, and Nietzsche, and political theorists such as Marx, Proudhon, and Lenin. But as the shared experience of French education removed the need to rely on Chinese and Japanese informants for their perceptions of European and American civilization, radicals apprehended Western morality, ethics, history, politics, and science in ways that substantially departed from the neo-Confucian imaginations of the Reform movement.

Young radicals assumed that their quest for self-knowledge and self-realization would in time bring not only national liberation but also transformations of the meanings accorded to personhood. Far more diffuse than the Reform movement in its overarching vision, however, radical thought articulated the relationship between new sources of Western-inspired knowledge, the shifting behaviour of individuals, and the coming of revolutionary social, cultural, and political change in eclectic and sometimes elliptical ways. Self-consciously experimental and iconoclastic, radical thought was never firmly anchored in a body of shared principles. Unlike the unifying experience of the traditional academies, with their emphasis on common Confucian values, the impersonal structure and more diverse curriculum of the French educational system left radical thought fragmented. The practices of French colonial censorship, which placed real limits on the ability of young radicals to extend their investigative studies of Western civilization to an analysis of Vietnamese conditions, only reinforced these inclinations.[16] Though eager to debate a wide range of issues, young radicals never formed a consensus on a single set of guiding ideals to bring change to Vietnam. Nor did the diffuse inclinations and leadership of the movement leave its members well placed to organize unified anti-colonial political action.

In the absence of an integrative vision for Vietnam's future, the disparate radical search for individual and societal transformation rested on an almost romantic belief in revolutionary heroism. It was expressed most forcefully in the numerous didactic biographies authored by student radicals that were among the dominant modes of indigenous publishing in the late 1920s. Vietnamese leaders of past resistance struggles against the Chinese, and contemporary Asian nationalists such as Sun Yixian and Gandhi, received substantial biographical attention, as did European individuals ranging from Columbus and Napoleon to Catherine the Great and Florence Nightingale. American figures also received biographical treatment, including George Washington, Abraham Lincoln, Benjamin Franklin, and Thomas Edison.[17]

The celebration of individual voluntarism in biographies of these Asian, European, and American figures served as a central vehicle through which radicals sought to realize their vision for fundamental change in Vietnam and the critical role that individuals, both elites and masses, would play in that transformation. In part these biographical accounts did bear similarities to the neo-Confucian past, perhaps more than young radicals might have cared to admit. Radicals used biographical forms to glorify the triumph of individual will over historical destiny, and sometimes ascribed Confucian virtues to their subjects. But these biographies also emphasized the role of political, economic, and social forces in shaping individual experiences, and their intended audience looked far beyond the neo-Confucian elites that were the focus of reform discourse on civilization. Often highly emotional in tone, radical biographies urged readers to emulate the personalities of the heroes they described—almost literally to become these heroes—in the belief that these figures offered exemplary models not only for collective action to overcome the impersonal political and social forces of French colonialism that had brought about the subjugation of the Vietnamese, but also as blueprints for how individuals could transform themselves and their relationship with society.

A 1929 biography of Abraham Lincoln[18] illustrates the rhetorical conventions of the genre. Lincoln's life is presented through a didactic series of vignettes interspersed with 'commentary' (*phe-binh*) designed to explicate the appropriate lessons for Vietnamese readers. The biography concludes with a 'general lesson' (*tong-binh*), calling upon young Vietnamese to learn the story of Lincoln to acquire the behaviour and morals necessary to transform themselves and society:

From the story of Lincoln, we know that fate does not control individuals if they know how to establish and show their resolve. From the story of Lincoln we know that any misery can be reduced if the politics of one's own country are democratic. From the story of Lincoln we know that his accomplishments were in all cases due to his inner virtue. If we aspire to the accomplishments of Lincoln we must first develop his virtues.[19]

The biographical literature of the 1920s provided the most forceful articulation of the radicals' shift in focus from the reform generation's efforts to cultivate a new set of elite virtues to calls for a revolutionary transformation of individual thought and behaviour at all levels of society.

Vietnamese Communism and its Political Rivals

Within this radical intellectual milieu, Ho Chi Minh founded the Vietnamese Revolutionary Youth League (Viet Nam Thanh Nien Kach Menh Hoi) in 1925. The Youth League served as the forerunner of Vietnamese communism and provided much of the movement's top leadership and its ideological orientation over the rest of the century.[20] Its membership included Pham Van Dong and Truong Chinh, who, along with Ho Chi Minh, would oversee the Democratic Republic of Vietnam after 1945. Both were students shaped by the radical politics of the 1920s, as were many other League members. Only Vo Nguyen Giap, who led the DRV's army in the French war and formed the third member of the leadership troika under Ho after 1945, was not a member of the League. He was, however, an active participant in the radicalizing events that shaped his generation.

—Ho Chi Minh was central to the establishment of the Youth League and its ideology. A few decades older than the student membership of the League, Ho was born sometime between 1890 and 1894 in central Nghe An province to a poor scholar-gentry family. Through his father, a minor scholar-official deeply involved in anti-colonial activities, he came to know many of the leaders of the reform generation. He left Vietnam for Europe in the summer of 1911, embarking on an intellectual and political odyssey that took him to Europe, northern Africa, and the United States, and through which he turned from more gradualist anti-colonial ideas and strategies to Marxism. After President Woodrow Wilson ignored a petition calling for Vietnamese self-determination drafted by Ho and other Vietnamese exiles in Paris for the post-First World War peace conference, he became a founding member of the French Communist Party in 1920. In the early 1920s Ho became a student at the University of the Toilers of the East in Moscow and a leading spokesman for the anti-colonial cause at the Fifth Congress of the

Communist International in 1924. Sent to China as a Comintern agent in 1925, he began the organizational work that resulted in the establishment of the Youth League.[21]

The ideology of the Youth League was most fully expressed in *The Road to Revolution* (*Duong Cach Menh*), prepared by Ho Chi Minh in 1927 as a training manual for the organization's members.[22] Marxism, particularly its Leninist formulations, occupied a dominant place in the work. It provided an expansive framework to universalize the Vietnamese colonial experience and an organizational path to realize the League's anti-colonial aspirations and envisioned transformations of Vietnamese society. But in *The Road to Revolution* Ho emphasized the immediate imperative of the 'national question' rather than 'social revolution' or class issues, borrowing as much from indigenous political discourse and the ideas of Jefferson, Gandhi, and Sun Yixian as he did from Marx and Lenin. He also freely mixed Confucian maxims with Leninist rhetoric from *What Is To Be Done?* to explicate the virtues necessary for young revolutionaries to bring about Vietnamese independence.

Ho's larger revolutionary vision in *The Road to Revolution* was not rendered in conventional Marxist terms as a dictatorship of the proletariat. While he offered the 'courage' and 'spirit of sacrifice' of the Russian revolution as one model, he borrowed a Confucian rather than Bolshevik idiom to articulate the aims of the Vietnamese revolution. Ho suggested 'the great unity under heaven—that is a world revolution', a characterization that both recalled the reform generation's use of the Confucian utopian peace to denote Vietnam's idealized post-colonial future and revealed radical efforts to recast and transform traditional categories of analysis for revolutionary purposes. In the end, Ho envisioned progressive elites and peasant masses united through patriotic ties and the desire for social reform coming together to throw off French colonialism.

The Youth League quickly counted many young student radicals as members, and by the end of the 1920s was considered by the French colonial state as the gravest danger to its control of Vietnam. These fears were heightened in February 1930 when Ho founded the Vietnamese Communist Party, for which the Youth League provided much of the initial membership. At the same time, unrest broke out in central Vietnam as angry peasants rioted following a sharp drop in rice prices sparked by the onset of the international Great Depression of the 1930s, which further eroded the already troubled colonial rural economy. In Nghe An and Ha Tinh provinces, local communist organizers worked with discontented peasants to form what they termed 'soviets', modelled on the worker committees of the 1917 Russian revolution. They replaced the local colonial administration with peasant associations, which reduced land rents and redistributed land to poor villagers. The eagerness of the Vietnamese communists to address peasant concerns represented a sharp break from the more elitist traditions of Vietnamese anti-colonialism and the beginning of communist efforts, intensified during the 1940s, to foster strong rural support. The Nghe–Tinh soviets themselves, however, were short-lived; they were brutally suppressed by French colonial forces in the spring of 1931.[23] In the wake of these and other incidents of anti-colonial agitation in the late 1920s and early 1930s, the French incarcerated many former Youth League members, including Pham Van Dong and Truong Chinh. Ho Chi Minh was arrested in Hong Kong but managed to escape, only to begin a desultory exile in Moscow.

The most important rivals to the Vietnamese communists in this period met a similar fate. The Vietnamese Nationalist Party (Viet Nam Quoc Dan Dang, VNQDD), founded in 1927, drew inspiration from the Guomindang in China, emphasizing the establishment of a Western-style republic. Anti-communist in outlook, it also shared Phan Boi Chau's conviction that anti-colonial violence offered the only sure means of ending French colonial rule. The party enjoyed only limited success at organizing and mobilization, in part because its social base remained rooted in a relatively small number of urban elites rather than in the countryside, where their focus on patriotism over economic reform gave the party little sustained traction. French capture and execution of party leaders before a planned uprising in 1930 severely weakened the VNQDD, though it remained a limited political force in the 1930s and later.[24]

✳   Vietnamese Francophile nationalists who urged collaboration with the French to promote indigenous economic and social improvement were also active in this period. They were made up of the few groups who directly benefited from French colonial rule, including large landowners, urban economic elites, rural notables, and Vietnamese Catholics. The most prominent example in the 1920s was the Constitutionalist Party. Made up of affluent urban professionals in the South, it sought more meaningful political participation for the Vietnamese in the colonial system and eventual independence under some sort of colonial union with France. These efforts were severely hindered by the lack of any meaningful French political and economic concessions. More generally, Francophile nationalists were viewed with some suspicion by rural peoples, who believed they sought to advance their own economic and political self-interests rather than the needs of the countryside.[25] The weaknesses of non-communist political parties in Vietnam during the colonial era would persist and complicate French and American efforts to establish viable alternatives to the communists after 1945.

The 1930s, however, did not prove receptive to Ho Chi Minh's desire to build a communist movement shaped by a broad-based patriotic and nationalist coalition. Vietnamese communists, influenced by a broader shift to more class-based revolutionary strategies within the international communist movement in the late 1920s, began to splinter into contending factions. In the absence of Ho and those Youth League members most closely associated with his ideas, a group of Moscow-trained proletarian internationalists was left to run what was now termed the Indo-Chinese Communist Party under an ultra-leftist banner emphasizing class struggle, proletarianization, and social revolution rather than the inclusive nationalism of the Youth League. In southern Vietnam, the party was increasingly mired in ideological division and endemic infighting by students returning from France who had been active partisans in debates between French Stalinists and Trotskyists. The adoption of the Popular Front policies in 1935 and its lack of emphasis on the international communist movement's concern with class struggle relegitimized aspects of Ho's ideological orientation, but Vietnamese communism remained fragmented and diffuse. The fall of the Popular Front government in France in 1939 and the onset of renewed colonial repression in Vietnam further dimmed the immediate revolutionary prospects of the Vietnamese communists.

Alternative Visions

The rise of mass politics in the 1930s did not foreclose the articulation of other paths to the post-colonial future by diverse individuals and groups operating outside the more formal political sphere. If the leadership of the Indo-Chinese Communist Party focused on collective rather than individual interests, some radicals continued the effort to redefine a more individualized sense of what it meant to be Vietnamese. The decade also marked the reassertion and reworking of Confucian and Buddhist conceptions of Vietnamese identities. While none of these formulations directly addressed the problem of overthrowing French rule, they spoke to deeply felt concerns about dislocations under colonialism. The alternative visions they offered for the post-colonial reconstruction of Vietnamese society continued to resonate after 1945 among many patriotic Vietnamese and remained in tension with the increasing commitment by Vietnamese communists to socialist revolution.

Many middle-class advocates of radicalism in the 1920s were wary of the class-based turn of Vietnamese anti-colonialism in the 1930s. They preferred what one scholar has termed an 'oratorical progressivism'[26] that opposed mass violence and class conflict but remained committed to the radical transformation of self and society. Vietnamese reportage (*phong su*) literature, authored by progressives and appearing with great frequency in the indigenous press of the 1930s, provides one iteration of the persisting concern with radical conceptions of the self and society. *I Pulled a Rickshaw (Toi keo xe*, 1932), an influential example of reportage by the northern Vietnamese journalist Tam Lang, is a first-person account of the difficult lives of Hanoi rickshaw drivers. One day, Tam Lang tells his readers, 'I borrowed a set of working clothes from a labourer, put them on, and adventurously went looking for work in the rickshaw trade.'[27] His disguise was more than a pose. The genre of reportage enabled him to imagine and articulate a new sense of social organization and the responsibilities it carried for individuals.

At one critical point in I Pulled a Rickshaw Tam Lang rhetorically asks his readers, 'Who is to blame for the class of people in our society that works like animals pulling other people?' To which he replies:

> I dare say you would answer honestly as follows: 'Society is to blame.'
> According to its strict meaning, 'society' is all of the people who come from the same origins and who all live together under the same system, and that includes you and me.
> Yes, you and me, all of us are equally at fault.[28]

Tam Lang's need to articulate what society (xa hoi) meant suggests the continuing novelty as late as the 1930s of an individualistic and egalitarian conception of social responsibility. It also marks a deepening effort to reshape radical visions of the self and their relationship to social order. Like much Vietnamese reportage of the period, I Pulled a Rickshaw sought to awaken its readers to reflect critically on the world around them and to recast individuals, whether writers, characters, or readers, as purposeful agents in the making of their own histories.

Novels and poetry associated with the Self-Reliance Literary Group (Tu Luc Van Doan), founded in 1933, shared the emphasis in progressive Vietnamese reportage on moral individuals, but also built on the romanticism that shaped aspects of the radical vision in the 1920s. Nhat Linh, the pen-name of Nguyen Tuong Tam, who founded the group, wrote perhaps the most celebrated Vietnamese novel of the 1930s. In Breaking the Ties, the heroine, Loan, becomes a vehicle through which Nhat Linh put forward claims for the individual over what he saw as the persisting constraints of conservative neo-Confucian familial order. Loan is forced to marry a man she does not love and comes to live with her demanding mother-in-law, Mrs Clerk. They spar over the use of Western medicine for Loan's son, who dies after Mrs Clerk takes him to a

Taoist practitioner. Her husband has an affair, and when the girl becomes pregnant Mrs Clerk insists he formally take her as a second wife or concubine, deepening Loan's estrangement from her husband and his family.

One night, during a fight with her husband that turns violent, Loan accidentally stabs and kills him. She finds herself on trial for murder. At her trial, the prosecutor scorns Loan for her 'romanticism' and for having forgotten the 'heaven-mandated roles of being devoted daughters-in-law and gentle wives, of being pillars of the family like the virtuous women in old Vietnamese society'. To this Loan's lawyer replies:

We can see that nothing that has happened is the fault of any one individual, but rather it must be blamed on the fierce conflict between the old and the new. . . . It is the French who have come here carrying Western culture with them. It is the French who have taught people new ways of reasoning, who have given people new concepts of life. . . . Vietnamese society today is not the Vietnamese society of the nineteenth century. . . . These people [like Loan] who have absorbed the new culture have been imbued with ideas of humanity and individual freedom, so quite naturally they seek escape from that system.

'Free Loan', he concluded, 'and you will perform an act of justice.'[29]

In the end the French colonial court finds Loan not guilty, a verdict Nhat Linh ascribes to the triumph of the modern spirit over the shackles of traditionalism. The individualistic sensibilities of *Breaking the Ties* infused the work of many of the writers associated with the Self-Reliance Literary Group, for whom the Confucian past was a primary source of present Vietnamese weaknesses.

Confucianism was not without its defenders among colonial Vietnamese elites. Some were collaborators with and apologists for French colonial rule. But others were given a more respectful hearing. In 1933 the scholar Tran Trong Kim published *Confucianism (Nho giao)*, widely regarded as the most important book on the subject to appear in the colonial period. Kim argued that Confucianism was like a 'very beautiful old house, which no one had repaired for ages'. It 'was senseless to let it fall into ruin', but no one 'had sketched a map for future generations to know' it. Kim sought to do so. Deeply critical of reformers and radicals for their haste in embracing modernity, he argued the Vietnam was losing 'the essence that had kept our society enduring for several thousand years'. Kim was particularly concerned with the spiritual rather than political decline of Confucianism, what he termed its 'inner spirit', and stressed the continued relevance of Confucian morality for everyday life.[30] Although an often elliptical work, it offered consolation to many Vietnamese, even those inclined towards radical modernist paths to the future, who continued to find meaning in Confucian virtues such as rectitude and filial piety.

A Buddhist revival among educated elites and the florescence of popular Buddhism, particularly in the southern Mekong delta, in the 1930s were further efforts to give meaning to the dislocations of colonialism. New forms of Buddhist thought and practice sought to provide compelling answers to the spiritual and material upheavals of French colonialism for many Vietnamese. Those most involved in the elite-led Buddhist revival were concerned with moral and spiritual decay under French rule and sought to disseminate more accessible versions of Buddhist sacred texts and sutras. By the early 1930s, the movement linked monks, nuns, and lay believers throughout the Mekong delta in Buddhist study associations. The explosion of colonial era popular Buddhism, more focused on practice than texts, centred on salvation and rebirth in a new millennial era that would transcend the troubles brought by French colonialism. Dozens of heterodox religious sects emerged in the South during 1920s and 1930s.[31]

The intensification of an eclectic religiosity and the emergence of Buddhist-inspired apocalyptic millenarian movements were especially prevalent in the western part of southern Vietnam. These sparsely inhabited western borderlands had always attracted political refugees, along with vagabond mystics and monks. The Seven Mountains (Chau Doc) on the current Vietnamese–Cambodian border was a gathering place for religious pilgrims and practitioners who believed the Maitreya Buddha would be reborn there. Huynh Phu So, the founder of the Hao Hao sect in 1939, who claimed to be the reincarnation of the Buddha, lived in this area. The Hoa Hao sect, shaped by folk Buddhist practices, favoured lay worship at home and prohibited elaborate ritual and temple-building. Another southern religious sect, the Cao Dai, was founded in the 1920s among civil servants in Saigon but later spread to rural areas near the Cambodian border. Considerably more colourful and exuberant than the Hoa Hao, the Cao Dai drew on strands of Buddhism, Christianity, and Confucianism and was structured on the model of the Catholic Church, with a diverse pantheon of saints from Sun Yixian to Victor Hugo. Both sects combined millennial spiritual messages with socio-economic reforms including welfare programmes, communal markets, and an independent court system that directly addressed the problems French colonialism posed for the livelihoods of rural people. At their peak, the Cao Dai and Hoa Hao commanded the allegiance of several million followers in the South.[32]

Towards the August Revolution

In many ways the Vietnamese were no closer to transforming indigenous society and achieving independence at the end of the 1930s than the Reform movement had been early in the century. The experiences of the Second World War, however, fundamentally shifted the fortunes of Vietnamese anti-colonialism, most particularly those of communist radicals. Japan occupied Vietnam for most of the Second World War, creating an ever larger political and military vacuum in the country. In part, the occupation humiliated the French and gave a psychological boost to Vietnamese nationalists as evidence of the possible defeat of the European powers by Asian peoples. More practically, the Japanese dismantled critical aspects of the French colonial security apparatus, allowing easier recruitment to the anti-colonial cause in Vietnamese villages. The Japanese occupation also imposed severe economic hardships on the population, intensifying radical demands for change. A terrible famine in the winter of 1944–5 in northern and north-central Vietnam killed as much as 20 per cent of the population

(2 million people). In fostering a potentially radical political environment, Japanese occupation of Vietnam created critical preconditions for the communist rise to power in the August Revolution of 1945.[33]

The Vietnamese communists embraced a series of policies that sought to take full advantage of this promising situation. Perhaps most important was the adoption of the policy of all-class nationalism and the establishment of the Independence League of Vietnam (Viet Nam Doc Lap Dong Minh Hoi), more commonly known as the Viet Minh. Ho Chi Minh, returning to Vietnam for the first time since the early 1930s, gathered the party together in May 1941 at the Sino-Vietnamese border for the Pac Bo Plenum. Here the policy of all-class nationalism first emerged, one which sought to tone down Marxist ideas of class struggle and emphasize Vietnamese patriotic traditions to unify all sectors of the Vietnamese population against the French and the Japanese. It recalled the more inclusive radical vision for the Vietnamese communist movement that Ho Chi Minh had advocated in the late 1920s, and marked, at least for the moment, the retreat of the class-based politics ascendant in the 1930s. Notably many of the communist leaders of the 1930s, particularly from southern Vietnam, were not present at the plenum as the French had imprisoned or executed them in the harsh campaigns of repression in 1939 and 1940. The Viet Minh became the institutional mechanism designed to implement these new policies, an organizational front under communist control that sought to include workers, poor and rich peasants, landlords, women, Buddhists and Catholics, urban elites, and intellectuals in a series of interlocking national salvation associations.

The formulation of the Viet Minh had important implications for the party's wartime diplomacy. The plenum's resolutions called for a policy of 'more friends and fewer enemies' in the international sphere, with a particular focus on improving relations with the Allied powers, including nationalist China, the Soviet Union, Great Britain, and the United States. The leadership of the Viet Minh, particularly Ho Chi Minh, devoted substantial efforts to deepening ties with China and the United States from 1943. Ho and his deputies met repeatedly with Chinese and American officials in the southern Chinese city of Kunming, pledging the Viet Minh's support for the Allied cause against Japan and in turn asking for support in the struggle against French colonialism. If official Chinese and American responses were muted, the Viet Minh did begin to enjoy a relationship with members of the US Office of Strategic Services (OSS) who were posted to southern China and northern Vietnam in early and mid-1945. Indeed, for a time Ho became OSS Agent 19, or Lucius, and reported regularly on Japanese troop movements in Vietnam. Later, in September 1945, Ho would make great efforts to foster close relations with OSS officers in Hanoi, sharing a draft of the declaration of independence with one to ensure that the words he borrowed from the American Declaration were accurately rendered.

The Pac Bo Plenum also adopted the use of guerrilla warfare strategies and revolutionary base areas. If, in the 1930s, the party had viewed its rise to power as the result of a single uprising modelled on the Bolshevik revolution, party strategists by the time of the Pac Bo Plenum recognized the necessity of prolonged struggle. Inaccessible and rugged rural areas, not cities, would provide the base for a full-time guerrilla force guided by the party. Influenced in part by news of Mao's military strategies in China, which had first circulated in Vietnamese radical political discourse in the late 1930s, they also reflected local conditions and Vietnamese experiences. These policies were put into practice through the development of base areas in the mountainous northern region of Vietnam near China known as the Viet Bac. Here the party, under the auspices of the Viet Minh, gained the support of upland minority peoples as well as, by 1944, many Vietnamese peasants living in the upper Red River delta. Base areas became the springboard for the Viet Minh's rise to power and played a critical role in Vietnamese strategy in the French war.

More immediately, the Viet Minh were the only effective force to combat the famine that gripped north and north-central Vietnam in the winter of 1944–5. The French and the Japanese largely ignored the famine, as did most other Vietnamese political groupings. But the Viet Minh jumped in to help, organizing raids on Japanese granaries, using ration cards to equalize food distribution, and supervising emergency rice-plantings. These efforts won them the allegiance of many desperate peasants. They also reassured landlords, as the Viet Minh's approach to famine relief did not include calls for land redistribution.[34]

Throughout the Second World War, the Viet Minh sought to portray themselves in Confucian and patriotic terms that they believed would resonate with wide sectors of the Vietnamese urban and rural population. The leadership consciously drew on Confucian models of personal ethics and selfless sacrifice to society. Ho Chi Minh's carefully crafted public persona projected all the desirable qualities of the Confucian 'superior man': rectitude, sincerity, modesty, courage, and self-sacrifice. Village-level cadres were asked to emulate these behaviours, hoping to draw the same kind of respect from the peasantry that the Confucian scholar-gentry had enjoyed in the pre-colonial period. Viet Minh political writings frequently resorted to the use of Confucian motifs and ideas. Cadres were required to read Ho's translations of a Chinese work on Confucian political morality, and songs like 'The Viet Minh Policies' ('Chinh Sach Viet Minh'), used to train military recruits, conveyed a sense of Confucian moral strictness. The Viet Minh also sought to align their struggle with Vietnamese traditions of patriotic resistance against Chinese invaders. The manifesto of the Viet Minh and its newspapers made frequent reference to such patriotic heroes as the Trung Sisters, Ngo Quyen, and Le Loi, who had led celebrated efforts to resist the Chinese in the pre-colonial period.

Given the origins of the Viet Minh in the Marxist-inflected radicalism of the 1920s and 1930s, and its distaste for both the pre-colonial Confucian order and French colonial rule, it may seem curious that the movement turned to Confucianism as part of its appeal. The decision to do so was more than simple expediency. Although the Confucian emphasis on natural hierarchies separated it from Marxist concerns with revolutionary equality, the two worldviews shared an emphasis on the problems of social organization, the need for an elite to guide the masses, and the primacy of self-sacrifice for the collective.[35] For the Viet Minh's more educated audiences, these intellectual continuities may have made the Marxism at the core of the Viet Minh movement easier to embrace. The turn to Confucian motifs in the Viet Minh's wartime organizing and propaganda also reflected a prevailing view among its leadership that the Confucian moral order had always been at its strongest, and most sincere, not among elites but in rural villages, where it continued to hold sway.

The Japanese coup of 9 March 1945 transformed the political climate in Vietnam and triggered the August Revolution, which brought Ho Chi Minh and the Viet Minh to power. The Japanese disarmed French troops and abolished the French colonial administration in less than twenty-four hours. They put in its place a puppet Vietnamese government without any real urban or rural support or independent military power. The Viet Minh used its expanding bases of support and developing military to take full advantage of this power vacuum. The Vietnamese Liberation Army under the leadership of Vo Nguyen Giap, along with local militias, successfully seized increasing amounts of territory in the Red River delta, and more and more northern villages pledged their loyalty to the Viet Minh. Aware of the likely victory of the Allied forces led by the United States in the Pacific War, Ho Chi Minh and the Vietnamese communist leadership were intent on seizing control of major Vietnamese cities before the Allied forces arrived in Vietnam to take the Japanese surrender in hopes that they could gain recognition from the Americans, British, and nationalist Chinese who were to oversee the surrender. The time was right, they believed, to launch a general uprising.

At a meeting of Viet Minh representatives in Tan Trao, a small village 200 kilometres north of Hanoi, in early August, Ho Chi Minh issued a public appeal for a general uprising:

Dear Fellow Countrymen! The decisive hour has struck for the destiny of our people. Let all of us stand up and rely on our own strength to free ourselves. Many oppressed peoples the world over are vying with each other in wresting back independence. We should not lag behind. Forward! Forward! Under the banner of the Viet Minh, let us valiantly march forward![36]

Moving out from the countryside, the Viet Minh took Hanoi on 19 August. Within days they seized control of Saigon and the imperial capital of Hue. On 30 August the last Vietnamese emperor, Bao Dai, abdicated. The imperial dynastic order, and the colonial order, appeared to be at an end.

The success of the Viet Minh in the August Revolution of 1945 was in many ways remarkable. Just five years before, neither the communists nor any other anti-colonial political movement appeared to have a chance at overthrowing French rule. The efforts of the Indo-Chinese Communist Party to capitalize on the changed circumstances of Japanese occupation in order to build the Viet Minh movement, an independent military force, and the support of so many Vietnamese—north, centre, and south—were extraordinary. Among the appreciative crowds who listened to Ho Chinh Minh's Independence Day address on 2 September 1945, which at 400,000 were more than double the size of Hanoi's population, there was palpable excitement. Buddhist monks and Catholic priests led their flocks to the ceremonies, where they were joined by a cross-section of Hanoi's population and large numbers of rural people and contingents of ethnic minorities, some of whom had walked hundreds of kilometres to attend. As one observer of the day's events wrote, trying to capture the feeling of crowd: 'The souls of the earth and water [traditional symbols of the Vietnamese nation] have returned to the former capital on this imperishable day, and all social strata of the Ascending Dragon Citadel [the imperial name for Hanoi] have just demonstrated the brave spirit of a people who have decided to retake their free life.'[37]

And yet, the Viet Minh faced serious external and internal challenges. The attitude towards the new Vietnamese state of the Chinese military forces that had been sent to Vietnam to take the Japanese surrender in the North was unclear. Viet Minh strength was far weaker in the South than it was in northern and central Vietnam because the Communist Party's southern leadership had been decimated in the severe French repression of the early 1940s. At the time of the August Revolution, the southern leader of the alliance who formally declared independence in Saigon, Tran Van

Giau, was not officially affiliated with the Viet Minh, but was part of a rival regional committee in southern Vietnam. Moreover, the future goals and strategies of the Viet Minh were also in some doubt. If in wartime all class nationalism and national independence had displaced the primacy of social revolution, factions within the Vietnamese Communist Party continued to debate the way forward. Some argued for more moderate social reform to maintain the broad based Viet Minh coalition. Others sought immediate and radical socialist transformation of Vietnamese society.

What would emerge in the colonial aftermath was also far from certain because so many Vietnamese actors saw the elusive post-colonial future through a very different lens from the Vietnamese communists. As one leading scholar has argued, 'many local groups calling themselves Viet Minh had almost no idea what the organization stood for'.[38] Contemporary Viet Minh reporting itself reflected considerable doubt about popular meanings ascribed to the August Revolution. One cadre complained that Ho Chi Minh's Independence Day address was believed by some to be the realization of a prophecy by a sixteenth-century Vietnamese Buddhist monk.[39] Others reported deep suspicions of the Viet Minh among a variety of political and social actors, despite widespread admiration for their winning independence. Middle-class urban Vietnamese were sometimes shocked to see who were among the followers of the Viet Minh, claiming, 'They looked liked robbers.'[40] Among the religious sects in the South, Catholics in the North, Francophile nationalists, Confucian traditionalists, and the remnants of political parties like the VNQDD, suspicion quickly turned to antipathy. Even among people most supportive of the Viet Minh, often those who had come of age during the radical moment of the 1920s, a lingering commitment to individualism as well as independence prompted concerns about the Viet Minh's collectivist ethos. In the coming wars for Vietnam, and even in their aftermath, the competing visions for the remaking of Vietnam that had emerged under French colonial rule would always remain close to the surface.

Ho Chi Minh observes a battle between French and Viet Minh forces near
Dong Khe, 1950

2
THE FRENCH WAR

'I unsystematically record the often aching doubts of a shedding of the skin,' the northern Vietnamese poet Nguyen Dinh Thi wrote in December 1947 just as the first year of the French war came to a close; 'the old body falling without fully separating, the newly grown young skin not yet strengthened, bleeding at the slightest touch.'[1] Nguyen Dinh Thi sought to articulate the soul-searching dilemmas of many Vietnamese intellectuals who supported the Ho Chi Minh government in its war against the French. Deeply sympathetic to the state's calls to use their talents to represent the struggles of peasants, workers, and soldiers in the French war, Thi and other patriotic intellectuals found it difficult to know how to place their art in the service of state politics and at the same time maintain a sense of themselves as creative artists.

The sensibilities of Nguyen Dinh Thi's 'aching doubts' capture the discomforts and ambiguities that hovered over the French war from 1946 to 1954. In one telling, the war is bounded by an eight-year narrative with a definite beginning, middle, and end. When war broke out in December 1946 between the Democratic Republic of Vietnam (DRV) and France, it began as a colonial war that pitted the newly independent Vietnamese state against France's ultimately failed efforts to turn back the clock on the August Revolution. The colonial war became a part of the emerging global cold war in 1950 when the People's Republic of China and the United States intervened. The Chinese communists supported the DRV with advisers, aid, and *matériel*; the US did the same with the French-backed Associated States government, led by the former Vietnamese emperor Bao Dai. In May 1954 the

French war came to an end with the Vietnamese defeat of the French at the climactic battle of Dien Bien Phu.

But that story, as important as it is, can obscure a host of tensions among the war's central actors, from internal Vietnamese and French doubts about the visions driving the war to bitter divisions with their external allies in Beijing and Washington. While the fledgling Vietnamese state showed surprising strength against the more powerful French, the war did not go well for the Vietnamese or the French in its initial years. Neither the partnership between the Vietnamese and the Chinese nor the one between the French and the Americans was especially harmonious. As the war progressed, many Vietnamese were increasingly uncomfortable with the radical and authoritarian directions of DRV political and social policy. Even the Vietnamese victory at Dien Bien Phu produced anxieties about future contours of Vietnamese state and society. In the end the outcomes and legacies of the French war—and its crucial transformation from colonial war to cold war—were considerably more uncertain than the apparent Vietnamese victory in 1954 would suggest.

Problematics of Independence

The independence Vietnamese revolutionaries wrested in 1945 from French colonial rule was extremely tenuous. If Ho Chi Minh and the DRV commanded considerable prestige because of popular support for the Viet Minh's anti-French and anti-Japanese struggle during the Second World War, its authority remained tenuous in many urban areas and in the countryside. At the same time the regime confronted an underdeveloped, war-ravaged economy and fears that some of the conditions that had contributed to the devastating famine in the winter of 1944–5 could re-emerge. While trying to build a new post-colonial state and economy from the ground up, the government also faced the post-war occupation by Chinese and British military forces who were to take the Japanese surrender, and the resurgence of French colonialism. The French desire to retake its colonies rested on efforts to restore

its Great Power status after the wartime devastations and humili-
ations experienced by France during the Second World War. It was
also prompted by perceptions of the economic role Vietnam could
play, particularly the southern rice and rubber industries, in rebuild-
ing the shattered post-war French economy. These pressures at
home were augmented by the strong desire of French colonists
and elements of the French bureaucracy in Vietnam to reassert
imperial control.

The DRV embarked on a two-pronged strategy to consolidate
its power, one that downplayed its communist origins and accelerated the turn during the Second World War to graduated rural
reform and an inclusive nationalism. The government launched a
controlled social revolution in the countryside aimed at increasing
peasant support and administrative control which involved
reorganization of the communal land system, tax and debt reform,
limitations on rents paid to local landowners, and selection of village
notables through election. It also spearheaded mass literacy drives to
teach rural people the Romanized Vietnamese script (*quoc ngu*). To
foster support among urban and rural elites, the regime continued
the policy of all-class nationalism. The results were dramatic increases in DRV strength in late 1945 and early 1946 in northern and
central Vietnam.[2]

Ho Chi Minh and the DRV also employed inclusive political
strategies to deal with nationalist Chinese military occupation in the
North. Some leaders of the Chinese forces had formed close relationships with Vietnamese nationalist groups like the Vietnamese
Nationalist Party (Viet Nam Quoc Dan Dang) and wanted to see
them gain some power in the emerging structures of the new
Vietnamese state. The situation was especially fraught given
Vietnamese historical memories of past Chinese conquest and
occupations. In an effort to reduce escalating tensions, Ho Chi
Minh sought to prohibit local militias from attacking Chinese forces
and agreed to provide a substantial number of seats in the new
National Assembly to parties unaffiliated with his government even
if elections results might not have allowed them to hold the seats. In
November 1945 the Indo-Chinese Communist Party was officially

disbanded. This move was more apparent than real as the party continued to operate in clandestine fashion and would be formally reconstituted in the middle years of the French war. But together these efforts did help to allay the suspicions of Chinese occupiers, who allowed the DRV government to continue to function and, most importantly from the Vietnamese perspective, refused French requests to introduce its forces into the North.[3]

The situation was a bit different in southern Vietnam. Here the DRV was the largest political authority on the ground, loosely holding as much as half the land and a third of the population of the South. But it was comparatively weaker than in the North, the result of both geography and history. In the notoriously fractious and independent-minded political culture of southern Vietnam, the DRV was unable to control fully the actions of the southern leadership of the August Revolution or many of the southern militias which had pledged their support to the Viet Minh. The South had also escaped the famine that gripped north and north-central Vietnam (the South in fact remained a rice surplus area), which gave agents of the Vietnamese state less opportunity to penetrate the southern countryside and win peasant support. Regional rivals like the Cao Dai and Hoa Hao challenged the regime's peasant appeals while moderate nationalists and radicals hostile to the DRV did the same in urban areas.

The occupation of the South immediately after the Second World War by British forces sympathetic to French colonial aims further complicated the DRV's position. British occupying forces showed little sympathy to the new Vietnamese government, a reflection of broader British concerns with holding their own colonies in South-East Asia and fears that Vietnamese independence could unleash anti-colonial movements elsewhere in the region. When British forces arrived in Saigon in early September 1945, they were accompanied by a detachment of French troops. The British commander refused to deal with the DRV-affiliated committee that had taken power in the South, declaring martial law and rearming 1,400 French soldiers who had been detained by the Japanese. On the morning of 23 September, French soldiers and civilians ran

amok, beating and detaining almost any Vietnamese they encountered in the streets. This provoked a severe backlash the following
evening. In the escalating chaos, fires enveloped whole neighbourhoods in Saigon, civilians fled the city, and by early October
most armed Vietnamese associated with the DRV had retreated to
the countryside. Word of the French assaults spread quickly.
Spontaneous outbursts of support followed, often without DRV
official sanction, from local people in the North and centre, including the sending of troops, food, and medicine for the emerging
anti-French resistance.[4]

Although under pressure from southern revolutionaries as well as
harder-line voices within his own government and the now clandestine Communist Party to move towards war, Ho Chi Minh
opened negotiations with French representatives in Hanoi.
Vietnamese negotiators insisted on unification of the entire country
and immediate self-government under the control of the DRV,
while the French sought to maintain control of the South, where
their economic interests and the pressures of French colonists and
denizens of the imperial order were greatest. In March 1946 the two
sides reached a preliminary accord. The French agreed to recognize
the DRV and the Vietnamese formally acknowledged a French
right to maintain an economic and cultural presence in the North,
including the stationing of some 15,000 troops to protect its interests there. On the status of southern Vietnam, France pledged to
hold a national referendum to decide whether Cochinchina would
rejoin the North and centre in a reunited Vietnamese state or
remain a separate French territory. The agreement sparked sharp
criticism by some militant Vietnamese, but it was approved by the
DRV's newly formed National Assembly. Talks with the French
were scheduled in the spring and summer to finalize the details of
the referendum.[5]

While efforts at diplomatic settlement continued, a darker side of
the Vietnamese revolution accompanied the more positive appeals
of the DRV government to win local support in both northern and
southern Vietnam. Throughout the late colonial period, the communists often organized opposition to French rule secretly, since

the colonial security police met open opposition with fierce repression. This dimension of the party's activities could involve intimidation, coercion, and sometimes assassination. These practices re-emerged in 1945 and 1946, when agents of the DRV killed hundreds of its domestic political opponents. Perhaps the most dramatic case was the assassination and dismemberment of Huynh Phu So, the spiritual leader of the Hoa Hao. Moderate and radical nationalists who opposed the Viet Minh were targeted in both the North and the South, some of whom were sent into exile in China and France. Others were murdered. To an extent, the political killings in this period were less the official policy of the state than a reflection of its continuing inability to control local forces associated with it. They nonetheless contributed to the tense political environment throughout Vietnam, hastening the departure of more moderate elements from the DRV government and increasing French suspicions of Vietnamese militancy.[6]

Much of 1946 was taken up with ultimately frustrated diplomatic efforts to mediate the conflict between Vietnamese and French national self-assertions. In negotiations held in the mountain resort of Dalat and at Fontainebleau, outside Paris, the two sides were unable to come to terms over the status of southern Vietnam. At Dalat the newly appointed French high commissioner Georges Thierry d'Argenlieu was a strong support of the *ancien* colonial *régime* and firmly resisted plans for a referendum on the South. In the meantime, a new French government was elected in Paris, one considerably less inclined to compromise on colonial matters, and negotiations at Fontainebleau floundered. Emboldened by these developments, d'Argenlieu packed a second Dalat conference with conservative colonial officials and colonists, who voted to create a separate Republic of Cochinchina under French control. Outraged, the Vietnamese delegation at Fontainebleau walked out of the conference in protest. Ho Chi Minh, aware of the continued weakness of his own government and its armed forces, finally accepted a compromise, in which both sides agreed to avoid armed conflict and promised to return to the negotiating table at the beginning of 1947.[7]

By the time Ho Chi Minh returned to Vietnam from France, the prospect for such a settlement looked grim. Initially the ceasefire held, but armed clashes between Vietnamese and French military forces soon began and in late November the French seized the northern port city of Haiphong. The Vietnamese government turned to fortifying Hanoi from attack, encouraging tens of thousands of non-combatants to evacuate the city, and began to establish safe zones (*an toan khu*) outside the city with communication links and defence works. Throughout early December, Vietnamese and French officials remained in contact about a settlement, but by mid-December the French position had again stiffened and radicals within the DRV pushed more strongly for war. On 19 December the Vietnamese made the decision to fight, but not before they had sought one last opportunity to meet with the French negotiator in Hanoi; he refused to meet the DRV representative. When Ho was told the news, he reportedly paused and said: 'Huh! Then we fight.'[8]

At 8.03 p.m. on 19 December, the lights went out in Hanoi. Workers at the city's power plant loyal to the DRV had successfully detonated the explosives they had smuggled past French guards. At the same time Vietnamese military forces attacked French installations throughout the city. With the battle for Hanoi, the French war had begun.

Early Years of War

The DRV immediately called the war against France a 'people's war', confidently predicting, in the words of the party's general secretary, Truong Chinh, that 'the resistance will win'.[9] In raising the banner of people's war, the Vietnamese consciously drew upon Maoist models then being applied by the Chinese Communist Party in the ongoing civil war in China. Although some of the leadership of the Vietnamese and Chinese communist movements had come to know one another as early as the 1920s, Maoist political and military thought first entered Vietnamese revolutionary discourse in the late 1930s and was influential in shaping the mass mobilization and guerrilla warfare strategies that shaped the Viet Minh's rise to power in the August Revolution of 1945.[10] To envision how the French war would unfold, the Vietnamese adapted Mao's three-stage people's war to local conditions: a defensive period (*phong ngu*) marked by temporary withdrawal from cities and the creation of liberated base areas in the countryside; an equilibrium phase (*cam cu*), when revolutionary forces would attack vulnerable French positions; and a final counter-offensive (*tong phan cong*) in cities and rural areas that would bring about French defeat and a unified Vietnam under DRV control.

If the Chinese model was a source of future optimism, initially the war went very poorly for the Democratic Republic, which quickly lost control of major cities including Hanoi. Beginning in mid-February 1947, the French launched a major offensive in the northern countryside that broke Vietnamese rural defences and put in danger the safe zones the government had established the previous year. Far from the defensive stage of people's war, these reversals better reflected what the Vietnamese military commander Vo Nguyen Giap termed a 'collapsing front' (*vo mat tran*): 'A collapsing front is entirely different from circumstances where our forces decide to retreat....Many units lose contact. Vacillation invades the thinking of cadres and soldiers. Some cadres run far, some soldiers suddenly desert. The people also became irresolute, believing the enemy is too strong.'[11]

Although the Vietnamese government was able to retain a loose control over rural northern Vietnam even after this French offensive, the fragile state apparatus it constructed in 1945 and 1946 largely ceased to function. As one contemporary critic in the government argued, 'plans were slow in coming out' and 'orders and instructions were not complete'. Each rural community, this critic continued, 'simply followed its own developments concerning tactics and organization. At the same time the way our cadres worked was also poor so that each time an order to set something in motion needed coordination it seemed to be too difficult.'[12] Communication beyond northern Vietnam was even more challenging. Some use was made of wireless radios, but more commonly governmental decisions were transmitted by couriers, who made the two- to three-month trip between Hanoi and Saigon partly by boat and partly on foot. The crisis faced by the state was compounded by Vietnam's isolation from its potential allies in the communist world. Despite the importance of Maoist models and the efforts of Vietnamese diplomats to press their case with the international communist movement, there is little evidence of financial and technical assistance from the Chinese communists, or from the Soviet Union and the French Communist Party, in the initial years of the war.[13]

In part, the Vietnamese state sought to meet these challenges by looking inward. In April 1947 a central party cadre conference issued a directive calling for an immediate intensification of guerrilla warfare tactics to meet the fierce French military challenge. As part of this shift, villages were instructed to establish self-defence militia units, and sustained training in guerrilla warfare began in liberated areas of the North. Domestic weapons manufacturing also increased, with the establishment of several major factories and numerous local arms workshops to produce bazookas, grenades, pistols, rifles, and machine guns. At the same time, the state sought to sustain and build popular support through renewed efforts at moderate land reform and intensified literacy campaigns.[14]

Looking outward, the DRV engaged in regional diplomacy in an effort to capitalize on the widespread professions of moral support the Vietnamese had received from nationalist leaders in India and South-East Asia who opposed French efforts to regain its colonial control in the area. Through its diplomatic mission in Bangkok and later in Rangoon, the Vietnamese state sought to establish closer ties with Thailand, Burma, Indonesia, India, and the Philippines, as well as more informal ties with radical nationalists in Malaya. Vietnamese diplomats were active in the 1947 Asian Relations Conference in India and the establishment of the South-East Asia League, which aimed to formalize networks of nationalist regional cooperation. The DRV also launched an initiative in the spring and summer of 1947 with American diplomats and intelligence operatives in Bangkok to win US political and economic assistance and support for mediation of the war with the French.[15]

Although these efforts brought few immediate material rewards, they served to foster ties of nationalism and anti-colonialism in the region that made possible the organization of clandestine networks to obtain arms, military supplies, and medicines needed for the war against the French. Bangkok initially served as the centre for an underground network that sent arms and supplies into Vietnam, though eventually these were expanded to include clandestine arrangements with sellers in Burma, Singapore, and the Philippines, and arms purchases from nationalist Chinese military commanders in northern Vietnam. While available evidence makes it difficult to draw precise conclusions about this arms traffic, Vietnamese documents captured by the French in this period suggest it was vital to the Vietnamese war effort. With the exception of arms produced in local armament factories and those captured from the French, the Vietnamese state's regional arms networks were the only major source of military equipment and supplies in this period.[16]

Despite substantial Vietnamese weaknesses, the French were not able to take full advantage of them in the early years of the war. In part, French troop strength in Vietnam remained limited given the numbers of French regiments involved in the post-war occupation in Germany and in quelling colonial unrest in the French colonies of Algeria and Madagascar. Even a massive French offensive in the fall of 1947, which inflicted heavy losses on the Vietnamese and came close to capturing Ho Chi Minh and his high military command, failed in its ultimate objective to isolate and crush DRV forces.[17] There were also important divisions within the French state over the prosecution of the war in Vietnam. On one side were centre-right Gaullist political groupings, right-leaning members of the Socialist Party, and military and colonial administrators in Saigon who defended French sovereignty over its empire and believed France should fight to return to the *status quo ante* in Vietnam. The hardliners were opposed by left-leaning Socialist Party and French Communist Party reformers, who advocated negotiation and liberalization of French rule in Vietnam. French public opinion towards the war reflected these divisions, with polls suggesting that as many favoured negotiated settlement or an immediate withdrawal as favoured a continuation of the war effort. More than 20 per cent of those polled in 1947 expressed indifference to the war entirely.[18]

Internationalizing a Colonial War

Given their internal divisions and weaknesses, proponents of the war within the French state increasingly looked to Great Britain and the United States for support and assistance, a process that would slowly, if fatefully, draw a hesitant United States closer into the war. These French efforts centred around seeking international support for what was called the 'Bao Dai solution'. It sought to use the former Vietnamese emperor, widely viewed in Vietnam as a toady and a puppet, to provide a fig leaf of legitimacy for the construction of an indigenous Vietnamese state that would remain under strong French influence if not direct control. Perceptions in London and Washington of French entreaties and apprehensions of the post-colonial moment in Vietnam reflected an interlocking set of dilemmas facing Euro-American states in the aftermath of the Second World War as nationalist movements in Asia, Africa, and the Middle East challenged colonial control. Whatever its own internal problems, the DRV's successful harnessing of the forces of indigenous anti-colonial nationalism was an element of this powerful global decolonizing phenomenon, which appeared to mark the end of the imperial order. These local and transnational developments shaped and complicated British and American thinking. Should assertions of immediate independence like those of the DRV be opposed or supported? Or could alternative scenarios like the Bao Dai solution make more gradual the transformation from colony to independent state?

The British adopted a pro-French neutrality in the first years of the war, one prompted by their own need to foster economic recovery after the Second World War and what was seen as the

necessity of unimpeded access to rubber and tin in their colony in
Malaya to advance these British economic interests. But while the
Labour government was broadly supportive of the restoration of
French colonial control in Vietnam, it was nonetheless constrained
by domestic politics and the attitudes of its own colonial subjects.
The Labour Party itself was divided on foreign policy. A substantial
number of Labour backbenchers who were advocates of colonial
self-determination expressed sharp criticism of British policy
towards the French war in Vietnam and effectively muted more
vigorous British support for it. Moreover, considerable hostility
among nationalist groups in South and South-East Asia to French
suppression of Vietnamese nationalism complicated British policy-
making as the Labour government was fearful of upsetting Asian
nationalists while Britain was negotiating delicate transfers of power
in India and Burma.[19]

American officials also tilted towards the French in the first years
of the war. From the time of the August Revolution to the outbreak of the French war, Ho Chi Minh and other Vietnamese
representatives made sustained appeals to the United States for
recognition and support of the DRV. The Truman administration
largely ignored them, acquiescing in the French return to Vietnam
in the fall of 1945 and declining to mediate the escalating Franco-
Vietnamese tensions in 1946. There were, however, significant
internal divisions among American policy makers about the war
and US policy towards post-colonial Vietnam. Asianists in the
State Department believed aggressive French policy in Vietnam, if
unchecked and supported by the United States, could produce a
destabilizing climate throughout South-East Asia and potentially
estrange America's future allies in Vietnam and the decolonizing
world. The Europeanist wing of the State Department stressed the
overriding importance of France in the construction of a stable
post-war order in western Europe and enthusiastically supported
the French position in Vietnam. Underlying these divisions,
however, was a shared and deeper sense of the problematic nature
of what all these policy makers regarded as an archaic French

colonialism and the potential dangers of an indigenous Vietnamese political regime.[20]

Their views recalled perceptions of Vietnamese inferiority, French colonial incompetence, and the certainty that the United States could do better that emerged among American observers of Vietnam as early as the 1920s. The Vietnamese were often rendered through a racialized lens as a backward and primitive people. As one American wrote in 1937, 'The Annamite dreams a perpetual melancholy reverie uncontrolled by any critical faculty. His thinking is confused and indecisive ... incapable of separating the essential from the trivial.'[21] Few believed the Vietnamese were capable of self-government or concerted political action of their own accord. Vietnamese nationalist agitation against the French was generally attributed to outside, usually Soviet, direction. Similarly, French colonial rule in Vietnam was judged to be an administrative, economic, and moral failure that had done little to arrest persisting Vietnamese inferiority and stagnation. Laced through these perceptions was the sense that superior American political, economic, and social models could do significantly better in transforming the Vietnamese.

Franklin Roosevelt's plans during the Second World War for placing Vietnam under some form of international trusteeship in the post-war period had rested on the widely shared belief that the Vietnamese were too backward to help themselves and that the necessary change could only come with external, American-engineered direction. But Roosevelt's oft-stated anti-French sentiments—he argued that Vietnam 'should not be given back to the French empire after the war' and 'that the French had done nothing to improve the lot of the people'[22]—were quite different from the kind of post-colonial visions that drove Vietnamese actors. Had plans for trusteeship for Vietnam not died with Roosevelt in April 1945, its fundamental premiss that Vietnam might require as long as twenty-five years of tutelage would have been unlikely to sit well with Vietnamese revolutionaries already in the process of establishing an independent state.[23]

Enter the Cold War

The escalating Soviet–American cold war rivalry in Europe and Asia in the late 1940s introduced a new urgency into American policy towards the French war. US policy makers watched with alarm as eastern Europe came under Soviet control, communist parties made advances in western European states, and the Soviets intervened in the Greek civil war and launched the Berlin blockade. The victory of Mao Zedong's communist forces in China in 1949 over the American-backed nationalist forces of Jiang Jieshi brought US cold war concerns more directly to Asia. Together European and Asian cold war tensions created a climate of domestic uncertainty and fear in the United States, producing a militant anti-communism at home and abroad. It was manifested in the hysteria of McCarthyism and a reassessment of US national security policy, which increasingly saw the US engaged in a zero-sum game against the fanatical forces of the Soviet Union and international communism.

These cold war developments powerfully affected American thinking about the French war in Vietnam. The need for a stable France and strong French support for the emerging US policy of containment in western Europe made American policy makers somewhat more amenable to French efforts to promote the Bao Dai solution as an alternative to Ho Chi Minh's Democratic Republic. So, too, did rising concerns among US policy makers about keeping South-East Asia open to the economies of Great Britain and Japan. The communist insurgency in the British colony of Malaya in 1948 alarmed US policy makers, who shared the British belief that access to Malay tin and rubber was central to arresting the devastation to the British economy induced by the Second World War. They also feared that communist success in Vietnam would further embolden the communist insurgency in Malaya, threatening this critical British economic interest. Similarly, American policy makers came to see Japan rather than China as the major US strategic ally in Asia as communist forces grew closer to victory in the Chinese civil war, and reversed immediate post-war policies designed to keep the Japanese state and economy weak. As part of this transformation, Americans increasingly viewed markets and resources in South-East Asia—including Vietnamese rice, rubber, and coal—as critical to building up the Japanese economy. Communist control of Vietnam potentially threatened those efforts.[24]

In promoting the Bao Dai solution, the French were quick to present the Americans with evidence of the communist ties of Ho Chi Minh and the top leadership of the Vietnamese state. American policy makers were aware of these linkages as early as 1944, but they had not previously attached overriding significance to them. In the changed climate of the late 1940s, their perceived importance grew. The racialist lens through which the Americans viewed the Vietnamese heightened the strategic importance of the French war for American cold war diplomacy. If the Vietnamese were incapable of self-government and susceptible to external direction, as most US policy makers believed, evidence of the communist orientation of the leaders of the Democratic Republic meant they could be little more than puppets directed from Moscow or Beijing, with alarming implications for the American cold war rivalry with the Soviet Union. 'The Annamese are attractive and even lovable,' one State Department observer contended, but 'essentially childish. . . . under the present government . . . [Vietnam] would immediately be run in accordance with dictates from Moscow'.[25]

Even so, American policy makers in the late 1940s had trouble articulating a definitive policy towards the French war in Vietnam. A telling cable from Secretary of State George Marshall in 1947 captures persisting American misgivings and discomfort. While Marshall acknowledged that the US had 'fully recognized France's sovereign position' in the area, he could not understand 'the continued existence of an outmoded colonial outlook' and the inability of the French to recognize the realities of a post-colonial future. Equally concerned by Ho Chi Minh's communist connections, Marshall also argued that it 'should be obvious that we are not interested in seeing colonial empire administrations supplanted by a philosophy emanating from and controlled by the Kremlin'.

Confounded by the perceived impossibilities of choosing between a radical political regime and an antiquated colonial one, Marshall could offer no clear American policy towards the French war. 'Frankly,' he concluded, 'we have no solution of the problem to suggest.'[26]

By 1950, however, a dramatic shift in the international climate pulled the United States directly into the conflict and transformed the colonial war in Vietnam into a central battleground of the emergent cold war. In January both the Soviet Union and Mao's China extended formal diplomatic recognition to the Ho Chi Minh-led Democratic Republic of Vietnam. Within weeks, diplomatic recognition of the Vietnamese state came from the governments of Poland, Romania, Czechoslovakia, Hungary, Bulgaria, Albania, and Yugoslavia, all of whom were now reliable and relatively pliant allies of the Soviet Union. With Chinese recognition of the DRV also came large numbers of military advisers and substantial amounts of military equipment and supplies for the Vietnamese state's war against the French.

The American response was swift. In early February 1950 the United States announced its recognition of the French-backed Associated States of Vietnam, led by former Vietnamese emperor Bao Dai, quickly followed by Great Britain. In May the Truman administration allocated $15 million in military and economic aid to the French and the Bao Dai government. The figure increased to $100 million by the end of year, stimulated in part by the ways in which the outbreak of the Korean war in June 1950 and direct Sino-American military confrontation on the Korean peninsula further heightened the geopolitical significance of the French war in Vietnam for US policy makers. At the war's end in 1954, the United States had paid as much of 80 per cent of its cost, some $1 billion.[27]

Tensions and Ambiguities

The transformational events of 1950 affected the subsequent course of the French war in Vietnam in complex and sometimes surprising ways. If they finally brought the French the expansive external support they believed would decisively turn their fortunes in the war against the Vietnamese, the relationship between France and its allies was not a smooth or harmonious one. Among American policy makers, derisive attitudes towards the French and negative assessments of Vietnamese capabilities persisted. Within months of the Truman administration's decision to recognize the Bao Dai government, tensions quickly emerged over the political, economic, and social construction of the new Vietnamese state. In the fall of 1950, Americans began to voice substantial doubts about the capability of the Bao Dai regime and its leadership to inspire allegiance in urban and rural Vietnam, as they did criticisms of French military abilities and persisting colonial controls on the Vietnamese economy. But the larger problem, most Americans agreed, was the continuing limits the French placed on the Bao Dai government. As one State Department report from the field argued, 'concessions to nationalist sentiment, leading to full sovereignty for the Bao Dai government, have been forthcoming so slowly and with such seeming reluctance on the part of the French' that the government has not 'won a strong nationalist following in any quarter'.[28]

Dissatisfaction with the Bao Dai government and French policies towards Vietnam continued to animate official American discussions on Vietnam after 1950, echoing the debates that had infused official debates throughout the late 1940s. As increasing amounts of US military and economic aid entered Vietnam, American scorn for French colonial methods intensified and provoked bitter disputes between French and American officials over how US aid in Vietnam should be spent. The organization and command of the Vietnamese army was a major source of concern for many American officials who advocated direct Vietnamese control against strong French opposition. From the US perspective, French efforts to dominate the Vietnamese army prevented the latter from acting to instil the notions of political community and citizenship that Americans believed were essential for the construction of a viable post-colonial state.[29]

The French were able to achieve some military success in southern Vietnam in the early 1950s, reversing the gains the DRV had made in the Mekong delta in the first phase of the war. The intensification of DRV land reform programmes in the delta from 1947 to 1949 helped the regime expand its authority in the rural south; as much as 30 per cent of the land in the South was taken from absentee landlords and French collaborators and given to poor and landless peasants. With increasing local support, the DRV began to control the political economy of the South, including an economic blockade of French zones, and to build and expand its political authority and military forces. But beginning in 1950, in the wake of US commitments of support, the French redoubled their efforts in the South. They successfully fortified the thousands of posts and watchtowers they had earlier built in the countryside, and launched an aggressive series of sweeps into the delta. By late 1952 even the DRV acknowledged that through these efforts the French had regained control over much of the delta.[30]

This reversal of Vietnamese fortunes, however, would be short-lived, undermined by the very French policies that had brought it about. The French campaign in the South rested in part on a series of alliances with the military forces of the Cao Dai and Hoa Hao, themselves increasingly hostile to the DRV. But when the French sought to build up Bao Dai's National Army in 1952, Cao Dai and Hoa Hao forces were not keen to surrender their autonomy and relations with the French broke down. One Hoa Hao commander pulled his forces out of the National Army, but not before burning the posts they had been assigned to guard. Increasingly the sectarian militias and armies would go their own way. Greater brutality also accompanied these campaigns, with both French and militia forces burning village houses, raping women, and arresting and killing men believed to be loyal to the DRV. The French return of land that the DRV had redistributed also meant the reprise of older patterns of economic exploitation by absentee landlords. DRV forces were quick to take advantage of these weaknesses, and there was a revival of their authority in the rural south by 1954.[31]

— If French alliances with local actors and their external supporters could be tense and sometimes counter-productive, ambiguities and tensions within the international communist world shaped the DRV's often fractious relationship with the Soviets and the Chinese after 1950. Despite its formal recognition of the DRV, the Soviet Union ceded a more direct military role in the conflict to the Chinese. Its broader relationship with the Vietnamese state remained as limited after 1950 as it had been before. Soviet hesitations appear to have been shaped by Stalin's long-standing distrust of Ho Chi Minh. During his stay in Moscow from 1934 to 1938, Ho underwent severe criticism for his alleged nationalist proclivities and sympathy with the bourgeoisie. Reports that Ho was put on trial while in Moscow remain unconfirmed, but given the widespread paranoia and terror of this period it is not impossible.[32] In 1945 the leader of the French Communist Party reported that Stalin continued to doubt Ho's reliability and had openly criticized his willingness to undertake initiatives involving American and British intelligence operatives during the Second World War without Soviet advice and consent. Along with the low priority Stalin accorded to the decolonizing world compared to Europe in the post-war period, these sentiments help to explain why the Soviet Union provided little more than rhetorical support for DRV efforts against the French. Stalin gave Ho Chi Minh a very cool reception in Moscow in 1950. The presence at those meetings of Mao, who was favourably inclined towards Ho, was critical to Soviet willingness to provide the support that it did in the French war. But the persistence of Soviet distancing from Ho Chi Minh's government is reflected in the fact that the USSR did not appoint an ambassador to the DRV until 1954.[33]

From 1950 Mao's China made substantial contributions to the Vietnamese war effort against the French. The Chinese provided military and political advisers, who worked closely with their Vietnamese counterparts in planning tactics and strategy. They also gave large quantities of military and non-military supplies. Although the best estimates suggest the Americans provided the French and Bao Dai with as much as seventeen times the amount of external aid the Chinese gave to the Vietnamese, Chinese military support was clearly critical to the Vietnamese given their international isolation in the early years of the war. The proximity of the Chinese communist state also shifted the strategic dynamics of the war in ways that ultimately favoured the Vietnamese. With the Chinese communists to the north, the Sino-Vietnamese border became a safer one for the Vietnamese and considerably shortened the DRV's supply lines. The successful Vietnamese military campaign in September 1950, in which a DRV force attacked and routed French military installations in the mountainous area near the Chinese border, was one early manifestation of the shift in Vietnamese military fortunes. Much of the rest of the French war was fought in the North, largely to the advantage of the DRV as the military and political strength of the Ho Chi Minh government remained weaker in the South. Empowered by Chinese assistance, the Vietnamese hoped the equilibrium phase of people's war had been reached, and that they could soon move to the final stage of a general offensive.[34]

But if Chinese communist support for the DRV war effort was significant, it also brought with it deep tensions between the Vietnamese and Chinese. At the most basic level, the massive influx of Chinese advisers, weapons, and supplies for the war effort as well as a Chinese political advisory group that sought a role in DRV domestic policy often seemed to overwhelm the Vietnamese. The fragile and underdeveloped Vietnamese state apparatus underwent serious strain as the leadership of the DRV worked to absorb Chinese support and advice. Disputes over military tactics and strategy quickly emerged, particularly after the failure of the Chinese-inspired military campaigns of 1951. In the wake of the successful 1950 border campaign, the Vietnamese launched what they hoped would be a successful general offensive again the French. Using more than 15,000 troops in Chinese-style human wave tactics, the DRV attacked French forces in the Red River delta near Hanoi. The result was a disaster. The French quickly called in reinforcements to hold their positions and launched air attacks using napalm bombs supplied by the United States. In the wake of the offensive, more than 6,000 Vietnamese soldiers were dead and the Vietnamese military leadership were left increasingly sceptical of Chinese military advice.[35]

Personal antipathies between General Chen Geng, the senior Chinese military adviser and representative to the DRV, and Vo Nguyen Giap, who commanded the DRV's army, accentuated tensions between the Vietnamese and Chinese communists. In his recently discovered diary Chen Geng described Giap as 'slippery and not very upright and honest'. More broadly, he castigated the Vietnamese for 'their fear of letting other people know their weaknesses' and lack of 'Bolshevist self-criticism'. Seemingly unaware of the problematic impact his tone might have on his intended audience, the diary also conveys his great surprise that the Vietnamese often appeared resistant to his critiques.[36]

The fragile contours of Sino-Vietnamese relations in this period were shaped by the manner in which Chinese national and geostrategic interests sometimes clashed with and superseded fraternal ideological ties. Mao's willingness to support the Vietnamese during the French war, leading historians of Chinese policy argue, was in large measure prompted by fears of an American-led invasion into southern China at a time when Mao felt his fledgling regime remained vulnerable. These national interests could promote cooperation with and support of the Vietnamese, but they could also prompt policies inimical to Vietnamese state interests. Chinese suspicions that Vietnam aimed at regional dominance in Cambodia and Laos, areas Mao sought to control to protect Chinese state interests, significantly strained Sino-Vietnamese relations.[37]

The shifting international contours of the French war also had a critical impact on the DRV's wartime policies in the domestic sphere, accelerating the Vietnamese state's turn in the late 1940s to a more open identification and intensification of its communist origins. One measure of this transformation was the increase in membership of the Vietnamese Communist Party, which went from approximately 5,000 in 1945 to 110,000 in 1947 and over 776,000 in 1951. As these numbers grew, the policies of all-class nationalism and moderate socio-economic reform that characterized the early war years were gradually abandoned. In February 1951 the Vietnamese Communist Party reconstituted itself as the Vietnam Worker's Party (Dang Lao Dong Viet Nam), and for the first time since the formation of the Viet Minh in 1941 a more public commitment to socialist revolution shaped its rhetoric and activities. Beginning in 1952, a campaign to purify the party was launched that eventually targeted middle-class veterans of the war and eliminated them from leadership posts. Increasingly the party and the state began to marginalize many of the rural landholders and urban elites whose support it had once sought. It also fostered deeper alliances with peasants, workers, and ethnic minorities through more radical land reform and the promotion of an increasingly hierarchical and class-bound vision of state and society. The result was a more authoritarian politics with considerably less room for dissident voices.[38]

Among poorer and landless peasants, the turn to more radical forms of socialist rural reform was quite popular. As one poor peasant from the South, who joined the party during the French war, remembered: 'When I heard that socialism would grant rights and material benefits to everyone, and would bring material benefits to the people, I was bowled over, and thought that socialism was a correct doctrine. . . . I liked this very much. I was poor, and I liked the idea of bringing material well-being to all people—all the poor liked this idea.'[39]

But for many urban elites who had initially embraced the August Revolution of 1945 and the war against the French, the DRV's growing antipathy towards them and its embrace of socialist internationalism presented painful choices. As state pressures intensified in the late 1940s, some elites, mainly the affluent Saigon bourgeoisie and Catholics, shifted their support to the French-backed Bao Dai government. Others found themselves uneasily suspended between the new hostility they encountered from the DRV and what they continued to see as the illegitimacy and sycophancy of the Bao Dai regime. If they were reluctant to embrace Ho Chi Minh, they also saw Bao Dai as a puppet of the French. In a reflection of these prevailing sentiments, an article in a Haiphong newspaper of the period lampooned the reach of Bao Dai's power, arguing that the government was only allowed to regulate the most petty issues like the activities of vendors in the market who sold goods from 'bamboo trays and baskets'.[40] Behind Vietnamese figureheads, many observers recognized, the French remained in charge.

Even elites who remained loyal to the DRV continued to struggle with the pressure they faced from the state to serve its turn to revolutionary socialist imperatives. The case of To Ngoc Van, a prominent pre-war Vietnamese painter and intellectual who enthusiastically joined the August Revolution and the war against the French, illustrates these acutely felt dilemmas. He oversaw the establishment of the state's school for the arts in the northern resistance zone during the French war. Teaching both drawing and the fundamentals of Marxism–Leninism, the school and its artists produced paintings, posters, stamps, and other visual emblems for the Vietnamese state and its war against the French. To Ngoc Van died in 1954 of injuries he suffered at the battle of Dien Bien Phu and was honoured by the state as a revolutionary hero and martyr. But despite his prominence and work as an agent of the state's cultural production, he repeatedly expressed deep misgivings about official efforts to define wartime art through its effectiveness in serving the goals of national independence and socialist revolution. He was particularly concerned about tensions between the state's politicization of art and his capacity as a creative artist. In a 1949 essay, 'Study or Not?', Van wrote: 'Here lies the principal point, the torment of my soul: how to make the self that serves the nation and the masses and the self that serves art—the artist of course cannot forget this responsibility—not come into conflict or even worse betray one another.'[41]

Ultimately in his art To Ngoc Van appeared to resolve his own creative dilemmas in ways that satisfied both him and the dictates of the state. His 1954 watercolour *Militia Woman* (see Plate 5) suggests the ways in which Van navigated these competing state and private demands. On the one hand, the mood of the watercolour and its gentle representation of a woman who served the state in the French war followed the state's preference for depicting the wartime sacrifices of ordinary people and what the state's cultural tsar Truong Chinh called 'correctly expressing the feelings of the masses that are pure, sincere and exceedingly warm'.[42] At the same time, however, its flowing lines, the delicacy of the central figure, and its gendered subject also recall his pre-revolutionary work in the 1930s and early 1940s, which often depicted bourgeois women and female beauty in similar ways. Indeed the parallels between his 1944 oil *Two Young Girls and a Child* (see Plate 4), representative of his pre-revolutionary work, and *Militia Woman* are striking. If the social class of the woman in Van's wartime painting fits state demands, its sensibility betrays Van's larger, and very personal, artistic vision. Others who shared To Ngoc Van's unease with the growing radicalism and pressures of the DRV state, however, would be less able to resolve comfortably the dilemmas he posed in his writings, and came under official attack when the war came to a close.

Denouement

Although the period after 1950 did not bring a string of unbroken Vietnamese victories over the French, momentum did begin to shift in their favour. Chastened by the failure of the 1951 offensive, the DRV turned to a more gradual military strategy, hoping to disperse French forces into defensive positions that the Vietnamese could then attack sequentially, slowly wearing down French resolve. Over time, the DRV exerted more control in the crucial northern and north-west military zones near the Chinese border. These efforts were advanced by a growing war-weariness among the French. By 1953 total French casualties had reached 150,000 and war accounted for as much as half of the country's defence expenditures even with increasing US aid. Low morale, an officer shortage, and limited air power undermined French military efforts in Vietnam, and at home concerns increased about the war's human and material costs and its protracted nature.[43] In a poll taken in May 1953 about what many French observers had begun to call the 'dirty war', or *la guerre sale*, 15 per cent of French people favoured giving

Vietnam up altogether and another 35 per cent advocated negotiations with the DRV; only 15 per cent favoured sending additional
French forces.[44]

With rising popular calls for a settlement from across the political
spectrum, the French government sought to prepare for negotiations by improving its military position on the ground in Vietnam.
Henri Navarre, the recently appointed French commander in the
field, was instructed to show a new aggressiveness. The much
publicized though sketchy Navarre plan called for as many as ten
new battalions to augment French troop strength in Vietnam,
massive increases in the size of Bao Dai's National Army, and
more forceful offensive operations aimed at a general offensive
against the DRV in 1955 and 1956. Navarre privately doubted
whether more than a draw was possible, but nonetheless initiated
a series of raids against DRV positions in the Red River delta in the
summer of 1953. Meanwhile, the DRV intensified efforts to mount
a major operation in the north-west and into French-controlled
Laos, believing the French would feel forced to beat it back and in
the process extend long supply lines over territory controlled by the
DRV army. Navarre decided to try to stop the Vietnamese by a
massive landing of French airborne units in late November at Dien
Bien Phu, a valley near the Lao border about 200 miles west of
Hanoi. He hoped to draw the Vietnamese into a conventional
battle there, believing superior French artillery and air power
would prevail. The Vietnamese, with the active encouragement
of their Chinese military advisers, decided to fight the French at
Dien Bien Phu, certain that its hilly terrain would favour them
rather than the French.[45]

Meanwhile, international sentiment for a negotiated settlement
was growing, prompted in part by a shift in the Soviet and Chinese
positions towards the French war. Stalin's death in March 1953 and
the emergence of a new Soviet leadership led to a reconsideration
of the Soviet Union's foreign policy, a part of which produced hints
in the Soviet press of support for a negotiated settlement to the
French war. The Chinese, anxious in the wake of the Korean
conflict to relax international tensions and turn their attention to

domestic matters, also spoke favourably of a peace settlement modelled on the terms of the recent armistice in the Korean war. The
French government indicated its own willingness to come to the
negotiating table at Geneva. In November 1953 the DRV did too,
a decision shaped by substantial Chinese pressure as well as
Vietnamese war-weariness. Although some within the DRV
opposed negotiations, Ho Chi Minh and other moderates were
well aware that without Chinese support the DRV would not be
able to withstand the French. Only the United States remained
implacably opposed to peace talks over Vietnam.[46]

The move towards negotiations, which were to begin in May
1954 in Geneva, significantly heightened the stakes of the coming
Franco-Vietnamese clash at Dien Bien Phu. Most observers
believed a decisive victory by either side would shape the terms of
a settlement. In early 1954 the Vietnamese began to move substantial numbers of troops into the hills surrounding Dien Bien Phu and
drew upon the assistance of local people, including women porters
in what was termed 'the long-hair army', to bring in the firepower
necessary to trap and defeat the French in the valley below. The
formal battle began in March 1954, with the Vietnamese initially
following the advice of their Chinese advisers to employ the
'human wave' tactics the Chinese had used against American forces
in the Korean war. But the strategy brought limited results and very
high casualties. After what were reportedly heated disputes with the
Chinese, the Vietnamese shifted tactics in late March to a prolonged
siege, digging in artillery units in trenches and tunnels. They
pounded French forces and gradually made the airfield unusable.
The French had initially believed the hills to be impenetrable.
But as the siege took hold and French forces became trapped
and isolated, it became clear that the French had severely
miscalculated.[47]

In late March the French government desperately approached
President Dwight Eisenhower to provide direct US military assistance in support of its embattled troops as defeat at Dien Bien
Phu loomed. Discussions within the Eisenhower administration
focused on the possibility of massive American bombing raids,

including the potential use of tactical nuclear weapons. But as a condition for giving the French anything more than limited air support, Eisenhower insisted on French promises to grant fuller independence to Vietnam, joint military action with the British, and full Congressional support of US intervention. Paris, London, and the US Congress failed to give their assurances, with strong opposition to military intervention voiced by the British government and many on both sides of the aisle in Congress. In the absence of American support, and as Vietnamese forces assaulted French troops trapped at Dien Bien Phu, the French surrendered on 7 May 1954 just as the peace negotiations opened in Geneva.[48]

The battle of Dien Bien Phu marked the final defeat of French colonialism in Vietnam, but the peace agreement signed at Geneva produced a limited victory for the DRV. The Geneva agreement temporarily partitioned Vietnam at the seventeenth parallel, giving the DRV control of northern Vietnam and the Bao Dai government authority in the South. Reunification was to come in 1956 with elections sponsored and overseen by an international body. With their dramatic victory at Dien Bien Phu, it might seem curious that the DRV was willing to settle for less than full control of Vietnam. The regime was under strong and, in some DRV quarters, deeply resented pressure from the Chinese to compromise in what many Vietnamese saw as another instance of China's national interests trumping its ideological ties to the Vietnamese. In this case the Vietnamese were suspicious that the Chinese were more concerned with using Geneva to foster their Great Power status and establish their own supremacy in the region than with the war in Vietnam. The Chinese were in fact instrumental in brokering the compromises that structured the Geneva agreement. In meetings with the DRV leadership, including Ho Chi Minh, in June and July 1954, the Chinese repeatedly emphasized the dangers of American intervention in Vietnam if talks at Geneva broke down: 'if we ask too much' at Geneva, the Chinese leader Zhou Enlai argued, 'and if peace is not achieved, it is certain the U.S. will intervene, providing...Bao Dai with weapons and ammunition, helping ... train military personnel, and establishing military bases there'.[49]

For its part, the DRV shared Chinese concerns with keeping the United States out of the conflict even if some in the leadership distrusted Chinese motivations. They also recognized that while France had suffered a huge military setback at Dien Bien Phu, the French still had more than 470,000 troops in the field and continued to control major cities like Hanoi, Saigon, and Hue. The Vietnamese military commander Vo Nguyen Giap estimated it could be two to five years before the DRV won a final military victory. By pushing too hard at Geneva, he suggested, the Americans might commit ground troops in Vietnam and further complicate the Vietnamese position. But if some were disappointed by the limitations of the Geneva accords, most of the DRV leadership believed the settlement would only delay rather than prevent their final victory. They were confident, when the promised reunification elections came in 1956, that the DRV would win.

In the event, the elections were never held. Instead the growing clash between communist insurgency in southern Vietnam and the US-backed Ngo Dinh Diem government in the late 1950s and early 1960s would bring another war.

Legacies

Without question the Democratic Republic of Vietnam emerged from the French war with enhanced prestige. The regime had defeated the French—an outcome almost unimaginable to many contemporary Western observers when the war began—and had built a strong and seasoned military force. Ho Chi Minh became an almost larger-than-life figure. Even those Vietnamese who opposed his socialist regime acknowledged his political skills and could not deny the larger symbolic resonances of the victory at Dien Bien Phu. The successes of the French war would provide the template for an emergent state narrative of 'sacred war' (*chien tranh than thanh*) that sought to give Vietnam a unified revolutionary history and to foreground the power of the socialist state in shaping Vietnam's post-colonial future. This effort to recast the Vietnamese past began at the moment of French defeat in 1954 and quickly focused on valorizing the self-sacrificing 'fighting spirit of the Vietnamese' (*tinh than tranh dau*) to foreign aggression throughout Vietnamese history. The French war became one of a series of didactic lessons in the necessity of collective sacrifice through which the Vietnamese state sought to legitimize its authority and mobilize for struggle.

Victory in the French war and the narrative purposes put to it by the state, however, elided the tensions within Vietnamese society that emerged during the war and the internal challenges and problems the Vietnamese state faced in its aftermath in what would be a massive project of transforming northern Vietnam from a war-ravaged territory into a functioning socialist state and economy. The destructive impact of the war on the Vietnamese economy manifested itself in serious reductions in rice production, limited internal trading, and a damaged irrigation system. As internal government reports of the period suggest, the devastation of the war was felt acutely in rural northern Vietnam. Many homes were burned or damaged by the war and unfit for habitation; so many water buffalo and oxen had been killed that villagers had to pull their own ploughs to prepare their fields; many impoverished families no longer had basic farming tools. Pockets of famine-like conditions appeared in central Vietnam, but food shortages were common throughout the North, with many destitute villagers eating only rice gruel and others living solely on a diet of vegetables and bran.[50]

To deal with these war-induced developments, and to launch the socialist revolution that, along with the independence struggle, had driven the DRV forward in the French war, the Vietnamese state undertook a radical land reform programme in 1955. Unlike more moderate efforts to redistribute land in the mid-1940s, the land reform targeted both large landowners and rich peasants and drew upon support and advice from Mao's China. If the land reform was initially popular among poorer villages, the process was divisive and often violent and its excesses unleashed further chaos in the northern countryside. Land reform teams were instructed to identify abusive landlords and rich peasants even when a village had none. Some villagers made false accusations against neighbours to settle old scores. Many households were wrongly classified and punished. A campaign of terror against rural people identified as 'wicked and tyrannical' landlords led to public trials and executions. Estimates vary, but agents of the state executed between 3,000 and 15,000 people during this period. By early 1956 hostility to the project was so great that Ho Chi Minh was forced to make a public confession of its failures.[51]

The state's other ambitious social engineering efforts also encountered resistance at the local level. A series of experimental collective agricultural cooperatives was established in the mid-1950s, a precursor to the full-scale collectivization of agricultural production in the North later in the decade. One state investigative team reported back to Hanoi that many peasants 'had divided minds . . . arguing among themselves and one another' about the 'individual, private way of work, which was familiar to them, compared to the collective and public good way of thinking, which was still immature and green'.[52] As many as 42 per cent of families who decided to join the experimental cooperatives had left them by mid-1957. At the same time, the state's cultural house (*nha van hoa*) project, which sought to further class-based socialist culture in individual villages by providing a physical locus for the dissemination and discussion of socialist books and newspapers, was largely unsuccessful. A Ministry of Culture report from 1956 reported, 'Activities are very haphazard and content is poor. There are even localities that built cultural houses worth more than a million piastres only to close them down . . . and a cultural house in Son Tay in which buffaloes and cows were allowed to sleep.'[53]

The end of the war also brought renewed tension between intellectuals and the state. In the *Nhan Van Giai Pham* affair northern writers and artists raised the banner of 'art for art's sake' against authoritarian state cultural policies. Perhaps the most important single expression of open intellectual dissent in the North during the post-colonial period, it was tolerated only briefly before the state launched a severe crackdown against it. The experience of the writer Tran Dan illustrates the broader dynamics of the affair and the ways in which it was in part shaped by contestations over the meanings of the French war.[54] At one level, Tran Dan might be viewed as an agent of the state's cultural policies towards the war. He joined the Vietnamese army and Communist Party in 1948, was trained in Chinese thought reform techniques, and led rectification courses in 1951 for fellow intellectuals and performing arts troupes on how better to support the state's war against the French.

In the spring of 1955 his novel *Men upon Men, Wave upon Wave* (*Nguoi nguoi lop lop*) appeared in Hanoi to great official and popular acclaim. The first major novel published in northern Vietnam after the end of the French war, it told the story of the battle of Dien Bien Phu. Tran Dan's novel was concerned less with the formal military dimensions of the battle than with capturing the heroic voluntarism of ordinary Vietnamese from all walks of life who contributed to the Vietnamese victory over the French. In the wake of the novel's success, Tran Dan was invited by the state to write the narrative for a commemorative film on Dien Bien Phu, which was later widely disseminated throughout northern Vietnam. Like Tran Dan's novel, the film's portrayal of the battle as a lesson in the need for collective self-sacrifice to achieve national liberation and socialist revolution closely matched official state narratives of the French war.

By 1956, however, Tran Dan had been arrested by the state as a reactionary, and he attempted suicide while imprisoned. Always a risk-taker and an iconoclast, Tran Dan's relationship with the state and its emerging strictures on cultural production was a compli-cated one throughout the French war. During the war he clashed with General Nguyen Chi Thanh, the head of the army's political department, over demands for creative freedom. He also incurred the displeasure of the army, which had the right to approval marital unions, over his choice of a bride. A Catholic and a businesswoman, she represented many of the dangerous and corrupting social influences the DRV believed were inimical to the revolutionary state. At the same time as the publication of his war novel, Tran Dan voiced increasingly public criticisms of the literature and poetry that had received official approval for its depiction of the war. His arrest was ultimately provoked by the publication of a long poem in one of the periodicals associated with the Nhan Van Giai Pham movement. Entitled 'We Must Win', it expressed his ambivalence over the meanings of the war and the immediate post-war period. The doubts and uncertainties of the poem's refrain mark a sharp contrast to the official post-war optimism of the Vietnamese state:

> I walk on
> seeing no street
> seeing no house
> Only rain falling
> upon the red flag.[55]

The case of Tran Dan was not an anomaly. After the French war, the Vietnamese state in the North increasingly sought to marginalize and silence voices who viewed the war and its meanings in ways that challenged the state's vision of it.

These legacies, and the ambiguities of victory in the French war, would powerfully affect the coming war in the South. The DRV's post-war position in southern Vietnam remained something of a question mark. With so much of the French war after 1949 fought in the North, the regime had less sustained military experience in the South and its support remained somewhat weaker than in the North. Southern cadres often voiced impatience at the DRV's insistence on building socialism in the North in the immediate post-war period before turning to the situation in the South. The DRV also emerged from the war uncertain about its relations with the Soviet Union and China and the support it might receive for nation-building or a future war. The disastrous experience with land reform, in which Chinese advisers had been central to its conception and implementation, heightened Vietnamese concerns about Chinese aims and motives. These complications only increased with the coming of the Sino-Soviet split and the resultant pressures on the Vietnamese to take sides in the dispute. Whatever the regime's immediate post-war prestige and confidence, the devastations of war, the problems of state-building in the North, lingering weaknesses in the South, and fissures in the international communist world left open a window of opportunity for constructing an alternative non-communist state in the South.

It was an opening the United States seized upon almost immediately. Against the hopes of the Vietnamese and Chinese that a negotiated settlement at Geneva would diminish the American threat to the Vietnamese revolution, the US commitment to Vietnam vastly accelerated in the aftermath of Dien Bien Phu and Geneva. Some observers have noted the restraint of the Eisenhower administration in the waning days of the French war, suggesting Eisenhower's ultimate refusal to come to the support of the French marked a rare moment between 1950 and 1970 in which US involvement in Vietnam did not grow deeper. But with the French defeat at Dien Bien Phu, American reticence quickly gave way to massive support for the political, economic, and military construction of the American-backed Diem government in southern Vietnam. Despite the fact that non-communist alternatives to the Ho Chi Minh government remained as weak after 1954 as they had been in the late colonial and French war periods, the US policy makers came out of the French war sure that they could do better.

The outcome of the French war in Vietnam was always a contingent one. At key moments, French policy makers might have made different choices: slow disengagement, immediate withdrawal, or a commitment to an enduring negotiated settlement. In the domestic realm, the Vietnamese communists might have curbed rather than quickened the trend to a more authoritarian politics, drawing on the traditions of iconoclastic radicalism in the 1920s that had initially shaped their vision of the Vietnamese revolution. That they did not, or felt they could not, reveals how the complexities of decolonization in Vietnam, and the growing constraints of the cold war, were central to the ways in which the war unfolded. The terms *lap truong* and *thac mac* first came into common usage in Vietnam during the French war. *Lap truong* gave expression to state demands for uniformity of belief and behaviour. By contrast *thac mac*— literally, 'to be still unclear about a point', 'to worry, to be uneasy', or 'to be at cross-purposes'—became the primary means for expressing divergent apprehensions of the world around them.[56] As the Vietnamese state and society navigated the local and global tensions that shaped the war and the multiple uncertainties that came at its end, the 'often aching doubts of a shedding of the skin' Nguyen Dinh Thi had first identified in 1947 continued to hover over the meanings many Vietnamese accorded to post-colonial independence.

Thich Quang Duc, a Buddhist monk, burns himself to death on a Saigon Street, 11 June 1963, to protest persecution of Buddhists by the South Vietnamese Ngo Dinh Diem government

3
THE COMING OF THE
AMERICAN WAR

On the morning of 11 June 1963, more than 300 Buddhist monks and nuns marched through the streets of Saigon. At the head of the procession was a blue Austin Westminster sedan carrying the 76-year-old monk Thich Quang Duc. Born in the central Vietnamese village of Hoi Khanh in 1897, he was ordained as a monk at 20 and played an active role in the Buddhist reform movement of the late colonial period, supervising the construction of more than fifty new temples in central and southern Vietnam. The marchers stopped at the busy Saigon intersection of Phan Dinh Phung Boulevard and Le Van Duyet Street. Thich Quang Duc emerged from the car along with two other monks. One placed a cushion on the road. The other opened the trunk and took out a gasoline can. As the marchers formed a circle around him, Thich Quang Duc seated himself in the lotus position and his colleague poured gasoline over his head. He struck a match and dropped it on himself. The American journalist David Halberstam, who witnessed the event, later wrote: 'Flames were coming from a human being; his body was slowly withering and shriveling up, his head blackening and charring. In the air was the smell of burning human flesh....As he burned he never moved a muscle, never uttered a sound, his outward composure in sharp contrast to the wailing people around him.'[1]

Thich Quang Duc's dramatic self-immolation points towards the complexities of southern Vietnamese politics and society in the years between the French and American wars. This ten-year period witnessed sustained and often bloody contestations between a variety of Vietnamese and international actors over the future of the South. In the wake of the Geneva settlement, Ngo Dinh Diem came to rule southern Vietnam. An unlikely figure to lead the construction of the fledgling South Vietnamese state, who had spent much of the French war outside the country, Diem enjoyed vigorous backing from the United States, which continued to see developments in Vietnam from a cold war perspective. At the same time, Ho Chi Minh's Democratic Republic and its supporters in the South hoped for the peaceful unification of Vietnam under communist control, as did their allies in Moscow and Beijing. It was not to be.

Throughout the late 1950s Diem unleashed a series of campaigns aimed at consolidating his hold on power. These often heavy-handed and always relentless efforts to crush opposition to his government brought some immediate success but ultimately alienated wider swaths of the rural and urban south. They gradually prompted DRV support of a growing southern communist insurgency, one that by the early 1960s had launched an increasingly successful military and political challenge to Diem. The authoritarian and dictatorial nature of Diem's government also produced widespread opposition from the urban middle class and the Buddhist protests in 1963 in which Thich Quang Duc's self-immolation played a critical role.

The fall of the Diem government in November 1963 brought escalating political chaos in the cities and the countryside. By the end of 1965 southern and much of central Vietnam was engulfed in a military struggle the Vietnamese would come to call the 'American war' (*chien tranh My*). It pitted the combined forces of the southern communist insurgency and North Vietnam, along with rearguard Soviet and Chinese support, against the South Vietnamese and American military. The lines of battle, however, would seldom be that clear on the ground for many Vietnamese bystanders and civilians, and even for some partisans of the communist insurgency and the South Vietnamese state. Relations among the alliance partners on both sides of the American war—whether between Saigon and Washington or between the southern insurgency and Hanoi, Moscow, and Beijing—were also highly unstable and fraught with tensions. In this difficult environment, infused by competing visions of state and society, the American war in southern Vietnam would unfold.

The South after Geneva

A massive flow of people between northern and southern Vietnam was among the most striking developments in the year that followed the French war. The Geneva accord provided for what it termed the 'regrouping' of military forces during the first 300 days of the agreement, as well as the movement of civilians who wished to live on one or the other side of the now divided Vietnam. As many as 100,000 southerners came north, largely DRV loyalists and party members who had fought against the French. The youngest were placed in training schools by the DRV with the possibility of infiltrating them back into the South at some later point. Even more dramatically, some 800,000 people made their way south. The majority were Vietnamese Catholics, whose initial fears about how they would be treated by the DRV in the post-war period were inflamed by propaganda campaigns that claimed 'the Virgin Mary is moving south'. Often entire northern Catholic villages and their priests moved south together, usually by sea in a refugee resettlement effort overseen by French and American officials as well as international voluntary associations. Some non-Catholics, including urban middle-class professional elites, also joined the exodus south.

The southern Vietnam these refugees came to in late 1954 and early 1955 was full of political unrest and uncertainty. If the DRV faced its own set of internal challenges in the period immediately following the French war, it had the advantage of more than eight years of experience in governance, albeit under difficult wartime conditions. By contrast, the embryonic South Vietnamese state had almost none as the Bao Dai-led government during the French war had largely been a fiction through which France continued its rule of Vietnam. Local authority was diffuse in the immediate post-war period. The leadership of the National Army, itself the creature of the French, sought to play a political role. The sectarian armies of the Cao Dai and Hao Hoa had become alienated from the French in the later years of the war and were not keen to relinquish power over the substantial territory they held in south-western Vietnam. The Binh Xuyen, a mafia-like group, dominated Saigon itself, controlling the police force in Saigon as well as much of the revenue flow into the city. Substantial portions of the southern economy remained in the hands of the French, who continued to own and operate expansive rubber, tea, and coffee plantations, and the overseas Chinese, who oversaw the lucrative rice export trade. A variety of smallish southern political parties made up of urban educated elites sought a role in whatever new government emerged. Despite the flow of many DRV and Communist Party supporters northward, as many as 15,000 partisans of the French war remained in the South. Some worked as members of local peace committees to promote the holding of reunification elections, while others organized and maintained political and paramilitary networks in urban and rural areas.

In constituting a new government in this fractious and fragmented environment, Bao Dai turned to Ngo Dinh Diem. The Ngo family, who had converted to Catholicism in the seventeenth century, had a long tradition of public service. Diem's father served at the highest levels of the Vietnamese imperial court, his eldest brother was a colonial provincial governor, and another brother was one of the first Vietnamese Catholic bishops. Diem himself became an official in the imperial administration and a province chief in his late twenties. He served as the interior minister in a reformist cabinet established by the then emperor Bao Dai in 1933, but earned a reputation for independence and resolute nationalism when he resigned in the face of French intransigence over real political and administrative reform. Diem remained active in court politics in Hue in the 1930s and under Japanese occupation during the Second World War, but he refused a position in the puppet government established by the Japanese in March 1945. To his reputation as a nationalist, Diem would soon add anti-communism. Invited by Ho Chi Minh to serve in a government of national reconciliation in early 1946, he refused. His antipathy towards communism was both ideological and personal; the Viet Minh had assassinated another of Diem's brothers in the early 1940s for what were called his repressive tendencies as a provincial official.

If his nationalist and anti-communist credentials contributed to his appointment as prime minister in June 1954, Diem was not a major player on the Vietnamese political stage during much of the French war at home, where his abilities were viewed somewhat sceptically. He spent most of the war years out of the country in Japan, Europe, and the United States. From 1950 to 1953 he lived in a Maryknoll seminary in New Jersey and came to impress a number of influential American political figures, including Cardinal Spellman, Senator John Kennedy, Supreme Court Justice William O. Douglas, and Senate Majority Leader Mike Mansfield. On his return to Paris in May 1953, he launched a somewhat quixotic campaign with his brother Ngo Dinh Nhu to lead the Bao Dai state. Only when French forces had collapsed at Dien Bien Phu and it became clear that American rather than French power would be more critical in the post-war era did Bao Dai turn to Diem, though his support for him would always be lukewarm. 'I knew that Diem had a difficult character,' Bao Dai wrote in his memoirs. 'I was also aware of his fanaticism and his messianic tendencies. But in that moment there was no better choice. . . . Washington would not spare him its support.'[2] Although the Eisenhower administration appears to have played no direct role in pressuring Bao Dai to appoint Diem, US Secretary of State John Foster Dulles was impressed by Diem. He told the French, 'the kind of thing Diem stands for is a necessary ingredient to success and we do not see it elsewhere'.[3] American diplomats in the field, and most French observers, were more critical of his appointment, with the US ambassador in Saigon noting the prevailing belief that 'Diem is a political dodo.'[4]

As he returned to Vietnam, Diem faced daunting obstacles in his efforts to construct an independent South Vietnamese state.

Government structures were in disarray, much of the countryside remained in the hands of the Cao Dai and Hoa Hao or communist forces loyal to the DRV, hundreds of thousands of Catholic refugees from the North needed to be resettled, French-trained officers hostile to his appointment dominated the military, and many local political elites in Saigon would become deeply disappointed by Diem's unwillingness to offer them a role in his regime. General Nguyen Van Hinh, who led the National Army, threatened a coup against Diem in the summer of 1954 and another in the fall, staved off largely by US pressure. But the most serious obstacle to his consolidation of power was the growing opposition of the Cao Dai, Hoa Hao, and Binh Xuyen to what they termed the 'Diem dictatorship'. In March 1955 these groups formed a united front and issued an ultimatum to Diem. Accustomed to running their own affairs, they were unwilling to surrender their power to Diem without gaining a prominent voice in his government. When Diem refused to address their demands, sect armies and the Binh Xuyen waged open warfare with government forces in the streets of Saigon.

As the political situation slid into bedlam, Diem remained intransigent about broadening his government, much to the distress of American diplomats in Saigon. Eisenhower's personal representative in Vietnam now reported to the president that Diem lacked 'the executive ability to head a government' and returned to Washington to urge his removal. In late April 1955 a reluctant Secretary of State Dulles sent a series of top-secret cables to the American embassies in Paris and Saigon withdrawing US support for Diem. Six hours after the cables had been sent, however, word reached Washington that new fighting had broken out in Saigon and might finally resolve the stand-off between Diem, the sects, and the Binh Xuyen. Dulles again wrote to Paris and Saigon, asking that they disregard his earlier messages for the moment. The week-long battle in Saigon was fierce, involving heavy artillery as well as small arms and mortars. House-to-house combat turned parts of the city into a free-fire zone and obliterated portions of some Saigon neighbourhoods. Several thousand of Diem's army and the Binh Xuyen were killed, along with 5,000 civilians; as many as 20,000 people were made homeless. Slowly Diem gained the upper hand, decisively defeating Binh Xuyen forces on 2 May 1955. Many Cao Dai and Hoa Hao forces rallied to Diem, but others retreated into the countryside, where some would form an uneasy alliance with the southern communist insurgency.[5]

Diem followed up his victory over the sects with an election to assure his predominance as the head of state. On 23 October 1955 voters in southern Vietnam arrived at the polls and were handed a ballot. They were asked to tear off the half representing the candidate of their choice. This was not the reunification election that had been promised by the Geneva accords. Ho Chi Minh was not on the ballot, but instead Bao Dai, whom Diem now sought to push aside. The left side of the ballot was framed in green, a traditionally unlucky colour, and contained a picture of a bloated Bao Dai in imperial garb above a text which read: 'I do not depose Bao Dai and do not recognize Ngo Dinh Diem as the Chief of State of Vietnam with the duty to organize a democratic government.' The right side of the ballot, bordered in an auspicious red colour, displayed a vibrant and smiling Diem walking among the Vietnamese people above the text 'I depose Bao Dai and recognize Ngo Dinh Diem as Chief of State of Vietnam with the duty to organize a democratic government.'[6] In Saigon's tightly censored media, supporters of the former emperor were unable make a public campaign on his behalf. Bao Dai himself remained at his home in Cannes while Diem campaigned vigorously in the weeks before the plebiscite. When the results of the election were announced, Diem had won an eyebrow-raising 98 per cent of the vote. In several areas, including Saigon, Diem's vote tallies exceeded the number of registered voters.

With Diem's victory in the sect crisis, and despite a bit of embarrassment over the tactics that had produced his lopsided election success, the United States gave Diem its warm official embrace. Officials of the Eisenhower administration and the American popular press began to call Diem 'a miracle man' and 'the Winston Churchill of Asia'. The South-East Asian Treaty

Organization was established under US auspices as a security alliance through which the Americans promised support against communist attacks in South-East Asia, including Vietnam. US support grew throughout the late 1950s, including more than $200 million per year in military and economic aid, which by 1960 accounted for as much as 70 per cent of South Vietnam's budget. More than $1 billion in subsidized US exports flowed into the South between 1956 and 1960 to ensure the availability of inexpensive consumer goods in urban areas. American military advisers retrained the Vietnamese army while civilian advisers offered help with governmental structure and economic development. The size of the US aid programme and its embassy in Saigon was second only to the American commitment to South Korea.[7] If this massive US support and aid undermined claims about Diem as an independent-minded patriot, American officials were primarily concerned about the larger cold war struggle against the Russians and the Chinese. They believed the Diem government offered a powerful and effective bulwark against international communism in South-East Asia.

Constructing Diem's Vietnam

Diem's bases of support within Vietnam were considerably slimmer than effusive contemporary American characterizations suggested. While the 1955 referendum was obviously rigged, the strong support Diem did have from several social groups within Vietnamese society allowed him to build a functioning state but one many Vietnamese would increasingly view as illegitimate. Large landowners with ties to the former French colonial regime quickly rallied to the Diem government. Their hold on land had been threatened during the French war, and many had fled to the cities. As absentee landlords, they were unable to collect rents from peasant tenants. After the war, many of them returned to the countryside and began to demand payments of both current and back rent. The remaining southern communists and supporters of the DRV urged peasants not to pay. But the Diem government championed elite interests, providing immediate redress and support to landlords while at the same time instituting new rural policies that severely limited any redistribution of land and placed large landowners and traditional elites back in charge of village governance. The Vietnamese Catholic community in the South, now much enlarged after the exodus from north to south following the Geneva accords, also put its strong support behind the Diem government. The new arrivals from the North were well provided for by Diem, and often allowed to settle on land already occupied by non-Catholic southerners. Although only about 10 per cent of the total population in the South, Vietnamese Catholics came to hold a much larger share of political power and filled many government posts after the departure of French colonial bureaucrats.

While landlords and Catholics provided critical support for the government, Diem relied on his family in ways many Vietnamese came to resent. His reclusive and semi-literate brother Can lived in Hue and built a clandestine network of supporters for the regime in central Vietnam, while another brother, Thuc, served as the archbishop of Hue. His brother Nhu oversaw an increasingly powerful security police, whose personnel were largely drawn from the somewhat shadowy Labour (Can Lao) Party he had formed to mobilize support for the regime. He also provided much of the eclectic ideological grounding for the regime. Like Diem, Nhu was a devout Catholic and staunch anti-communist. He was attracted to the ideas of the lay Catholic philosopher Emmanuel Mounier, who rejected liberal individualism and Marxist materialism in favour of the spiritual and social development of the total person. What Nhu and Diem called 'personalism' (*nhan vi*) became the guiding ideal behind the South Vietnamese state, though its actual meanings remained abstruse if not almost completely unintelligible for most Vietnamese.[8] Because Diem never married, Nhu's wife, Tran Le Xuan, served as a kind of unofficial 'first lady' for the regime. The daughter of a wealthy landlord, she became known as the notorious Madame Nhu for her oft-quoted reference to the Buddhist self-immolations of 1963 as 'barbecues'—'let them burn', she told one interviewer, 'and we shall clap our hands'—and her prudish efforts to combat vice in southern Vietnamese society, including prohibitions on public dancing.

The narrow social bases of the regime and its familial character, along with Diem's tendency towards obstinacy and an unwavering certainty in his own virtue and wisdom, produced an authoritarian government intolerant of dissent that was willing to suppress its opponents brutally. With the sect crisis and referendum behind him, Diem repudiated the reunification elections promised by the Geneva accords and turned his attention to what remained of southern communist forces and partisans of the DRV. He launched the Denounce the Communists (To Cong) campaign in 1955 to root out subversive elements throughout the southern countryside. Those arrested were sent to detention camps, where some were tortured and executed. Vietnamese communist sources report that 25,000 suspected communists were arrested and as many as 1,000 killed during the first year of the campaign. These efforts succeeded in severely weakening communist networks in the South, but the anti-communist campaign came at the cost of growing rural and urban opposition to the regime. Many of the arrests were arbitrary, with corrupt local officials using the law to carry out brutal private vendettas in which the innocent had to pay large bribes to avoid arrest.[9] One villager recalled that

the families who had relatives working for the resistance movement had to display black boards in front of their homes. Others were allowed to display white boards. All the persons who had black boards . . . lost their civil rights. During that period, families who did not want to display black boards had to present bribes to the hamlet chief.[10]

The heavy-handed censorship that accompanied the campaign, and numerous arbitrary arrests, also deepened suspicions of the Diem government by non-communist urban elites, as did his efforts in 1956 to shape a constitution that put most state power in Diem's hands and outlawed oppositional political parties.

Diem intensified his efforts to suppress southern Vietnamese communists, to whom the regime began to attach the pejorative label Viet Cong. The regime established what it called agrovilles (*khu tru mat*) in the southern countryside in an effort to defend villages from communist infiltration and control. The agrovilles were presented as a way of bringing development and the amenities of urban life to the rural south, but the real motivation was rural security and population control. Peasants were relocated into new settlement areas of about 2 square kilometres and forced to provide the labour for their construction. This often meant the villagers had to dismantle current homes near their rice fields and build new ones in the agroville much farther from their fields. Existing fields were sometimes dug up to create new networks of transport canals, meaning some peasant families lost their livelihoods. The agrovilles were easier than traditional villages for the government to defend but alienated many peasants, a number of whom came to support the southern communists as a result of their experience in them.[11]

Diem also rapidly expanded the state's military forces, the Army of the Republic of Vietnam (ARVN). His forces received extensive training and substantial numbers of weapons from US military advisers. Divisions did emerge between Diem and his American advisers over the organization of the Vietnamese military. The Americans, drawing on recent US combat experience in the Korean war, urged the development of a large conventional army with heavily armed divisions to defend against an attack from the North by the DRV. Many of Diem's generals sought a leaner fighting force, including the development of special forces and local infantry battalions that could conduct anti-guerrilla and civic action operations. Diem, who ignored most US advice that went against his own inclinations, uncharacteristically bowed to American pressure, though ARVN forces were augmented by the creation of local paramilitary militias such as the Self-Defence Corps (Ton Doan Dan Ve), Youth for the Defence of the Countryside (Than Hein Van Ve Huong Thon), and the Republican Youth (Than Nien Cong Hoa). The establishment of the latter was tied to broader efforts by Diem's brother Nhu to create forces loyal to the regime rather than the state. A rapidly expanding ARVN was staffed in part by volunteers, but the Diem regime increasingly turned to conscription and longer tours of duty, with drafted soldiers accounting for as much as 65 per cent of the army's total troop levels. Beginning in 1957, this large American-trained fighting force began a series of campaigns to occupy strongholds of the southern communists in the north-central and north-western portion of the Mekong delta.[12]

In May 1959 the Diem government sharply increased its political repression with the issuing of the draconian Public Law 10/59. The law dramatically widened the meaning of political crimes to virtually any form of political opposition, which was now equated with communism and treason. Roving tribunals circulated throughout the countryside to try, convict, and execute those accused of subversion. Public Law 10/59 also increased the power of local officials, who could summarily imprison for life or put to death anyone they designated as a 'communist' opponent of the regime. Corrupt officials intensified the practices of bribery that had become common under the earlier Denounce the Communists campaign. The repression that accompanied Law 10/59 did severely curtail the activities of communist activists. The size of the Communist Party in the South declined to as few as 5,000 members by the end of 1959. Threats of life imprisonment and execution instilled real fear among peasants about the stakes involved in opposing the government. But the extreme measures of the Diem regime under Law 10/59 tended to embitter many urban and rural peoples, who questioned the legitimacy of a government whose claim to rule appeared more and more to rest on force.[13]

In April 1960 a group of leading southern moderate political figures issued a manifesto of grievances to Diem. They complained that 'continuous arrests fill the jails and prisons to the rafters', the government and military was shaped by 'favouritism based on family connections', and 'public opinion and the press are reduced to silence'. None of the signatories were especially sympathetic to the communist movement and their tone was respectful of Diem; some in fact had earlier served in the Diem government. The manifesto did not ask Diem to resign but warned that in the absence of reform the 'truth shall burst forth in irresistible waves of hatred on the part of a people subjected for a long time to terrible suffering'.[14] Middle-class professionals in Saigon, including doctors, lawyers, accountants, teachers, and lower-level government functionaries, increasingly shared their views. Like those who signed the manifesto, they objected to Diem's reliance on his family and Catholics to run the most important posts in government, were concerned about arbitrary limits on freedom of expression, and opposed the lack of protection for the rights of the accused in Law 10/59. These middle-class families also resented their sons being drafted and killed in Diem's army for a regime in which they had little confidence and which marginalized their own voices.

Diem chose to ignore these pleas for a more open political process, clamping down even further on political dissent and closing most opposition newspapers. Urban discontent with the practices of the regime simmered, and in November 1960 a group of prominent army officers led several ARVN battalions in an attack on government installations in and around Saigon. They, too, called not for Diem's resignation but instead for political reform. Typically, Diem reacted with force, sending many of the insurgent leaders into exile or jail. For good measure, he imprisoned all those who had signed the April reformist manifesto.[15] The limits to the expression of popular dissent, beyond clandestine communist organizing, were becoming ever narrower in southern Vietnam.

The Path to Revolution

As Ngo Dinh Diem worked to consolidate his power and control over the state and society in the late 1950s, southern communists and the leadership in the DRV watched with mounting alarm. By the end of 1960 they endorsed armed struggle in the South and had put in a place a new structure for the southern communist insurgency. But these decisions came slowly and were marked by discord among and between northern and southern communists and their allies in Moscow and Beijing.

When the French war came to an end, the DRV was unsure if the elections promised in the Geneva accords would actually come about. Although aware of the vagaries of the post-war situation, Ho

Chi Minh among others reportedly thought the elections would take place. Although some were more sceptical, all of the top leadership believed that, with Ho's popularity and the Democratic Republic's defeat of the French at Dien Bien Phu, they were certain of victory. But even after Diem had repudiated the Geneva-mandated election processes, much of the northern leadership continued to advocate a peaceful, if protracted, struggle for national reunification. As one party source put it: 'Our goal, then, was not to overthrow the enemy government . . . but to force it, by means of struggle, to improve social welfare and carry out freedom and democracy. In this way the enemy administration would be changed gradually, and favourable conditions for the realization of independence . . . would come about.'[16]

Part of these calculations reflected post-war uncertainties and dislocations in the North, including the problems of economic reconstruction and the political and social troubles produced by the failed land reform campaign. Northern reticence also reflected the continuing desire to move ahead with the building of socialism in the North, especially the collectivization of agriculture, and the need to modernize the army before returning to war. The inclination to go slow was reinforced by Soviet and Chinese policy at the Geneva conference. In pushing the Vietnamese to agree to a negotiated settlement, the Soviet Union and China made clear that, if war broke out again, the DRV might have to fight without their assistance.

Many southerners who supported the DRV during the French war saw things somewhat differently. They came from a variety of class backgrounds and political orientations. Some were communists who had been keen not only to fight the French but also to realize a full-scale socialist transformation of all Vietnamese society. Others were drawn to the DRV out of simple patriotism. Many wanted to see political and social reform in the post-war period but in less radical forms than were emerging in the North. Diem's repression in the mid- to late 1950s not only decimated the communist leadership in the South, but it embittered moderates who had hoped to find a place in the Diem government and were shut out of political life. Southern peasants who had supported the DRV during the French war and remained inclined towards the southern communist movement in its aftermath were both increasingly fearful of the Diem regime and embittered by its rural policies. A growing sense emerged among the embattled regional and local communist leadership in the South that peaceful political struggle needed to be augmented by the use of force.

If many party leaders in the North continued to believe that socialist reconstruction and full consolidation of the DRV's authority in northern Vietnam should come before armed struggle in the South, influential voices were beginning to take up the cause for a more forceful response to the actions of the Diem government. Most important among them was Le Duan. Born in central Vietnam and a party member since 1930, he was imprisoned by the French during much of the 1930s and the Second World War period for his political activities. By the time of the French war he was a member of the party's Central Committee and closely involved in the political and military struggle against the French in the South, serving as the deputy director of the Central Office for Southern Vietnam (COSVN). He became a vigorous spokesperson in the early post-war period for the rapid reunification of Vietnam under communist control. In the winter of 1955–6, as Diem launched his Denounce the Communists campaign, Le Duan started to warn northern party leaders that increased use of armed violence might be required to overthrow the Diem government and reunify southern Vietnam with the North.[17] Refugees from the South who came north after the Geneva accords and began to hold significant party and governmental positions also put pressure on the DRV to come to the aid of their compatriots who remained in the South. While not all southern communists agreed with Le Duan and the regroupees, many did and took matters into their own hands. Some local southern militias were formed in the Mekong delta and went on the attack against Diem's military forces. Campaigns of terror against local and provincial Diem officials were also initiated.[18]

The leadership of the DRV, however, continued to hesitate over its policy towards southern Vietnam. Their reticence was reinforced by a shift in the Soviet Union's foreign policy in January 1956, when the new leader, Nikita Khrushchev, announced a policy of 'peaceful coexistence', which downplayed violent class struggle in favour of more peaceful transitions to socialism. Soviet diplomats made clear to the Vietnamese that they saw this new policy as applicable to the post-Geneva situation in Vietnam. Party leaders in Hanoi were forced to navigate between these Soviet pressures and the deteriorating situation on the ground in the South. They began to acknowledge that armed struggle might be necessary in the future, calling for the consolidation of local militias and the development of revolutionary base areas, but continued to insist that for the moment the primary means of struggle should remain political to protect and further socialist advances in the North. In the summer of 1956 Le Duan sought to spark a reconsideration of northern policy by writing *The Path to Revolution in the South* (*Duong Loi Cach Mang Mein Nam*). Although his report supported the existing policy of political struggle, Le Duan advocated what he termed a more activist 'revolutionary war' that would allow southern cadres to protect themselves against Diem's repression. His position received some support from the DRV's allies in China, who were willing to encourage low-level armed struggle but told the Vietnamese that reunification could be a decade or more away. Soviet insistence on restricting revolutionary activities in the South and the Democratic Republic's own focus on the northern economy in 1956, however, made northern party leaders wary of any dramatic shift in southern policy.[19]

Diem's increasingly draconian repression in the late 1950s and its crippling effects on the southern insurgency gradually pushed the North towards armed struggle. Le Duan, who had left the South in 1957 to become the acting general secretary of the Communist Party in Hanoi, played a critical role in fostering this important shift. So too did southern party activists, who, despite Diem's anti-communist campaigns, worked to increase their military presence in the delta and the strategically important central highlands, launching attacks on district capitals and a US military base in mid-1958. Le Duan made a secret visit to southern Vietnam in late 1958 and returned to Hanoi to report that policy in the South required urgent clarification, noting the decline in party numbers as a result of Diem's policies and the demoralization of southern communist forces. More hopefully, he suggested, those same policies that had brought heightened peasant dissatisfaction with the Diem government had also begun to produce favourable revolutionary conditions in the countryside.

At the Fifteenth Plenum of the Vietnamese Communist Party in January 1959, the decision to allow the use of force in southern Vietnam was finally made. 'The fundamental path of development for the revolution in South Vietnam', the final plenum resolution stated, 'is that of violent struggle.' Some ambiguity about strategy remained: 'political struggle will be the main form', the resolution continued, 'but because the enemy is determined to drown in revolutionary blood . . . it will be necessary to a certain extent to adopt methods of self-defense and armed propaganda struggle to assist the political struggle'.[20] But if the North continued to express rhetorical qualms about the parameters of armed struggle, increasingly the preconditions for it were being put into place in ways that would powerfully challenge the Diem government. The construction of what became the Ho Chi Minh Trail began in the May 1959 to provide a route to transport weapons and supplies, and later troops, from north to south along the mountainous Vietnamese–Lao border. The first equipment moved down the Trail in late 1959, along with some of the southern regroupees who had been sent north after Geneva.

Beginning in the summer of 1959 and accelerating in the winter of 1959–60, local communist groups initiated a series of what were called 'concerted uprisings' (*dong khoi*) in central and southern Vietnam, taking control of portions of several districts in the central highlands and the Mekong delta.[21] As evening fell on 17 January 1960, the sounds of gongs and wooden bells began to echo in the villages of Ben Tre province in the Mekong delta of southern Vietnam. During more peaceful times in the delta, these sounds often emanated from village Buddhist temples in a call to prayer. That night the intensifying sounds of gongs and bells came at the instruction of the southern insurgency as the signal for local people to rise up against the Diem government and take control of their villages from 'rapacious' landowners and 'corrupt' local officials. Nguyen Thi Dinh, a leader of the uprising, remembers the evening like this: 'The people immediately tore up the flags and burned the plaques bearing their house numbers and family registers. On the roads, the villagers cut down trees to erect barriers and block the movement of the enemy . . . It was a night of terrifying thunder and lightning striking the enemy on their heads.'[22] The Ben Tre uprising was followed by others elsewhere in the delta. In some cases, such as Ben Tre, the Diem government was able to restore order. But in other provinces the uprisings were not as easily suppressed, adding to the territory and population controlled by the southern communists.

Over the next year efforts were made to unify the scattered military forces of the insurgency, which grew from 2,000 in 1959 to as many as 10,000 in early 1961, and put them under a central command. The new military organization was given the name the People's Liberation Armed Forces (Quan Do Nhan Dan Giai Phong, PLAF). Its structure followed the organization patterns of the DRV army in the French war, with local self-defence forces who had limited training and weapons defending individual villages, full-time regional guerrilla forces who were better armed and under district commanders, and elite uniformed main force units organized into battalions. The PLAF engaged Diem's forces with increasing success in the early 1960s. By mid-1961 the PLAF had pushed the ARVN out of much of the Mekong delta and were on the move in provinces west and north of Saigon. Only the south-central coastal area remained under firm ARVN control.[23]

The Rise of the National Liberation Front

Military efforts were accompanied by even more substantial plans to develop the political dimension of the struggle in the South. The

DRV and the southern insurgency drew on the principles guiding the broad-based Viet Minh front in the August Revolution of 1945 and the French war, including the ideas of all-class nationalism and more moderate approaches to the social and economic transformation of rural and urban life, to found the National Liberation Front of South Vietnam (Mat Ran Dan Toc Giai Phong Mein Nam Viet Nam, NLF) on 20 December 1960. Within a year the NLF had as many as 200,000 supporters in the South. The structure of the NLF is best seen as a series of concentric circles that sought to bring together a variety of progressive forces in southern society. At the centre was the COSVN, which made political and military policy along with the party and state leadership in Hanoi. The next ring oversaw the political activities of the Front. Although not formalized until 1969 as the Provisional Revolutionary Government (PRG), this dimension of the Front was immediately active and included leaders from the urban middle classes who were increasingly discontented by Diem policies, as well as radicals who had supported the DRV during the French war.

Moving outward from the centre were rank-and-file NLF cadres, usually young males, though sometimes women as well. In the outermost ring were a host of mass organizations that supported the Front. The most public face of the Front, they included associations of peasants, workers, writers, youth, students, women, Buddhists, Catholics, and ethnic minorities from the central highlands. These mass organizations, especially the Farmer and Youth Liberation associations, were also training grounds to identify those with the skill and fervour to make deeper commitments to political and military revolutionary struggle. The Women's Liberation Association was among the largest of the mass organizations, with as many as 1 million members by 1965, and became a central element in NLF strategies and tactics. Colloquially termed soldiers with long hair (*doi quan toc dai*), women in rural areas were active in combat operations only in limited cases. More often they were used to provide intelligence, communication, and support for male political cadres and PLAF forces.[24]

By some estimates the NLF controlled as much as half the population in southern Vietnam by 1963. The reasons so many people came to support the Front so rapidly varied. For many peasants, the Diem government failed to assure a minimal level of well-being and safety for their families while the NLF appeared to do so. Middle, poor, and landless peasants (*trung*, *ban*, and *co nong*) found little to like in Diem's land reform efforts. In deference to the regime's landlord (*dia chu*) base of support, it only redistributed land when holdings exceeded 250 acres, forced those who received land to pay for it, and tolerated land rents at 25 to 40 per cent of output. By contrast the NLF's land reform programme avoided the excesses of the northern land reform in the mid-1950s and returned to the moderate DRV policies of the 1940s. It set maximum rents at 15 per cent, limited total landholding to 15 acres, and redistributed land at a nominal cost. Similarly, the Diem government's regressive tax policy protected wealthy interests while the NLF's more progressive taxation, a return to earlier norms based on the ability to pay, eased the burden on rural peasants.[25]

The differences were immediately apparent, with peasants in NLF-controlled areas enjoying incomes two to three times higher than their counterparts in territory dominated by the Diem government. As one central Vietnamese villager recalled of the period:

The Liberation had answers for all the most important problems that we all knew. They had an answer about land reform, which was they would give land to the poor people. They had an answer about high taxes. They said that the Liberation would spend the taxes only for the people and would collect them without corruption. They also said that they would help the poor, and this was something else that made them popular, because many people in the village were very poor.[26]

The failure of Diem policies in the countryside and the ways in which they contributed to NLF rural support emerged most sharply in the regime's efforts to build more than 8,000 strategic hamlets (*ap chien luoc*), beginning in 1962. They were designed to create new villages the NLF could not infiltrate. Similar to the agroville project that preceded them, strategic hamlets went a step further in providing fortifications aimed to keep the Front out. Barbed wire and bamboo stakes surrounded the hamlets, with residents trained and armed for self-defence. As they had with the agrovilles, peasants resented being forced to build their new homes and village amenities with their own labour and very limited funds. Like the agrovilles, some strategic hamlets were located far from existing rice fields. The long walk to the family fields, often much further than from their original village, made everyday life more difficult; moreover, those who did not get home in time at night could be locked out. Nor was the programme successful in its goal of limiting NLF influence in villages. The ideas that shaped the strategic hamlets were borrowed from efforts to defeat a communist insurgency in Malaya in the 1950s. The Malay Communist Party consisted mainly of ethnic Chinese, which sometimes made it easier to differentiate them from ethnic Malays by sight. This kind of visual discernment was impossible in the more ethnically homogenous southern Vietnam, and in any event many villagers were willing to shield the identity of NLF partisans from the government. In the end, the Front was able to infiltrate as many as 80 per cent of the strategic hamlets constructed by the government.[27]

If the NLF offered more positive incentives to gain the support of rural peoples than did the Diem regime, it also utilized terror more effectively. The Front targeted the most competent and the most corrupt local officials of the Diem government, killing some 6,000 officials in the early 1960s. As many as 25,000 civilians were also murdered in this period, suggesting that the NLF did not always carefully discriminate between its targets. But once in control of an area, the Front generally did significantly reduce its attacks on civilians. NLF assassinations fell by 80 per cent between 1961 and 1965 as their control over rural southern Vietnam increased. At the same time, through Public Law 10/59 and more widespread authoritarian repression, the Diem government's use of terror against civilians was increasing and becoming ever more arbitrary.[28] In terms of both physical and economic well-being, many peasants saw the NLF not only as allowing them to get on with their lives but as providing the opportunity to improve them.

Economic and material calculations were not the sole motive for those who came to support the NLF. For some, the commitment to the Front was shaped by revolutionary nationalism as they saw it as a part of the longer struggle for national independence beginning with the August Revolution and the French war. The NLF was quick to reinforce these sensibilities, labelling the Diem government as the My-Diem regime. The 'My' in this equation referred to the United States, drawing attention to Diem's American backing and equating 'American imperialism' (de quoc My) with French colonialism in an extension of the sacred-war narrative the DRV had popularized during the French war. Illustrative of those who saw the struggle this way was Nguyen Thi Dinh, one of the leaders of the Ben Tre uprising in 1960, whose family had fought for the DRV against the French. Her family had been active in anti-colonial agitation since the 1930s and her brother had been arrested and tortured by the French. As she wrote in her memoirs, 'I began to understand that making a revolution was a good thing, since my brother continued to do it even though he had been jailed and beaten up for it.'[29] Nguyen Thi Dinh, a native southerner, was arrested and imprisoned by the French for three years during the Second World War, served as a Viet Minh organizer in the French war, became a rural organizer for the southern insurgency in the Diem years, and was a leading member of the PRG during the America war.

Others were attracted to the Front's emphasis on social justice even if they were not fully committed to the socialist internationalism of the DRV. Truong Nhu Tang, the son of a wealthy Saigon business family who joined the NLF leadership in the South, is one example of an urban professional alienated by Diem policies who saw the Front as a means towards progressive reform.[30] The Front's effective organizational and mobilizational techniques also help to account for those who were drawn into the movement. The NLF was especially skilled at drawing on ties of kin and family to build its rural and urban networks, as Nguyen Thi Dinh's own personal history suggests. Its relatively loose structure and attention to kinship relations allowed the NLF, through both positive and coercive appeals, to convince civilians to hide insurgents from government searches, to provide food and intelligence, and to get round official government bans on filling prescriptions for essential antibiotics and other medicines.

Young people provided the Front much of its strength in urban and rural areas. Joining the NLF as political cadres provided a short cut to power and prestige for youth in a society where age and wealth was usually determinative of individual and familial social status. In fact, for younger rural people in the late 1950s and early 1960s, the line between town and country increasingly blurred. Displacements under the French war in the Mekong delta—losing a father, a mother, husband, or a wife—led many young people to seek to make their own way in a changing world. Some left their villages for district or provincial cities, or for Saigon, to attend school, work in markets and the petty trades, or become servants in middle-class households. Urban sojourns were often temporary, but, as one scholar recently argued, exposure 'to the different costumes and gestures, sights and smells, work regimes and leisure patterns in the city served as ... reminders that other ways of living were possible. Schooling in the contingency of social arrangements did not make revolution inevitable, but it did help to enlarge the consciousness of a nomadic peasantry.'[31] When NLF land and social policies in the early 1960s began to challenge rural hierarchies that had become ossified under the Diem regime, they helped to launch a wider revolutionary debate across Mekong delta villages and cities about the nature of the southern political, economic, and social order. Youthful village-based militants were among the most engaged in these debates, and ultimately many chose to join the Front.

On the military side, NLF forces had increasing success in engaging Diem's army and came to control as much as three-quarters of the territory of southern Vietnam by the end of 1963. Perhaps the most dramatic NLF victory was the battle of Ap Bac in early 1963. PLAF forces had moved into Ap Bac, a village in the Mekong delta near the provincial capital of My Tho, in December 1962. Aware of these troop movements, Diem's ARVN went on the attack on 2 January 1963. But despite as much as a four to one advantage over the PLAF in troop strength and the presence of substantial American helicopter support, they suffered a huge defeat, with more than 450 ARVN soldiers killed and wounded by PLAF forces. American military advisers to the ARVN division at Ap Bac were both admiring of PLAF military prowess and sharply critical of the behaviour of Diem's officers and troops during the battle, especially of their reluctance to engage the PLAF forces fully. ARVN forces would later reoccupy Ap Bac and drive out the NLF insurgents, but the battle revealed the emerging strength of the Front's military capabilities, which allowed it to inflict heavy losses on the ARVN's numerically larger and technologically superior military force. After the battle of Ap Bac, the PLAF launched successful attacks in four additional Mekong delta provinces and increased the amount of territory under NLF control in other provinces because of tactical retreats by ARVN forces.[32]

Despite the escalating popular support for the NLF against the Diem regime and its military victories, internal tensions and uncertainties in the movement at the highest levels revealed its complicated relationship to the Communist Party in the North and the DRV state. At the height of the American war in Vietnam, the official US view saw the NLF as a tool of the northern Vietnamese communists. The American anti-war movement made almost the opposite case, calling the Front a southern grassroots movement. Neither view captured the complexities of relations between the NLF and the North. Without question, the Front had deep southern roots and spoke to profound discontent with the political and social order under Ngo Dinh Diem. It also quickly became dominated by Hanoi, a role that the North went to great pains to hide. For many in the southern movement who saw the NLF as a continuation of the larger struggle for Vietnamese independence and had given their allegiance to the DRV in the French war, this was not a particular problem. But for others it would be.

The very difficulties of getting the DRV to accelerate its support of the southern insurgency in the late 1950s, and the perception that it favoured northern interests over those of the South, introduced tensions into the relationship. Some in the Front leadership, like Truong Nhu Tang, who were more interested in individual justice than collectivist social revolution were quickly at odds with what they saw as more doctrinaire DRV cadres sent down from the North to advise them. On the ground in the village, local NLF cadres and supporters were not always of one mind on policy, with some believing revolutionary rural change could go further and others in favour of more moderate socio-economic reform. But whatever the differences within the Front and between it and the DRV—and they would continue to increase as the American war wore on and war-weariness emerged on all sides—the NLF provided a viable and popular means not only to challenge the Diem government but also to imagine an alternative state and society for southern Vietnam.

The Buddhist Crisis

The NLF channelled much but not all of popular discontent with the Diem government in the early 1960s. Thich Quang Duc's dramatic self-immolation in June 1963 represented another dimension of opposition to what many southerners saw as the authoritarian and dictatorial nature of the Ngo Dinh Diem regime. In fact it was the Buddhist protests of 1963 rather than the NLF that brought about the fall of the Diem government, an event marked by the grisly violence of the murder of Diem and his brother Nhu.

The Buddhist protest movement initially centred on calls for religious freedom. It began in May 1963 in a dispute over flags when Buddhists in Hue hung flags on homes and temples to honour the birth of the Buddha. The deputy chief of security for the province insisted they be taken down. Diem had passed a law in the late 1950s that decreed the South Vietnamese flag should always be larger and fly higher than other flags. The law was rarely enforced, and in fact earlier that spring the Vatican flag had flown as big and high as the South Vietnamese flag for ceremonies in Hue to mark the ordination of Diem's brother as archbishop. The predominantly Buddhist population of Hue, who had viewed the

Catholic cast of Diem's government with some suspicion, insisted on their right to fly the Buddhist flag as the Vatican flag had been flown, sending monks and laymen into the street on 8 May to make their protestations. The government's representatives in Hue ordered the police to fire on the protesters, who included older people and children. Nine people were killed, two of whom were children.

Further street protests brought demands not only to fly the Buddhist flag but for legal equality between Catholics and Buddhists, compensation to families of the victims, and an end to arbitrary arrests. Although Diem reluctantly agreed to pay compensation, tensions in Hue remained high. In late May and early June thousands of Buddhist protesters took to the streets in Hue. They were met by government attacks that used tear gas and dogs to scatter the demonstrators. As protest continued, Diem put Hue under martial law and a dusk-to-dawn curfew. Slowly street protests began to emerge in Saigon centred on Xa Loi temple, the most important Buddhist pagoda in the city. They accelerated in the wake of Thich Quang Duc's self-immolation, the first of what would be six self-immolations by Buddhist monks and nuns in the following weeks and months.[33]

Diem insisted that the Buddhist protests were the work of the NLF, but this broad-based and diffuse movement was not the creature of the southern communist insurgency. Buddhist leaders had been singled out as early as the 1950s by the Viet Minh as reformist monks antithetical to the goals of the party.[34] The protests are more accurately seen as a part of the larger twentieth-century revival of Vietnamese Buddhism, in which Vietnam's future was believed to rest in the revitalization of its Buddhist heritage. Moreover, as the movement gained momentum, it was transformed from a solely Buddhist protest to a larger campaign against Diem, led by discontented members of Saigon's middle class. At first it was high school and university students who led these wider protests. But when the government threatened marchers with military force, some soldiers, whose brothers and sisters were taking part in the protests, also began to participate, as did their grandfathers and grandmothers.

Diem remained unmoved as protests continued throughout the summer of 1963. But in late August he sent in military forces armed with rifles, machine guns, grenades, and tear gas to raid Xa Loi temple, arresting scores of monks, nuns, and lay people. Government troops and police stormed major temples in Hue. These raids were initially fought off by monks and nuns, but they were eventually overrun. In the end, about 1,400 were killed. Diem banned public gatherings and put the entire country under martial law. Defying bans on public protest, student unrest at universities and high schools in Saigon and Hue swelled. Diem responded by arresting students and eventually shutting down most universities and high schools. South Vietnam had fallen into political crisis.[35]

The Buddhist protests and the government's response had a powerful impact on Diem's patrons in the United States. When he came into office in 1961, President John F. Kennedy deepened the commitment of the Eisenhower administration to the Diem regime. Like Eisenhower, Kennedy saw Vietnam as a critical link in cold war efforts by the United States to contain and combat international communism. Concerned about NLF military advances and the faltering of American nation-building project in southern Vietnam, Kennedy rejected the advice of some of his advisers to commit American ground troops but did significantly increase the number of US military advisers in Vietnam from 3,200 in late 1961 to more than 23,000 in 1963. These advisers were directly involved in ARVN combat operations, flying Diem's troops into battle zones, as they did at the battle of Ap Bac, and advising on tactics and strategy in the field. Before the Buddhist protests began, some Kennedy administration advisers in the US Department of State had begun to doubt if Diem was really up to the task of defeating the southern communist insurgency, given NLF gains on the ground in 1962 and 1963. Diem's response to the Buddhist protest heightened their disenchantment with him, though top-level officials within the Department of Defense and Central Intelligence Agency (CIA) at first continued to support him.

As the Buddhist protests unfolded in the spring and summer of 1963 and images of the self-immolations circulated widely in the American and international press, Kennedy tried to put pressure on Diem to moderate his responses to Buddhists and their allies. But Diem, who had never been especially keen to listen to the advice of his American supporters, had just received another big instalment of US aid and saw himself as free to defy Kennedy's request. Unfavourable US attitudes to Diem intensified after the late August attacks on temples in Saigon and Hue, with a growing sense that the American anti-communist crusade in southern Vietnam would fail if Diem were not replaced. The Kennedy administration signalled its changing sensibilities by sending a new ambassador to Saigon, Henry Cabot Lodge, who was deeply critical of Diem's policies. By October, Lodge and several local CIA operatives were in contact with dissident generals in Diem's army, who were making plans for a coup. With some reluctance Kennedy gave his support to the coup at the end of the month. On 1 November 1963 anti-Diem elements in the army seized control of the government throughout southern Vietnam and stormed the presidential palace in Saigon. Diem and his brother Nhu fled to a nearby Catholic church to hide after Lodge refused to guarantee their personal safety. Captured by the leaders of the coup, Diem and Nhu were put in the back of an armoured car and shot dead.[36]

Decisions for War

The American expectation that Diem's removal would dramatically shift the political situation in southern Vietnam was an illusion. In many ways, the fall of the Diem government only made the situation in the South worse. Between 1963 and 1965 there were twelve different governments in the South as coup followed coup. The NLF took full advantage of this political instability to make further gains in territory and popular support. But the future path of the war in the wake of Diem's death remained unclear to the central protagonists.

In December 1963 the leadership in Hanoi debated the way forward at the Ninth Plenum of the party's Central Committee. There was now widespread agreement that some form of armed struggle was critical to achieving NLF victory in the South but vigorous disagreement about the nature of that military effort. Some favoured the use of regular troops from the People's Army of Vietnam (PAVN), the North's military force, to hasten the final collapse of the southern regime. Others argued for a more rapid build-up of the PLAF, the NLF's military force, which they believed should continue to take the lead in military efforts aimed at a general uprising in the South. These debates reflected uncertainties over future US intentions. With the assassination of John F. Kennedy in November 1963, party leaders were unsure whether President Lyndon B. Johnson would maintain Kennedy's policies of using American military forces in southern Vietnam primarily as advisers or introduce US combat troops to fight directly against the Vietnamese.[37]

Fears of an expanded US military presence were compounded by unease over heightened Sino-Soviet tensions and their impact on any decision to expand the war effort. The relationship between the Soviet Union and China deteriorated in the late 1950s over a series of ideological, political, and economic issues. Mao Zedong strongly objected to Khrushchev's project of de-Stalinization, arguing that it marked a revisionist capitalist restoration in the Soviet Union. Khrushchev's withdrawal of Soviet experts from China, his decision to reduce Soviet assistance and to support India in the Chinese–Indian border conflict of 1962, and his refusal to share nuclear secrets with China deepened these strains. By 1963 the split between the Soviets and Chinese brought open public criticism of each other's policies, part of which focused on support for revolutionary nationalist movements. The Chinese insisted that the centre of world revolution had shifted from Moscow to Beijing; the Soviets thought otherwise. As the Sino-Soviet dispute escalated, Moscow continued to advocate peaceful coexistence and remained as reluctant as it had been at the 1954 Geneva conference to support armed struggle in Vietnam. Soviet support in 1957 for the admission of both the DRV and the Diem government into the United Nations, much to the surprise and consternation of the Democratic Republic's leadership, was one sign of Soviet aversion to war in Vietnam. Vietnamese party leaders in 1963 were fully aware that a decision to introduce PAVN troops into the South risked a breach with Moscow.[38]

The escalating polemics of the Sino-Soviet dispute and a shifting domestic political climate did prompt a gradual change in Chinese policy towards Vietnam. At Geneva and in its immediate aftermath the Chinese had cautioned against further war, a sentiment that reflected the Chinese desire to focus on domestic politics at the end of the Korean war, worries about US intervention in Vietnam, and their diplomatic embrace of peaceful coexistence. Even as late as 1961, the Chinese made clear they favoured political rather than military struggle in southern Vietnam, though they took no active steps to oppose the acceleration of a militarized southern resistance, preoccupied in part by the mass starvation that followed Mao's disastrous Great Leap Forward policies at home. As domestic conditions improved in late 1962 and early 1963, Mao renewed his emphasis on class struggle and radical politics in the domestic arena and launched a series of very public attacks on Soviet 'revisionism', in which he called for confrontation short of war with the United States to advance the cause of global revolution. In May 1963 Chinese officials told Ho Chi Minh: 'We are standing by your side, and if war breaks out, you can regard China as your rear.' By December 1963 a Chinese delegation presented the Vietnamese with plans for assisting in the construction of defence works and naval bases in the North. The Chinese were not calling for full-scale war, which they feared might draw in the United States, but their support of guerrilla warfare along with heightened political struggle was clear.[39]

Prior to the Ninth Plenum, the DRV had tried to stand apart from the growing Sino-Soviet rift. To an extent the decisions of the plenum reflected a continuation of that delicate balancing act.

It rejected the use of PAVN troops in the South, sensitive to Moscow's likely opposition to such a policy and an American military escalation. But the plenum did not back away from armed struggle, calling for increased material aid from the North and intensified use of an expanded PLAF to achieve military and political victory in the South. If the Ninth Plenum brought determination to unite Vietnam by force, it also exposed internal divisions within the party and state, which deepened as the American war in Vietnam accelerated. One plenum resolution condemned 'revisionism'. While not mentioning the Soviet Union by name, it signalled growing tensions with Moscow and sympathy with Chinese ideological views.[40]

The condemnation of revisionism also brought significant changes in the northern Vietnamese domestic political scene. Intellectuals who had studied in the Soviet Union and eastern Europe became the primary victims of an anti-revisionist campaign in early 1964. Accused of being influenced by the same 'modern revisionism' Mao argued had overcome the Soviet Union, many were removed from government jobs and party positions, and jailed or put under house arrest. Ho Chi Minh's primacy within the top leadership shifted too. In a Christmas 1963 visit to the Soviet embassy in Hanoi, he announced his retirement from day-to-day political affairs. From then on, Ho's role was increasingly as an icon of the Vietnamese revolutionary state, while Le Duan emerged at the forefront of party and state power and decision-making in the North.[41]

In the wake of the new aggressive military strategy adopted at the Ninth Plenum, NLF military forces gained ground throughout the South in 1964, with a stable liberated zone emerging in large segments of central Vietnam and the Mekong delta. Only areas around major cities remained securely under the control of the Saigon government, and even there the southern insurgency was making inroads. In the spring and summer of 1964 the DRV began to mobilize its own forces for war, transforming the Ho Chi Minh Trail into a transportation network capable of handling large trucks and preparing PAVN units for infiltration into Vietnam. With increased northern material support, the PLAF grew to forty-five main force battalions, complemented by 35,000 guerrilla fighters and some 80,000 irregular troops.[42]

The formation of a new government in Saigon under ARVN general Nguyen Khanh in early 1964 to replace an ineffective junta did little to slow NLF advances. Continuing instability sharply eroded the Khanh government's already weak authority in the rural south and produced near-anarchy in Saigon and other major cities. ARVN losses increased from 1,000 a month in January 1964 to 3,000 in December. Spiralling ARVN desertion undermined the government's legitimacy, as did massive street protests after Khanh assumed almost dictatorial powers in August. Khanh was briefly overthrown by ARVN officers jockeying for power, and then returned to power in an uneasy alliance with younger army officers. By the fall of 1964 the legitimacy of the South Vietnamese government was in shambles.[43]

For American policy makers in the Johnson administration, the inability of the post-Diem governments to combat the southern insurgency and form a stable political state was deeply disturbing. Although aware that the Sino-Soviet split challenged long-standing cold war assumptions about a monolithic international communist movement, President Johnson continued to see holding the line in Vietnam as central to US foreign policy. But beyond increased military and economic aid Johnson was hesitant to shift radically the American military effort in Vietnam throughout much of 1964, largely out of concern about the impact escalation might have on his presidential campaign and his ambitious Great Society legislative agenda, which sought to provide sweeping social welfare protections at home. He did begin to put pressure on the DRV, aimed at limiting the infiltration of people and supplies from the North, approving a series of covert operations in northern Vietnam that included coastal commando raids by South Vietnamese military forces with the assistance of American advisers and ships. The administration also issued warnings through Canadian intermediaries that the Democratic Republic's support for the southern insurgency could bring American military retaliation against the North.

The Gulf of Tonkin incident in August 1964 marked a critical juncture in the coming of the American war in Vietnam. US naval patrol boats had begun to carry out electronic espionage near Vietnamese waters to support covert raids off the northern Vietnamese coast by the Khanh government. A group of DRV torpedo boats closed in on the destroyer USS *Maddox* on the afternoon of 2 August 1964. In a brief engagement, the *Maddox* opened fire and the Vietnamese ships launched several torpedoes before being driven away. Two days later, on the evening of 4 August, the *Maddox* and a second destroyer, the USS *Turner Joy*, were operating under heavy seas 60 miles off the coast of northern Vietnam and reported being under Vietnamese attack. Although evidence of the second attack was less than conclusive, and retrospective reconstructions make clear that it never took place, the Johnson administration authorized retaliatory air strikes against Vietnamese torpedo boat bases and nearby oil storage facilities. The incident also allowed Johnson to win the passage of a Congressional resolution that essentially gave his administration a blank cheque to take whatever military steps were necessary in Vietnam. In presenting the resolution to Congress, the administration engaged in deliberate deception, never mentioning the role of *Maddox* and *Turner Joy* in covert operations against the North and framing the attacks as 'open aggression on the high seas'. The resolution passed with virtual unanimity, opening the way for the US to play a larger military role in Vietnam.[44]

The Johnson administration's responses to the Gulf of Tonkin incident did not deter the leadership in Hanoi from escalating its support for the NLF. In September 1964 the first PAVN units were sent down the Ho Chi Minh Trail and would begin to engage in direct combat with the South Vietnamese military by the end of the year. The appointment of General Nguyen Chi Thanh, who favoured a strategy of high-level confrontation, as the military commander to lead an expanded military effort further signalled Hanoi's resolve. It also marked the eclipse of General Vo Nguyen Giap, who had led Vietnamese forces in the French war and had consistently advocated a more gradual and politically oriented strategy to guide the southern insurgency after 1954. Along with the use of PAVN forces in the South, Thanh sought to build up a liberated base zone in the central highlands, drawing on the primarily minority population of the area as a source of recruitment into the PLAF, and to push into areas of ARVN troop strength near Saigon. NLF resistance leaders also began to attack US installations and personnel, including a mortar attack on the US air base near Bien Hoa on the eve of the US presidential elections.[45]

In its escalation of the military conflict in the South, Hanoi increasingly had the support of the Soviet Union and China. The fall of Khrushchev in late October 1964 prompted a reassessment of Soviet policy towards Vietnam. The new joint Soviet leadership under Leonid Brezhnev and Alexei Kosygin backed away from Khrushchev's policies of peaceful coexistence. Though wary of a wider war in Vietnam, they promised to increase Soviet military assistance to Hanoi. In return, the Vietnamese agreed to stop their criticism of Soviet 'revisionism' and to work to keep the conflict from spreading beyond southern Vietnam. The NLF set up a permanent mission in Moscow, and an official visit by Kosygin to Hanoi was scheduled for early 1965. In the wake of the Gulf of Tonkin incident, China put its southern military forces in a state of combat-readiness and significantly increased its support of the DRV's air force. The Sino-Soviet dispute continued to hover over Vietnam's relations with its communist allies, and the Chinese took every opportunity to raise questions about the sincerity of the Soviets. But for the moment the DRV was able to leverage needed support and assistance from both sides.[46]

Amid continuing political crisis in Saigon and NLF advances in the southern countryside, President Johnson made a series of choices in late 1964 and early 1965 that would fundamentally shift the US commitment to Vietnam. They set the larger American war into motion by authorizing a bombing campaign against the North and sending what would become an open-ended number of ground combat troops to the South.[47] Operation Rolling Thunder began in March 1965, a graduated bombing campaign that targeted Vietnamese military installations in the North, along with infiltration routes along the Ho Chi Minh Trail. At the same time the first US combat troops arrived in the South as two battalions of Marines splashed ashore at Danang on 8 March. They quickly began to engage the PLAF and PAVN in combat. By late April nearly 40,000 US combat troops were in Vietnam.

The military and political position of the Saigon government, however, continued to deteriorate. When General Khanh finally left the political stage in February 1965, a renewed series of coups and counter-coups and a short-lived civilian regime finally produced a new government in June, led by the commander of the Air Force, Nguyen Cao Ky, and General Nguyen Van Thieu. It did not inspire confidence in many contemporary American observers, who were profoundly sceptical of the mercurial Ky's abilities. ARVN desertion rates, for instance, reached almost 50 per cent in mid-1965. To prevent what appeared to be an almost certain NLF military victory in the South, Johnson's military advisers pressed him to expand US ground troops and accelerate the Rolling Thunder campaign. After debates in the spring and summer of 1965 over the scale and scope of the US commitment to Vietnam, Johnson increased American military forces to 125,000, with the promise of additional troop deployments as recommended by commanders in the field. The Saigon government was never consulted on the decisions to bomb northern Vietnam and introduce ground troops. By the end of 1965 approximately 184,300 American ground troops were in southern Vietnam, a total that would grow to almost half a million within two years. Some 864,000 tons of American bombs were dropped on northern Vietnam by the end of 1967 in the Rolling Thunder campaign.

In what proved to be a fundamental miscalculation, President Johnson made the decision for war in Vietnam believing incremental increases in American bombing and troop levels would eventually push the DRV to abandon its support for the NLF. Against the views of some of his military advisers to go for broke in Vietnam, and a small minority of civilian advisers who urged him to withdraw entirely, Johnson's graduated commitment of US air power and ground forces—what he termed 'going up old Ho Chi Minh's leg an inch at a time'[48]—marked a conscious desire to place limits on the American war in Vietnam. His complex calculations in part reflected political concerns, especially his desire to keep the costs of the American commitment in Vietnam manageable enough for his Great Society programme to be fully funded and implemented. But it was also the product of his fears of Chinese intentions in Vietnam. Johnson and some of his advisers often spoke of the lessons of the Korean war, when the American decision to send military forces into North Korea to push back communism there triggered a massive Chinese intervention. If the US pushed too far and too fast in Vietnam, Johnson thought, it might provoke the Chinese to do the same in Vietnam and unleash a wider war.[49]

For their part the Chinese were also keen to avoid a direct war with the United States over Vietnam. China was quick to provide military equipment and supplies to the DRV as American bombing and troop strength increased, and it facilitated the movement of supplies south by organizing secret supply routes along the Vietnamese coast and through Cambodia. A substantial Chinese troop presence in northern Vietnam began in June 1965, including ground-to-air missile, anti-aircraft artillery, railroad, minesweeping, and logistical units. More than 320,000 Chinese troops were stationed in the DRV between June 1965 and March 1968, allowing the North to send larger numbers of PAVN forces to fight in the South. But the Chinese also hoped to avert a larger war, and signalled to the Johnson administration through intermediaries that Beijing would not increase its role further if the US limited the air war in northern Vietnam and did not attack China. For its part, the Johnson administration made clear its intention to avoid war with China when it publicly announced that the US had no plan to destroy the DRV as a viable nation or to invade China. Through these public and private signals, Beijing and Washington came to a tacit understanding concerning the limits of each other's involvement in the war.[50]

The Chinese willingness to limit its military support for the war in southern Vietnam introduced additional tensions into the Sino-Vietnamese relationship. But in the end, the US strategy of gradual

1 Transplanting rice near Haiphong, April–May 1916.

2 Hanoi, c.1940.

3 Dien Bien Phu, 1954.

4 To Ngoc Van, *Two Young Girls and a Child*, 1944.

5 To Ngoc Van, *Militia Woman*, 1954.

6 South Vietnamese President Ngo Dinh Diem, November 1955.

7 Along the Ho Chi Minh Trail, South Vietnam, 1966.

8 NLF cadres meet in the Nam Can forest on the Ca Mau Peninsula wearing masks to hide their identities from one another in case of capture and interrogation.

9 ARVN and NLF forces battle in the Mekong delta.

10 Saigon streetscape, 1967.

11 New recruits for the North Vietnamese army undergo physical examinations in Haiphong, July 1967.

12 Local militia and villagers in northern Vietnam camouflage a bridge with brush and banana leaves to hide it from American bombers.

13 Dang Thuy Tram.

14 Last page of Dang Thuy Tram's diary.

15 Signing of the Paris Peace Accords, 23 January 1973. Le Duc Tho (second from upper right) and Henry Kissinger (lower centre) initial the accords.

16 South Vietnamese President Nguyen Van Thieu.

17 Abandoned ARVN combat boots on highway outside Saigon, 30 April 1975.

18 Nguyen Manh Hung, *A Group of SU 22*, 2007.

19 Liza Nguyen, *Dien Bien Phu*, from the series *Surfaces*, 2005.

20 Dinh Q. Lê, *So Sorry*, from the series *Vietnam: Destination for a New Millenium*, 2004.

escalation worked in favour of Hanoi and the NLF as it gave them time to adjust to US bombing and develop tactics and strategies to blunt the impact of American ground forces in the South. Hanoi and the NLF responded to American escalation by confronting the US directly in the South. They saw the continuing weaknesses of the Saigon government and the ARVN along with the NLF's control of territory and population in the South as substantial advantages in an expanded war that worked to undermine American power. As Le Duan wrote in November 1965,

We all agree that the reason why the United States had to bring thousands of troops into the South is that they basically failed in the 'special war', and also failed heavily in the sabotage of the North. The fact that they brought further forces into the South makes it all the more clear that they are now in a passive political and military position not only in the South and in the North, but around the world as well.[51]

In December a confident leadership increased the infiltration of PAVN units into the South and ordered direct attacks on US and ARVN forces, as well as the acceleration of political struggle in the cities. The American war had come to Vietnam.

NLF hospital near the Cambodian border

4

EXPERIENCING WAR

In the spring of 1967 Dang Thuy Tram, a young woman fresh out of medical school in Hanoi, arrived in the mountainous central Vietnamese province of Quang Ngai to serve as the chief physician at a thatched-roof field hospital. In this lonely and remote spot, she cared for wounded North Vietnamese and NLF soldiers. Tram kept a diary: simple notebooks of five by seven inches, dull brown with cardboard covers. The diary is full of stories about amputating limbs and trying to avoid American planes and foot patrols, which sometimes forced Tram and her colleagues to move their clinic by carrying the wounded on their backs. The diary also gives voice to her youthful optimism, to moments of self-doubt, to how much she missed her fiancé back home, and to her deep animosity towards what she calls 'the American invaders'. It conveys her sense of betrayal that the Vietnamese Communist Party appeared unwilling to recognize her wartime sacrifices but also a steadfast resolution to redouble her wartime efforts for the party's revolutionary war for independence.[1]

Like millions of Vietnamese, Dang Thuy Tram was drawn into the American war and came to understand it in complex ways. This chapter pauses our narrative of the war to explore how the Vietnamese who made a revolution or resisted it, who fought the Americans or cooperated with them, or who endured and survived the war as it engulfed the world around them made sense of their own experiences. Between 1965 and 1967 the United States put nearly half a million combat troops in Vietnam, dropped more bombs than it had in all theatres of the Second World War, and spent more than $2 billion a month on the war. And yet by the end of 1967 the Americans and the Vietnamese faced a stalemate on the battlefield. Vietnamese on all sides of the conflict responded to these developments in myriad ways, from a profound war-weariness to a continuing willingness to make the individual and collective sacrifices they believed were necessary for eventual victory. But as they did so their visions of what the post-war peace might bring also began to shift, and to some extent narrow, as the capacious revolutionary and utopian hopes articulated throughout much of the century faced the limiting realities of states, societies, and peoples at war.

South Vietnam at War

The escalation of the American war brought further instabilities for the South Vietnamese state and a growing sense among many southerners about the futility of the conflict. The renewal of Buddhist-inspired demonstrations in 1966—which grew to include other opponents of the government including students, labour unions, and some members of the armed forces—returned southern Vietnam to the kinds of urban chaos unleashed by the Buddhist protests in 1963 and again threatened the government in southern Vietnam with collapse.

The protesters initially called for new elections and the resumption of a civilian government, but the more radical among them soon advanced a far-reaching attack on the war itself and the need for a coalition government that included non-communists who were a part of the NLF if lasting peace was to come to Vietnam. Massive protests emerged in Hue, Saigon, and other major cities in central and southern Vietnam in March 1966. In Danang the mayor supported a secessionist movement against the Nguyen Cao Ky government, as did some local ARVN officers. Large numbers of ARVN soldiers participated in the demonstrations in Hue. Civilian protesters in Hue and Danang, where US ground troops had landed a year earlier and prompted intense nationalist sentiments, had a strong anti-American cast. Signs calling for the 'End [of] Foreign

Domination of our Country' appeared in Hue and Danang. Protesters burned the American consulate in Danang, and local firefighters refused to help put out the fire. US forces came under fire from ARVN troops who supported the protests as well as ARVN units loyal to the government.[2]

Under strong pressure from the American government, which inaccurately believed that the Buddhist leaders of the protests were under the direction of the NLF, the Ky government deployed two loyal ARVN battalions in a surprise attack in mid-May, which successfully suppressed the protests in Danang. The protest movement continued elsewhere in the South, however, with large sit-down strikes and street protests organized in May in Saigon that met severe repression from the government. In late May and early June the first of what would be a renewed series of Buddhist self-immolations took place in Hue. At the same time, crowds attacked and burned the American consulate and sympathetic residents placed sacred family altars in the streets to block the passage of government troops.[3]

The South Vietnamese government prevailed in the Buddhist protests of 1966. Suppressing the street protests raging in Saigon in late May, it regained control of Hue by the end of June. Elections were held in 1967, which brought General Nguyen Van Thieu to power as president of South Vietnam, a position he held until 1975. Nguyen Cao Ky initially served as his vice-president but was quickly pushed out of power by Thieu. If Thieu's election brought a level of stability to the highest levels of the South Vietnamese government, popular support for it remained tepid. In the election Thieu had only managed to capture 35 per cent of the popular vote, mainly in outlying districts where ARVN commanders managed the electoral process on his behalf. This low plurality was surprising, given the severe constraints placed on the campaigns of Thieu's civilian opponents. A further demonstration of widespread antipathy to Thieu's military government was the finish in second place of a civilian candidate running on a peace platform who garnered 17 per cent of the vote. An embarrassed Thieu had him arrested, along with a number of other dissident political figures.[4]

The Buddhist challenge and prevailing scepticism about the Ky and Thieu governments emerged against the continual fraying of social and familial bonds within southern Vietnam. The intensification of the American war in the countryside brought many peasants into what were believed to be the safer sanctuaries of the cities and nearby refugee camps. As peasants fled, the South became more urban than rural in its demography. Land under cultivation, especially in the north-east around Hue and Danang, fell to below 50 per cent in 1967. Once among the largest rice exporters in the world, southern Vietnam became a net importer of rice by late 1965 and continued to import ever larger quantities as the war continued. Migration-induced growth of urban populations was exponential, with Saigon at four times its pre-war population at the end of 1966. The most conservative estimates put the number of urban refugees at 1.5 million in November 1966. Altogether an estimated 4 million Vietnamese in the South became refugees during the American war, roughly 25 per cent of the population. The existing urban infrastructure could not easily sustain this population movement, and large slums emerged in many southern cities to house refugees.[5]

Other war-induced migrants ended up in refugee camps, especially in the central coastal provinces and what was known as the Iron Triangle north-west of Saigon, where NLF support was especially strong. Here the American military and the South Vietnamese government established 'free-fire zones' in which artillery and air power, including the use of napalm, could be used indiscriminately to dislodge NLF forces. Toxic chemical defoliants were also used, as part of what was known as Operation Ranch Hand, to kill vegetation and deny the NLF cover, actions which left the lasting effects of high rates of cancer and birth defects among many southern Vietnamese families. Civilians in free-fire zones were often caught in deadly crossfire, and many villages were entirely destroyed. In the village of Ben Suc, for example, more than 6,000 civilians were forcibly evacuated, the village was bombed for four days, and two army divisions then moved in to complete the destruction.[6] The inhabitants of central Vietnam saw some of the worst brutalities of the war. For seven months between May and November 1967 the

US Army's 'Tiger Force' moved across the central highlands killing hundreds of unarmed civilians, in some cases torturing, mutilating, and raping them before they were shot. In March 1968 a US infantry company led by Lieutenant William Calley entered the central Vietnamese hamlet of Son May (known to the Americans as My Lai) and gunned down an estimated 150 elders, women, children, and babies.[7]

In the wake of these American-led operations in rural Vietnam, villagers were understandably terrified. But their options were limited and many were herded into squalid camps enclosed by barbed wire where basic needs for food and medicine went unmet. One contemporary observer of the Hoai An refugee camp in central Vietnam described the conditions in which as many as thirty people could share a single room:

The insides of the buildings smelled of stale food and urine and wood smoke from cooking fires burning indoors in the heat.... The sickest and most seriously injured lay on their backs on straw mats on the dirt floor looking with weak laconic eyes at the ceiling as if waiting to die.... There were no toilets. The stench was so strong it stayed in our noses when we left the building. Outside, on an arid piece of sand-covered soil, small individual piles of human excrement were arranged on the ground in neat, even rows decomposing in the sun, fertilizer for some future crop. There was not enough food.[8]

Some refugees were eventually impressed into military service, but most remained unemployed and the camps some became a primary source of recruitment for the communist insurgency.

Along with these massive civilian dislocations, perhaps no other group in wartime South Vietnam suffered more in terms of sheer numbers than the enlisted men serving in the ARVN and their families. The ARVN forces reached 685,000 in 1967 and over 1 million after 1969; one in six adult males served in the ARVN by 1968. The age of conscription shifted from 20–25 in 1964 to 18–34 in 1968, with the upper age for support personnel as high as 45. Three-year tours of duty during the initial years of the war were replaced by unlimited service in 1968. With most ARVN recruits drawn from peasant families, the rapid build-up of the army and length of required service posed severe problems for household agricultural production. As one Mekong delta farmer recalled, 'We lived through French imperialism, war against the fascists, a liberation war with the French, and never had we known such problems. In the days before the ARVN draft, if families needed labor they could always hire from local families with more sons. The draft took all our sons and made farming almost impossible.'[9]

Corruption and abuse in the deferment system further alienated rural peasants. ARVN desertion rates were exceedingly high, in large measure because of inadequate leave to meet family obligations, low rates of pay, and substandard medical care and food. With massive and escalating inflation the norm in southern Vietnam, an ARVN private saw his real pay drop from $77 per month in 1964 to $30 per month in 1972. Over time, as tours of duty became unlimited and the destruction of war made lives more difficult for their families, desertion numbers dropped and ARVN troops increasingly brought wives, children, and parents to live with them or in nearby base camps in makeshift shanty towns. With little investment in the aims of the South Vietnamese state, ARVN soldiers increasingly took refuge in efforts to ensure family survival.[10] In a further survival mechanism, and as the outcome of the war looked increasingly murky, it was not uncommon for families to send one son to serve in the ARVN and another with the NLF's armed forces.

American assistance to South Vietnam further widened levels of social and economic inequality and compounded the fragility of the state. Although the United States had provided exceptionally high levels of economic assistance to the Ngo Dinh Diem government, the sums became truly staggering as the war accelerated after 1964. The American economic aid programme in Vietnam accounted for one-quarter of the total aid the US provided throughout the world. Dollars were pumped into the Vietnamese economy at a much faster rate than it could absorb, severely distorting the domestic economy, prompting exceptionally high levels of inflation and ever wider forms of corruption. As much as 80 per cent of the budget of

South Vietnam came to be funded through American aid and a US-financed import initiative known as the Commercial Import Program (CIP). To make up the gap between American aid and government expenses, the South Vietnamese state often printed money; in 1965 newly minted currency made up about one-quarter of its budget. The CIP provided large windfalls for the government and importers alike. Local importers obtained licences, usually through corruption and bribery, and paid the government in US-provided dollars at higher than prevailing official exchange rates, which added substantially to government revenue, but at lower than black market rates, allowing importers to make an immediate profit on the exchange and sell their goods very cheaply. In the process, Vietnam essentially became a service economy. With declining agricultural and manufacturing production, the service and government sector accounted for 78 per cent of the southern economy in 1972.[11]

Inflation plagued the South Vietnamese economy. Prices increased by more than 100 per cent in 1965 and again in 1966, and rose even further as the war continued. One estimate suggests consumer prices in South Vietnam rose 900 per cent between 1964 and 1972, with the cost of rice rising more than 1,000 per cent. At the same time, the real income of salaries paid to government civil servants fell between 30 and 50 per cent, depending on rank and pay grade, between 1965 and 1968. Reductions in income relative to inflation were an invitation for routine looting and corruption, further reducing the government's tax revenues and its dependency on US aid. Positions in the government went to the highest bidder, compounding problems of corruption. To occupy a very junior post in the customs service at Saigon's Ton Son Nhut airport, for instance, required $2,000 in cash and daily kickbacks to more senior officials of $20, even though the official salary for the position was $35 per month.

Bribes were required in almost every dimension of daily life, including for work permits, driver's licences, visas, and passports. Government officials required their cut for any construction project, usually renting or selling land at vastly inflated prices. ARVN officers often asked for the payment of a 'tribute', sometimes tens of thousands of dollars, to ensure the safe movement of economic goods from one part of the country to another. Illegal currency exchanges were common, as was an open black market that sold American imports. Stolen goods could be seen throughout major cities, with irrigation pumps intended for agricultural development powering car washes and military generators illuminating private night clubs. In mid-1966 US official reporting suggested that theft, bribery, the black market, currency manipulation, and waste accounted for as much as 40 per cent of US aid funds and goods entering South Vietnam.[12]

The massive US presence in South Vietnam affected the fabric of southern society in other ways too. American goods and consumer culture flooded into Vietnam, challenging and sometimes reshaping the mores of the urban middle class and often pitting more conservative parents against their children, who eagerly embraced 1960s era fashion, hair styles, movies, and music from the United States. The author of a women's advice column in late 1968 for the Saigon daily *Quyet Tien* censoriously argued that the majority of women 'threw themselves into an excessively extravagant life' that caused 'grave damage' to the family and society. She asked:

In such a situation, what do we women do? Every day we still buy face powder, lip-stick, perfume, jewelry, blouses and skirts and silks of foreign countries.... Precisely because of the lack of conscience of the great majority of women about the future of the nation, we women have lost the virtue of thrift of the people of Vietnam that was so worthy of respect.[13]

Other observers were critical of how human relations, including romantic love, had shifted in the wake of American social and cultural influences. In his 1965 essay 'The Way of Loving Today', the well-known southern author Vo Phien wrote:

To avoid loneliness city people, men and women, search out each other, but not in a context of gentle breezes and soft moonlight, when they are relaxed and their hearts are at ease, but in the midst of the noise, dust, meanness and hurry of city life. The meetings are urgent, not relaxed. It's no longer about appreciating love but about escaping the sense that one has been abandoned.[14]

Southern Vietnamese concerns about changing sexual mores were heightened by the emergence of a wartime sex industry. Bars and brothels that catered to American servicemen sprang up near US bases and in many urban centres, giving rise to a culture of prostitution and drug abuse that drew considerable opprobrium in local society and further alienated many southerners from their American-backed government. The sex industry, which brought together American soldiers and usually poor Vietnamese women from the countryside lured into prostitution, contributed to the rise of mixed-race Amerasian children. Colloquially referred to as *bui doi* (dust of life), their parentage made these children virtual pariahs in wartime and post-war Vietnamese society.

Tensions also emerged between Vietnamese civilians and troops from South Korea, who had come to Vietnam under American auspices to fight along side US and ARVN forces. At the peak of its involvement between 1966 and 1970, South Korea maintained a combat force of 50,000 in Vietnam, about 10 per cent of its armed forces, with a total of 300,000 Korean soldiers serving in Vietnam between 1965 and 1973. Almost 5,000 were killed in Vietnam, a casualty rate as high as the United States, suggesting the South Korean role was as intense proportionally as that of the Americans. Additionally, as many as 18,000 South Korean civilians had come to work on development projects in Vietnam by mid-1968. Korean troops were in Vietnam as part of the American 'more flags' effort to provide international legitimacy for the war; in exchange for South Korean support, the US extended ever larger levels of American economic aid to the Korean government. But South Korean soldiers were not well received by the Vietnamese they were purportedly fighting for as they sometimes engaged in ruthless military tactics and massacres against unarmed civilians. Many individual Korean troops found themselves in the confusing position of going into battle against fellow Asians in a conflict many of them came to oppose.[15]

Among southern Vietnamese, a prevailing mood of war-weariness and scepticism towards the state was best captured in literature and the arts. Novels and poetry were far from heroic in their subject matter, often focusing on feelings rather than deeds and on the wartime failures to uphold the social order. The writer Nguyen Thi Thuy Vu's 1967 *Embrace of Fire* (*Loa vao lua*) was one widely read novel that told the story of a former teacher who tries to join the South Vietnamese military as a paratrooper. But in fact he is a physical coward and too fearful to jump out of the plane. Unlucky in love as well as on the battlefield, his girlfriend eventually jilts him. An essentially impotent figure, Vu's hero was a symbolic attempt to portray the larger forces contributing to the fragilities and moral failings of southern Vietnamese society as it encountered the onslaught of the American war. Other works, employing either veiled satire or blunt attacks, took on the invasive corruption at the village and national level.[16] Saigon daily newspaper columns of a variety of political persuasions were increasingly full of criticisms of the Vietnamese–American relationship, scorning what they saw as everyday American racism towards the Vietnamese and expressing the belief that a neo-colonial United States had put in place a parasitic ruling class in the South.[17]

For younger urban southern Vietnamese, the hugely popular anti-war songs of Trinh Công Son helped to define sensibilities about the war. Son came of age in the 1950s in central Vietnam and was a product of Hue's cosmopolitan intellectual milieu. Like many of his set who gathered in coffee houses to talk about existentialism and literary modernism, Son was especially influenced by the works of the French writers Jean-Paul Sartre, Albert Camus, and Guillaume Apollinaire, as well as the American novelist William Faulkner. One of his love songs from this earlier period, 'The Song of the Sand Crab' (Da trang ca), was clearly modelled on Camus's *The Myth of Sisyphus*. Others were inflected by Buddhist notions of impermanence and suffering through which Son and other southern intellectuals came to understand the wider meanings of existentialism. If the inspiration for his songs varied, their mood was, as one scholar recently argued, 'sad, dreamy and romantic' in ways that appealed to the Vietnamese ear and they quickly began to attract an appreciative audience. By the mid-1960s Son's work had turned to the American war. Songs such as 'Lullaby of Cannons for the Night' (Dai bac ru dem), 'Vietnamese Girl with Golden Skin' (Nguoi con gai Viet Nam da vang), and 'A Mother's Legacy' (Gia tai cua me) expressed sorrow at the destruction caused by war and asked listeners to transcend the present moment through expressions of familial love and love of country. In 'Lullaby of Cannons for the Night', Son evoked a prevailing climate of sadness and loss:

> Every night cannons resound in the town
> A street cleaner stops sweeping and listens
> Every night cannon shells create a future without life
> Cannons like a chant without a prayer
> Children forget to live and anxiously wait.

Son's performances of these songs at universities and their wide circulation through relatively inexpensive cassette tapes helped to make his music almost ubiquitous throughout wartime southern Vietnam. His modest and unassuming style and his efforts to avoid the draft further cemented his reputation among high school and university students and a growing public. Although the Thieu government in 1969 formally banned his work, it continued to circulate, and his anti-war message remained at the centre of wartime popular culture.[18]

Keeping a tight hold on power and ever wary of expressions of popular dissent, the South Vietnamese government under Thieu never experienced the kind of destabilizing protests led by the Buddhists in 1963 and 1966. No indigenous third force emerged at home in the years after 1967 that could have successfully challenged the southern Vietnamese state. The more radical leaders of the Buddhist peace movement did not recover from the government suppression of 1966, although some continued to operate clandestinely. An emergent moderate Buddhist leadership tended to avoid the public and political spheres. But the absence of more formal religious or secular political opposition to the Thieu government did not translate into widespread support for it.

Dispirited and weary, many South Vietnamese may have out-wardly acquiesced in state power, but they came to feel just as alienated from the American-backed southern government as they did from the NLF and North Vietnam. As the American war dragged on, it looked to them less like the earlier war against the French, and the choice between communism and anti-communism appeared increasingly hollow. One leading southern intellectual captured these emergent sentiments in late 1967, observing:

If the Southern Liberation Front truly was merely resisting 'American imperialist aggression', then why up until now has it not yet been able to stimulate . . . an ardent uprising among all of the people as in the 1945 period again the French colonialists? If a policy of opposing Communism has truly only been called into existence because of the aggression of the northern Communists, why has it not been able to stimulate a positive attitude of self-defense, why do we have indifference, desertions from the army, collaboration, escapes to the enemy army? . . . We cannot make a clear-cut choice but we have not found another way.[19]

Others looked beyond the state to familial and other social networks for ways to survive the continuing onslaught of war. The complexities of these networks could be dizzying and often cut against more formal political divisions in southern society. The case of a wounded ARVN officer's escape from a municipal hospital in Danang in 1969 provides one instance of how these cross-cutting ties operated in wartime Vietnam.[20] A nurse in the Danang hospital had a long-established network associated with the NLF. She gath-ered information from the wounded soldiers and smuggled out medicine, and was connected to a network of covert action through the daughter of a local pharmacist. The wounded ARVN officer was himself enmeshed in a highly covert network of officers and soldiers. He was in turn connected to a small network of friends and relatives outside his army life. The officer's elder brother, who was a clandestine NLF operative, had created this network. The patient in the bed next to the officer belonged to another counter-insurgency network. He was an informant hired by the South Vietnamese military intelligence, which was suspicious of the wounded officer's loyalty. The children who sold toothbrushes and towels to the patients had their own set of social connections. Their group belonged to a complex network of street children that incorporated orphans, children of prison inmates, old gangs of playmates, and children of refugee families.

All these networks, completely unknown to one another, became intertwined in the wounded ARVN officer's escape from the hospital in May 1969. The nurse was instructed to make contact with the wounded officer. She took his neighbour, the informant for ARVN military intelligence, to the examination room at an appointed hour late one afternoon. With the ARVN informant distracted, the wounded officer escaped to a Buddhist pagoda and was met there by the children he had seen in the hospital. They showed him a tunnel that had been dug underneath a tomb. In the early hours of the morning, a member of the officer's own network turned up and escorted him out to the riverside. From there, he was handed over to an unknown NLF liaison. Both the liaison and the wounded officer swam to the opposite side of the river and disappeared in the direction of the mountains.

That the wounded ARVN officer ultimately defected to the NLF is perhaps the least important part of this story, although it does suggest the comparatively more sophisticated and effective set of social and political relationships fostered by the southern communist insurgency. More significantly, it is one among many instances of the ways in which individuals and families looked beyond the state to navigate and survive the complicated terrain of wartime South Vietnam.

The American War and North Vietnamese Society

North Vietnamese society during the American war was, at least outwardly, considerably more unified than in the South. The political leadership in the North was generally quite stable, with none of the coups and counter-coups that plagued the South

Vietnamese government. Most of the leadership of the party and the northern state had been together since the 1930s. Even after Ho Chi Minh's death in 1969, a shared commitment to victory in the American war and to socialist revolution fostered a prevailing unity of purpose among the leadership. There were sometimes fierce debates over strategy and tactics for fighting the war, but they never produced the kinds of chaos that plagued southern political life. Throughout the war, the northern state carefully sought to foster popular support for the war and to keep military and civilian morale high. In part through these efforts, urban and rural society remained much more cohesive than in South Vietnam, despite the huge and often devastating impact of the American war in the North.

The American air war in northern Vietnam brought the first widespread dislocations for civilians. In the Rolling Thunder bombing campaign against the North from 1965 to 1968, US bombers flew 300,000 sorties over the DRV. Some 860,000 tons of bombs were dropped, an average of 32 tons per hour over three years. Approximately 52,000 civilians were killed as a result of Rolling Thunder. This graduated campaign, aimed at hitting the war-making capacity of the North and its ability to infiltrate men and supplies into the South along the Ho Chi Minh Trail, eventually targeted almost all of lowland northern Vietnam. Along with areas of the rural north, industrial cities were badly damaged. Vinh, a major staging area for the infiltration of troops and supplies into the South, was hit especially hard, with the centre of the city almost entirely destroyed. Attacks against bridges, oil and gas depots, power plants, rail stations and lines, roads, and radar and artillery posts brought the bombing into both rural and urban areas. Until late in the war, Hanoi and the port city of Haiphong escaped the worst of the bombing. There were sustained attacks throughout Rolling Thunder on Hanoi's electric and water supplies, its rail transportation network, and the Long Bien Bridge, the city's major link across the Red River. But if the physical devastation of the city centre in Hanoi was smaller than in other urban areas, the psychological trauma of years of air-raid alerts, bomb blasts, and the inevitable death and destruction that followed in their wake was considerable. Nor could people ever be sure that the bombing wouldn't suddenly intensify.[21]

To protect against the dangers of a wider American bombing campaign against Hanoi, the DRV evacuated many residents after the bombing of the city began in June 1966 in a practice that was also followed in other major urban centres. Children and elders, along with other civilians who did not directly contribute to the defence of the city or provide essential services, were sent to the countryside. The strain on divided families was intense, but parents reluctant to send their children away were confronted with the prospect of losing their wartime rice rations. For the many fathers whose work required them to remain in Hanoi, travel from the city to the countryside to visit family members was difficult as almost all motor vehicles were used for military purposes and the bombing seriously disrupted many transport routes. The evacuation reached its peak in 1968 when from one-third to one-half of the populations of Hanoi, Haiphong, and other major cities was relocated to rural areas. One estimate of Hanoi's population in 1971 placed it at 200,000 fewer than ten years earlier. Over time, schools were moved into the countryside, along with some government offices, and much of the urban industrial sector believed to be vulnerable to American attacks was dismantled and scattered throughout the rural north.

The wartime bombing and evacuations significantly shifted the familiar rhythms of urban life in Hanoi and its impoverished residents. No larger gatherings were permitted during daylight hours, leaving the streetscape deserted with barred doors and closed shutters during the day. A few authorized shops were allowed to open between six and eight in the morning and again after six in the evening. Street lights remained dim to protect against bombing raids, making the city seem, one Hanoi writer recalled, 'lonely, cold and deeply sad'.[22] Few consumer goods were available, and many central markets were closed. Rationing of rice and cloth was introduced; cloth rations allowed for only one change of shirt and trousers, increasingly the standard dress for both men and women, each year. Networks of air-raid shelters were built in Hanoi and other cities. Initially they were rough brick structures constructed above ground, but eventually individual holes were built underground, every 5 to 10 metres on Hanoi's main streets, topped with concrete pipes and lids.

Late in the war, Hanoi was dramatically affected by the resumption of US bombing. The single most devastating and intensive bombing campaign of the American war was Linebacker II, sometimes known as the Christmas bombings, from 19 to 29 December 1972. Over these eleven days B-52 bombers dropped more than 30,000 bombs in more than 1,500 sorties, with smaller jet aircraft using laser-guided 'smart' bombs. The official targets were military, communication, and industrial installations, but many of the attacks went astray. The physical damage to the oldest parts of central Hanoi was minimal, but more than a quarter of the city's housing stock in its outer rings and suburbs was destroyed, leaving tens of thousands homeless. Civilian casualties numbered around 2,000.[23] One Hanoi resident whose home was destroyed in the Christmas bombing later recalled:

I began to dig quickly, and found three bodies—my father, my younger brother, and my sister. My mother had been evacuated with the younger children. My older brother and sister-in-law I couldn't find. The next morning I found my brother's head. I never found my sister-in-law, nor one of my aunts. My uncle's body was found two months later, near the house. My neighbor Mr. Van, his wife and five children were killed, seven people.[24]

In rural Vietnam the sustained American bombing also had a severe impact. In many districts and provinces US bombs and rockets hit most villages, some several times over. Estimates suggest that, between 1965 and 1972, 70 per cent of the rural north was bombed, with 5 per cent of rural subdistricts almost completely obliterated. One 1967 report on the impact of the bombing contended: 'Water buffaloes and oxen have been killed, some land can't be ploughed and planted, various public works have been damaged, transportation is difficult... All of these have adversely affected agricultural production.' The destruction of irrigation and flood control systems compounded these problems. By 1968 many rural provinces reported that few 'irrigation works, large and small, remained intact'. Rural living conditions in the 1960s were at best stagnant and in many cases severely declined. Aggregate per capita food consumption declined by as much as 15 per cent. In one northern province during a period between harvests, 38 per cent of villages were malnourished in 1966; almost half were underfed at a similar point in the agricultural cycle three years later. Declining living standards were in part the result of the failures of the collect-ivization of agriculture in the North, but the major cause was the American bombing.[25]

Beyond the bombing, most northern families were directly affected by the escalation of the American war through conscription into the People's Army of Vietnam (PAVN). Sixty per cent of northern families had husbands, sons, brothers, or sisters directly involved in the war effort, many of them inducted into the PAVN. The northern army doubled to over 400,000 by the end of 1966 as a result of new draft laws that sought to match the escalation of American forces in the South. A year later, as fighting intensified and casualties increased, the DRV extended draft eligibility for men aged 18–25 to those aged 16–45. The PAVN's northern-based troops, augmented by large rural militia forces and urban self-defence forces, were detailed not only to protect the North against American bombing attacks and to restore the industrial and trans-port infrastructure in the wake of those attacks but also to provide the manpower to keep the wartime northern economy functioning. PAVN units operated some of the most productive state farms in the North, on which they raised rice, vegetables, and livestock, and oversaw projects for flood relief, water conservancy, and school-building. Those troops sent south travelled there on foot by way of the Ho Chi Minh Trail through the mountains of central Vietnam and southern Laos. The entire journey could take two to six months, with troops moving about 20 kilometres per day. Northern soldiers, termed *bo doi*, carried their own provisions, mainly a food ration of several kilos of rice supplemented with what vegetables and meat they found along the trail. As many as 20 per cent never made it south, and died from malaria, attacks by wild animals, drowning in rivers, or starvation if they became lost in the jungles. Those who reached the South were assigned to a PAVN unit, where they would fight alongside the NLF's People's Liberation Armed Forces (PLAF) directly against the Americans and the ARVN.[26]

PAVN units in both the North and the South were considerably more cohesive than their counterparts in the ARVN. The northern army drew on its experiences in the August Revolution of 1945 and the French war to interweave closely political and armed struggle. By contrast to the often opaque goals of the South Vietnamese state, the leadership of the DRV and the party carefully framed participation in the war, officially called the War of National Salvation against the Americans (Chien Tranh Chong My Cuu Nuoc), as patriotic and socialist contributions, in order to mobilize the population to fight. In a speech to an anti-aircraft unit in Hanoi in 1965, for instance, Party General Secretary Le Duan said, 'Saving the nation is a sacred obligation of the people.... We are determined to fight and win to keep our independence and freedom, secure our health and happiness, and to build the nation into a wealthy and beautiful Vietnam.'[27] PAVN itself had a dual command structure that combined military agents of the state and party political commissars. Basic training reflected both military and political goals, with political education continuing in the field. Political cadres were present at the unit level, and soldiers were regularly involved in political meetings and self-criticism sessions. Periodically throughout the war various moral exhortation campaigns were launched—with such titles as the Strengthen Revolutionary Discipline Movement and the Develop Good Qualities and Increase Fighting Strength Emulation Movement—to increase solidarity further.[28]

The northern Vietnamese state directed considerable effort at maintaining wartime morale among civilians, celebrating acts of self-sacrifice by soldiers and revolutionary cadres, patriotic workers and peasants, and heroic mothers, children, and grandparents to infuse a larger meaning onto the suffering and death caused by war. Officially sanctioned creative works in the North borrowed from Soviet and Chinese modes of socialist realism that accentuated the positive through the depiction of larger-than-life revolutionary heroes. Along with literature and poetry, film was a particularly important means through which the state imparted the meanings it accorded to the sacrifices of favoured social groups. The first feature-length northern Vietnamese film, *On the Same River* (*Chung Mot Dong Song*, 1959), told the story of two young lovers divided by the river that formed the Geneva-mandated boundary between north and south. They put aside the individual sorrows of their frustrated love to fight for the reunification of the country and the ideals of socialism.

On the Same River set the tone for wartime film-making, including such widely distributed films as *The Fledgling* (*Chim Vanh Khuyen*, 1962), in which a little girl is killed in her attempts to warn a revolutionary cadre of an impending enemy ambush; *When Mother Is Absent* (*Me Vang Nha*, 1969), which focused on a mother and her five children who responsibly take care of each other at home while their mother fights the enemy on the battlefield; and *Coal Season* (*Mua Than*, 1970), set among coal miners in the North who overcome constant bombardment by American jets to produce the fuel needed for the war effort. These sensibilities emerged most fully in the 1965 documentary *Victory at Dien Bien Phu* (*Chien Thang Dien Bien Phu*), released to coincide with the tenth anniversary of the battle. Cutting between black-and-white footage of the battle itself and vignettes that celebrated individual acts of heroism by soldiers in battle and by peasants and workers on the home front, the film presented what it called the 'spirit of Dien Bien Phu' as a lesson in the need for collective self-sacrifice to realize 'the struggle against American imperialists for independence, for the land of the peasants, for socialism'.[29]

As the concept of 'sacrifice' (*hi sinh*) came to embody the state's narrative of sacred war (*chien tranh than thanh*), the ultimate sacrifice was considered to be death in battle as a 'revolutionary martyr' (*liet si*). In late July 1967 the state launched its annual public commemoration of the war dead on War Invalids and Martyrs' Day (Ngay Thuong Binh Liet Si), with government officials holding ceremonies in Hanoi and localities throughout the North to express the gratitude of the state and offer small gifts to the families of martyrs. War cemeteries, or areas reserved for war dead in local cemeteries, were also created. Provincial and district authorities encouraged children to visit the graves to understand the sacrifice of the martyrs and learn to tend their graves. In one locality, officials decreed all marriage ceremonies should conclude with the placing of flowers on a war dead monument so that couples could express their gratitude to those who gave their lives in war. The families of the war dead (*gia dinh liet si*) received special privileges from the state, including an initial cash payment immediately after the death as well as preferential hospital admissions for family members, priority status for admission to schools and universities for their children, and easier access to government jobs and membership in the Communist Party. More generally, the state supported families of soldiers serving in the war through the creation of what were termed social policy officers (*pho ban chinh sach xa*). These local officials not only coordinated state benefits for families of war dead but looked after military families and veteran interests, including the provision of increased food rations to supplement economic dislocations caused by the war.[30]

Despite these efforts, there were considerable stresses and strains just below the surface in northern society. Peasants who were in rural agricultural cooperatives often complained about poor local party and state leadership and petty corruption by taking sly aim at government propaganda. In response to the state's Everyone Work as Hard as Two campaign, making reference to working on the cooperatives in support of the home and war fronts, one mocking peasant verse went:

> Everyone work as hard as two
> so that the chairperson can buy a radio and bicycle.
> Everyone work as hard as three
> so that the cadre can build a house and courtyard.[31]

The war also had a profound effect on gender relations as the state promulgated the 'three competencies' (*ba dam dang*) movement for women. As they had during times of peace, women shouldered most of the domestic duties in the household and served as the primary care givers to their children and elderly parents. But the mobilization of men to fight in the South meant women had to work outside the home in rice fields and factories to maintain agricultural and industrial production. Many women became more involved in party affairs by attending political meetings and study groups in a sharp departure from pre-war practices, when men dominated party affairs. Women were also drawn more directly into the war effort, serving as a home guard in villages and manning anti-aircraft guns in urban areas as American bombing campaigns against the North became more intense. All younger women were eventually required to join local militia and self-defence units. After 1966 they were permitted to go to the South, transporting food and weapons or serving as nurses and doctors in field hospitals at the front. Beginning in 1969, women were allowed to join the PAVN and become more actively involved in the fighting. Older women and those with families who remained at home continued to make indirect contributions to the war effort.[32] Along with prolonged absences of men for military service, new gendered responsibilities in fields and factories and for wartime service posed considerable stresses on family and household life. While the state portrayed the 'three competencies' of family, work, and war as a patriotic duty, many northern women privately resented it as a triple burden.

North Vietnam's tightly controlled public sphere made overt expressions of wartime dissatisfaction or dissent almost impossible. The complaints of northern soldiers, however, emerge in captured documents, among them the personal effects of troops killed in the South such as letters home, poetry, and diaries which talk of fear, hunger, illness, loneliness, and sometimes dreams of desertion, even as they take solace in official narratives of patriotic self-sacrifice. The everyday tensions of wartime service emerge in Dang Thuy Tram's diary. One of its themes is her discontent with the unwillingness of the local party officials, who were suspicious of her 'bourgeois' class background, to grant Tram membership in the party despite her self-sacrificing efforts to treat the wounded in the field. 'I have come to the Party with a devoted and open heart, but it seems the Party has not treated me in kind,' Tram wrote in the summer of 1968. 'No matter how sincere and honest you are, you will suffer to know that there are selfish people who would not hesitate to use tricks and clever maneuvers to cheat and rob you of every shred of credit.'[33] A more devastating critique of the party and state emerges in northern Vietnamese fiction published after the war written by veterans of the American war. These novels foreground the contradictions between the state's soaring rhetorical claims about the noble purposes of the war and the corrupt and self-serving wartime actions of many state actors. As the veteran narrator of one of these works says, 'The ones who loved war were not the young men but the others like the politicians, middle-aged men with fat bellies and short legs. Not the ordinary people. The years of war had brought enough suffering and pain to last them a thousand years.'[34]

If open critiques of state policies and actions could never have appeared during the war itself, there is evidence of an active underground group of writers and painters in wartime Hanoi who met in clandestine coffee houses to discuss their work, whose form and content sharply departed from those mandated by cultural authorities. Though never publicly exhibited during the war, the paintings of Bui Xuan Phai were especially influential in these circles and illustrate their wider sensibilities. Phai painted a series of desolate brown and grey streetscapes of wartime Hanoi which appeared to react against the depiction of wartime heroism in official art and instead drew attention to the deprivations of the population and the unmet promises of utopian socialism.[35] Poetry that circulated in similarly clandestine ways sometimes took on these issues too. A 1970 poem, 'Open Door' ('Cua Mo'), authored by Viet Phuong, the personal secretary to DRV prime minister Pham Van Dong, spoke to how ideology could blind the party and state to the realities around them:

It is clear, Soviet watches are a hundred times better than Swiss ones
That was our credo, our will, our pride,
The moon in China is much rounder than in the USA.
Our lyricism of the absolute rang with a strange naïveté.
Maybe after a quarter of a century we finally know
What it means to love, what it means to kill and to liquidate.[36]

In this case the identity of the poet became known and Viet Phuong lost his official position, but the phrases 'the moon in China is much rounder than in the USA' and 'Soviet watches are a hundred times better than Swiss ones' became ironic proverbs voiced behind closed doors by many Hanoi intellectuals.

Even at the highest levels of the party and the state in northern Vietnam, tensions simmered below the public façade of wartime unity. The Anti-Party Affair in the late summer and fall of 1967 brought the arrest of party members with ties to the Soviet Union for their alleged involvement in a pro-Soviet plot against the party and state. Those arrested were mainly middle-level cadres, includ- ing military figures, intellectuals, and journalists. Some were held until 1972, and then arrested again if they sought redress for their detention. The precise meanings of the Anti-Party Affair remain murky, in part because the Vietnamese government remains hesi- tant to discuss it. Some have argued that the timing of the arrests was designed to tamp down dissent within the government before a planned major escalation of the war that became the Tet Offensive of 1968. Available evidence suggests that the affair also reflected a jockeying for power among the top leadership in anticipation of Ho Chi Minh's death in 1969. Party General Secretary Le Duan and those around him apparently viewed General Vo Nguyen Giap as a serious rival for power. Giap, the architect of the Vietnamese defeat of the French at Dien Bien Phu, remained highly popular in the North and had expressed serious doubts about the scale and scope of northern military campaigns in South Vietnam. Giap was never arrested during the Anti-Party Affair, but many of those who were had close ties to the general.[37]

And yet, by comparison to South Vietnam, political and social cleavages in the North were far more limited in scope. The tensions that did emerge at the local level were often mediated by a population who continued to respect the North Vietnamese state's prosecution of the American war and the state's own ideological flexibility when confronted with the worst sufferings of war. The divergent public and private meanings of death in battle are a case in point. Official memorial services for northern war dead, reflecting the state's emphasis on carefully honouring wartime self-sacrifice, took place in individual homes at the intersection of the state and the family. The village's social policy officer presided. He presented white flowers to the family (white is the colour of mourning in Vietnam) and read a standardized statement of policy that framed their child's death as 'a loss for the fatherland and the people' and urged the family 'to turn its grief into activity for the revolution ... and to completely defeat the American enemy'. Following the ceremony, the officer gave the family $150 in cash as immediate assistance and an elaborately produced certificate that formally recorded the circumstances of the soldier's death and formed the basis for the family to receive the special privileges accorded them by the state because of their child's death in battle.[38]

But the death of a child in war posed existential problems for northern Vietnamese parents that these official services could not address. In Vietnam death in war, no matter how noble its purpose, is culturally conceived as a 'bad' death. For most Vietnamese the range of bad deaths include dying young without children, dying violently and far from home, and a mutilated or incomplete corpse; all of its forms held out the possibility that the soul would be unable to make its way to the 'otherworld' (*the gioi khac*). Instead the spirit would become a dangerous wandering ghost (*con ma*) who could take its anger out on the living. Because the deaths of soldiers in the American war included almost every possible combination of bad death and its anxiety-producing consequences, families throughout northern Vietnam faced a series of agonizing dilemmas. Traditional funerary rites had been severely circumscribed by the state in its broader campaigns against 'superstitious ritual' in the 1950s. But even the more circumscribed allowable practices had always centred on the physical presence of a corpse, which was often absent with the war dead. As the American war continued, villagers developed a complex set of private ceremonies of remembrance (*le tu niem* or *le tuong niem*) that fulfilled the perceived need to propitiate the soul of the deceased so that it would come to peace and enter the otherworld.[39]

The presence of what one anthropologist has called 'two distinct communities of remembrance'[40] did not necessarily mark a conflict or struggle between state and private practices over commemoration for the war dead in northern society. Rather, families were generally honoured to have their children's actions glorified by the state but, at the same time, were eager to employ alternative practices that spoke more directly to familial concerns for the fate of their son or daughter's departed soul. That the state was willing to acquiesce in these practices, despite its hostility to superstitious practices, suggests how differently the North responded to the human consequences of the American war than did state and society in the South.

The NLF at War

The many southern Vietnamese whose lives during the American war were shaped by their involvement with the National Liberation Front inhabited quite literally a liminal time and space. If it was 1 p.m. in an area controlled by the southern Vietnamese government, it was noon in NLF territory. Officially clocks and watches in South Vietnam were set one hour ahead of those in the North. The NLF followed northern time. For the Front's military and political cadres, the difference was often critical to carrying out their assignments for the Front. As one NLF liaison agent wrote, 'Normally, I started from Long Hung at noon (Saigon time) on my working days because the period of time from noon to 2:00 p.m. is the government soldiers' rest time. There were no patrols on rice fields and no movements of troops. I crossed back over the open rice fields and arrived at my hamlet at about 2:00 p.m. It was an easy job, with little risk or difficulty.'[41]

The NLF was exacting in the regime of time it attempted to impose on both its military and civilian branches. For many peasants who served in the PLAF, the Front's military forces, the close regulation of working hours—including when people rose in the morning and went to bed in the evening and ate their meals, as well as the division of mornings for 'military training' and afternoons for 'political study' and self-criticism (*kiem thao*)—marked a considerable departure from the agrarian rhythms that shaped much of rural southern life. Front time was solar time, with the Western calendar used to structure its military and political initiatives. Much of village time revolved around the lunar calendar. It structured the economic and social dimensions of the household agricultural cycle, most importantly the planting and harvest of rice, as well as the spiritual life of the agrarian population from the soteriological sensibilities of southern Buddhism to rituals honouring family ancestors and tutelary deities.

As the southern communist insurgency reconstituted itself in the late 1950s and early 1960s and into the first years of the American war, it was particularly effective at striking a balance between the potentially competing demands of the solar and lunar calendars. If the Front shared the northern regime's antipathy to 'superstitious practices', it nonetheless sought to minimize tensions between the commitments of cadres as family cultivators and political or military operatives. Unlike ARVN policies, soldiers and political cadres were granted leave to support their families at planting and harvest times when the need for agricultural manpower was at its greatest. The Front's progressive tax policies were also relatively light compared to those of the South Vietnamese state, more closely matched to the agrarian cycle and to the inevitability that some years would produce better harvests than others. Underlying all these practices was a prevailing sense of a quick victory in the war.

But as the war after 1965 began to look protracted and the fighting became fiercer and more destructive, the balance between solar and lunar time became more difficult to maintain and civilian confidence in the NLF started to decline. The bombing, shelling, and ecological warfare that characterized American military strategy in southern Vietnam took a huge toll on the fabric of rural society, literally depopulating huge swaths of the countryside as villagers moved to refugee camps and urban areas. Those who remained did not necessarily turn towards the South Vietnamese government, but they also blamed the Front for its inability to protect them from the American onslaught and were critical of the Front's shifts after 1965 to military conscription and more coercive taxation policies. Reporting on attitudes in a single Mekong delta village, one NLF cadre summarized these prevailing views of the Front and its agents:

they no longer welcome them warmly in their homes, wining and dining them as they used to do before. The people are no longer so respectful toward the cadres in their hamlets in their speech and behavior. Besides, they no longer comply with the cadres in civilian labor or paying taxes as they did before. In other words, the people are indifferent or even cold toward the cadres.[42]

Civilian war-weariness, even among those peasants most sympathetic to the NLF, would over time shift the dynamics of the movement. Along with patriotism, much of the early appeal of the southern revolution had been class-based, centring around the NLF's promises of village land reform. By the late 1960s, however, wealthier peasants had fled most NLF-controlled villages, and with land redistribution in place there was a levelling out of class tensions. Villages increasingly consisted of middle peasants (*trung nong*), defined as those who had enough land to support themselves and their families without hiring themselves out as labourers or hiring labourers themselves. As many of these new middle peasants had been poor or landless peasants in the past, their better fortune was the direct result of NLF land reform. But the elimination of landlordism and the large southern landless tenant class, which had been so critical to the NLF's early appeal, also posed problems. With the emergence of a rural middle class, peasant interest in revolution sharply declined. Though often more sympathetic to the Front than the South Vietnamese state, in part because of the debt they knew they owed to NLF land policy, many rural people were more interested in bringing the war to a close than in protracted revolutionary struggle. These attitudes also coloured the attitudes of a younger generation who increasingly led the NLF after 1967. Many in the revolutionary generation who launched the southern insurgency in the late 1950s were killed or disabled by the mid-1960s. Others quit the Front, or fled the war-torn countryside. Some cast their lot with the South Vietnamese government. For the younger generation of NLF leadership active in the final years of the war, the desire for peace was as important, if not for some more so, than bringing about social revolution.[43]

There were other tensions within the Front that increased as the American war escalated. Women played a particularly important role in the NLF. At its highest levels, Nguyen Thi Dinh was a founding member of the NLF and led its Women's Association throughout the American war, while Nguyen Thi Binh served as the foreign minister of the Front's Provisional Revolutionary Government. Many urban and rural women also served in more everyday military and civilian capacities as soldiers, cadres, porters, nurses, and intelligence-gatherers. But, like their counterparts in the North, they also carried the burdens of caring for their families and, in the war-ravaged southern countryside, became responsible for household agricultural production in ways that limited their upward mobility within the Front. The double standard through which women could be viewed within the Front is best illustrated in its reaction to sexual relationships outside marriage among its cadres. Officially the NLF insisted on chastity for both its male and female comrades, in part concerned about the impact of sexual promiscuity on the Front's relations with local peoples but also about maintaining a rhetorical commitment to gender equality. In practice, however, male indiscretions were often tolerated or excused while the affairs of female cadres, usually with men in the Front who outranked them, were viewed more sternly; in a number of cases they were forced to leave the movement altogether.[44]

There were also ambiguities over the relationship between class struggle and the American war both within the NLF itself and in its relationship with the state and party leadership in Hanoi. Many of the urban professionals who were attracted to the Front and became its public face never fully embraced socialist revolution but instead believed they could realize their more individualized commitment to social justice far better through the NLF than through the South Vietnamese state. These highly educated cosmopolitans chafed at NLF policies that emphasized class, and they increasingly resented the class politics of some of the political cadres sent down from the North to advise them. The Anti-Party Affair of 1967 in the North marked a further hardening of attitudes about class struggle among the top Hanoi leadership, which complicated the North's relationship with the NLF in the final years of the war. At the same time, the NLF's own policies around class issues and their implementation on the ground were sometimes at odds. The Front's 1965 effort to promote class consciousness through the Eliminate American Merchandise Movement (*phong rao bai tru hang My*) asked soldiers to burn clothes made with nylon or synthetic fabrics associated with American capitalism and gave them black pyjamas woven from rough cotton cloth made in a northern textile factory. The campaign, however, was unevenly applied, with many of the PLAF's most elite battalions allowed to dress in any way they pleased, suggesting the plurality of perspectives that shaped the Front's inconsistency on class issues.[45]

Whatever its internal tensions and setbacks and despite the emerging complexities of its relationship to rural civilians, the NLF retained considerable strength in southern Vietnam. An assistant squad leader with a PLAF unit vividly described the hardships facing the Front's military forces in this period:

During the rainy season, sometimes in the middle of night, water rushed down from Cambodia and covered the canal bank where we were sleeping. We were so tired and sleepy that we didn't bother to move, and continued to sleep in the water with only our heads above the water. One time we had to sleep near the pig pen of a liaison station and awoke at night to find ourselves drenched with the urine of pigs and sows. What's more, we were often strafed by helicopters and didn't have enough to eat. We never had fresh fruit to eat and our diet never varied; it was always rice with salt or fish sauce. Then the men began to long for all sorts of material things and to miss their families. There were few people in the areas where we lived, and we felt very lonely. In addition, the cadres didn't provide firm ideological leadership, and this was why many men deserted. Besides, there were no safe places where we could stay and we were strafed and bombed constantly.[46]

There were desertions from this unit, as many as twenty per month. But, perhaps more remarkably, most of its members held firm. NLF main force units and its irregular guerrilla forces, along with its rural civilian supporters and PAVN troops from the North, kept the American war to stalemate by the end of 1967.

The human costs of the American war in Vietnam were immense. More than 200,000 PAVN and PLAF soldiers were killed in action in 1968, when the war's casualties were at their height, along with 28,000 ARVN troops. Over the course of the American war, a little over a million PAVN and PLAF soldiers and almost 240,000 ARVN troops were killed, about 3 per cent of Vietnam's total wartime population. By way of perspective, had the United States sustained casualties at a similar percentage of its 1970 population, there would have been 6 million war dead instead of the 58,000 Americans who died in Vietnam. Furthermore, in the US civil war, which claimed the lives of more soldiers than any other American war, 620,000 troops were killed or a bit less than 2 per cent of the 1870 US population.[47] We simply do not know the exact number of Vietnamese civilians who died as a result of the war, with estimates ranging from between 1 and 4 million. Almost no Vietnamese family north or south remained untouched by the war.

   Dang Thuy Tram wrote the final entry in her diary on 20 June 1970. Most of her colleagues and the party cadre at the medical clinic in the Nai Sang Mountains of central Vietnam where she worked had fled in face of sustained American aerial bombing and ground attacks. An informer had given away their position. Tram remained, along with three female medics and five wounded soldiers. Their rice rations were nearing an end:

Until today, no one has returned. It has been almost ten days since they left and promised to come back. . . . We didn't think any one would leave us like this. . . . I am not a child. I am grown up, and already strong in the face of hardships. But at this minute, why do I want so much a mother's hand to care for me? . . . Please come to me and hold my hand when I am so lonely. Love and give me strength to travel the hard sections of the road ahead.[48]

Two days later Dang Thuy Tram was found dead, with an American bullet lodged in her skull.

South Vietnamese National Police Chief Brigadier-General Nguyen Ngoc
Loan executes an NLF cadre during the Tet Offensive

5

WAR'S END

At 2.45 a.m. on 30 January 1968, a team of NLF cadres blasted a hole in the wall surrounding the US Embassy in Saigon and dashed into the courtyard of the compound. For the next six hours, this potent symbol of the US presence in southern Vietnam was the scene of one of the most dramatic episodes of the American war in Vietnam. Unable to get through the heavy door at the main entrance of the Embassy building, the attackers retreated into the courtyard and took cover behind large concrete flowerpots, pounding the building with rockets and exchanging gunfire with a small detachment of military police. They held their positions until 9.15 a.m., when they were finally overpowered. All nineteen of the NLF cadres were killed or severely wounded. The attack on the American Embassy was a part of the Tet Offensive of 1968, known colloquially in Vietnam as Tet Mau Than, a massive coordinated assault by North Vietnamese and NLF forces against the South Vietnamese government and their American allies in major urban areas and the countryside aimed at bringing victory in the American war.

It did not, in 1968. Seven years would pass before the war came to an end. But in the wake of the Tet Offensive, the dynamics of the American war profoundly changed. Despite the spectacle of the NLF attack on the US Embassy, the Front emerged from the offensive far weaker in both the political and military spheres than it had been throughout most of the 1960s. An ever deepening warweariness in the South cut against subsequent efforts to rebuild its forces. After Tet the North Vietnamese army provided the military muscle for the southern communist insurgency in a struggle that would more and more pivot on conventional military battles rather than guerrilla warfare.

But who the northern army would face on the battlefield, and where, was also in flux. Notwithstanding its devastating impact on the NLF, the psychological shock of the Tet Offensive dramatically shifted American policy towards the war in Vietnam. US military forces in South Vietnam, which had reached their peak in 1967, were slowly drawn down. In their place the South Vietnamese army, whose troop strength reached over 1 million by 1972, would face North Vietnamese and NLF forces, backed by massive US airpower along with continuing and substantial military aid and assistance. The geographical contours of the war also grew wider, drawing in both neighbouring Cambodia and Laos, which experienced some of the most sustained and devastating US bombing campaigns of the American war. Efforts intensified, too, after Tet to find a negotiated settlement to the war in a process shaped by a larger transformation in relations between the United States, China, and the Soviet Union. The diplomatic search for peace, however, brought the North Vietnamese into more acrimonious conflict with their Soviet and Chinese allies, strained the already fraying bonds of the US–South Vietnamese relationship, and ultimately produced a settlement that marked no more than a pause in the fighting.

When military victory came for North Vietnam in April 1975, far more quickly than it had anticipated, its three-decade struggle for national liberation against France and the United States was at an end. But the twin goal of socialist revolution in a reunified Vietnam proved more difficult to realize. The shifting dynamics of the American war after Tet shaped not only the war's end but also the sometimes contradictory and surprising dimensions of the post-war peace.

The Tet Offensive

The decision to launch a general offensive in the South emerged through vigorous debates among the top Hanoi leadership in 1967.

During the French war, the DRV had seen the larger path to victory through a Maoist lens as a three-stage process that moved from defence to equilibrium and finally to a general offensive. For many in the party and state the American war appeared to be entering into a stage of equilibrium (*cam cu*) in 1967, though one they defined somewhat differently than they had in the past when such judgements rested on a sense of the numerical superiority of their own forces. The party leadership was aware of their own setbacks on the ground in the South since the introduction of American ground forces, and that more could come. They also acknowledged the continuing imbalance in firepower and numbers of regular troops on the ground between the two sides. But Hanoi believed that the inability of the American search-and-destroy missions and bombing campaigns to alter decisively the dynamics of the war, a growing domestic opposition to the war in the United States, and the continuing weaknesses of the South Vietnamese state offered promising openings to exploit the enemy's vulnerabilities. The time had come 'to prepare quickly on all fronts to seize the opportunity to achieve a large victory and force America to accept a military defeat' through a major military offensive and a popular uprising throughout southern Vietnam, what officially became known as the General Offensive and General Uprising (Tong con kich, Tong khoi nghia).[1]

The strategic and tactical contours of the offensive, however, were hotly contested, shaped by differing visions of how to fight the American war and by the complexities of Hanoi's relationship with its Soviet and Chinese allies. General Nguyen Chi Thanh, the commander of military operations in the South, urged the adoption of the strategy of high-level confrontation that had informed his aggressive policies since 1965 of engaging American and South Vietnamese troops in conventional battles with main-force units. As General Thanh wrote in early 1967, 'To attack unremittingly is the most active and most effective method to maintain and extend our control over the battlefield.'[2] But when Thanh's tactics began to produce exceptionally high casualties and failed to shift decisively the balance of military forces in the South, powerful forces within

the DRV, including the defence minister and general in command
of the northern army Vo Nguyen Giap, raised serious questions
about the efficacy of big-unit warfare. Giap saw the war in the
South as a protracted people's war, emphasizing that it could take as
many as fifteen to twenty years to achieve victory and strongly
advocating guerrilla warfare along with regular units and conventional battles.[3]

These internal debates were complicated by competing pressures
from the Soviet Union and China as the tensions of the Sino-Soviet
split intensified. The Soviets, who provided anti-aircraft artillery
and heavy weapons critical to fighting the Americans and whose
level of military and economic aid would shortly exceed those of
China, urged the Vietnamese to fight a more conventional war.
For their part the Chinese, who controlled the transport logistics
for both Chinese and Soviet aid and provided 320,000 troops to
man engineering and anti-aircraft units in the North, urged the
Vietnamese to follow a Maoist-style protracted guerrilla war. The
Chinese also feared that a large-scale offensive would further
increase North Vietnamese dependence on the Soviets for military
aid and weapons. As Mao told Vo Nguyen Giap at a meeting in
Beijing in early 1967,

We have a saying: 'if you preserve the mountain green, you will never
have to worry about firewood.' The U.S. is afraid of your tactics. They
wish that you would order your regular forces to fight, so they can destroy
your main forces. But you were not deceived. Fighting a war of attrition is
like having meals: [it is best] not to have too big a bite.[4]

The incremental and improvisational planning for Tet reflected
these internal and external divisions. Nguyen Chi Thanh's aggressive approach to the general offensive was scaled back in the early
summer of 1967, when a decision was made to rely more on
southern-based NLF troops rather than on those from the North
Vietnamese army and to put limits on where attacks in the South
would take place. Thanh's sudden death in early July prompted a
further scaling back of plans for the military offensive. At the same
time, plans moved forward to foment a general popular uprising in

the South, although they were communicated to southern NLF cadres in piecemeal and sometimes confusing ways. Throughout the fall of 1967, the North Vietnamese undertook a series of diversionary military moves in an effort to make the Tet Offensive a surprise. They attacked along the Cambodian border, the central highlands, and the demilitarized zone that separated North and South Vietnam to convince the Americans and the South Vietnamese government that Hanoi was intent on seizing the northern sectors of South Vietnam. The North also began to move troops into place near Khe Sanh, in the north-west near the Lao border, hoping to draw American troops out of southern cities and make urban centres more vulnerable to attack during Tet. Reports of these troop movements did alarm American observers, who feared Khe Sanh might be another Dien Bien Phu. President Johnson in fact had a scale model of Khe Sanh built for the White House situation room so that he could follow developments closely. The Americans redeployed as many as 50,000 troops from urban centres to Khe Sanh and the northern border region, weakening the defences of South Vietnamese cities in the way in which Hanoi had hoped. North Vietnamese troops initiated the battle of Khe Sanh on 21 January 1968, nine days before the beginning of the Tet Offensive, in what became one of the bloodiest battles of the American war, though ultimately of little consequence for the war's resolution.[5]

As North Vietnamese soldiers were put into place near Khe Sanh, planning for the Tet Offensive and the popular uprising continued. The timing of the offensive was carefully chosen, consciously drawing on a military tactic used by the Vietnamese in a late eighteenth-century battle against the Chinese. Tet is the Vietnamese lunar New Year, the most important holiday in Vietnam, when almost all work in the country comes to halt for a week of familial celebrations with many travelling back to their home villages. Throughout the war, both sides had honoured a ceasefire during Tet. Using the holiday, when ARVN was at half strength as so many soldiers had Tet leave to return home to their families, introduced a critical element of surprise. The cacophony of firecrackers and fireworks that herald the beginning of the New Year also provided useful cover for the gunfire that opened the Tet Offensive. On 30 January 1968 communist forces, mainly local units of the National Liberation Front's PLAF, attacked thirty-six of South Vietnam's forty-six provinces, sixty-four of the 242 district capitals, five of the South's largest cities, and countless numbers of hamlets and villages. In Saigon NLF units attacked Tan Son Nhut airport, the headquarters of South Vietnam's general staff and the presidential palace.

Just as Vietnamese willingness to engage in battle during lunar New Year had surprised the Chinese two centuries before, the Tet Offensive caught South Vietnam and the Americans off guard. But once the initial shock had passed, they quickly recovered. Most of the attacks in urban areas were reversed in three to four days, and the hope of a general uprising in the cities was quickly forestalled. Communist forces did hold the former imperial capital of Hue until late February. The liberation of that city involved intensive artillery fire, heavy bombing, and savage street fighting, which produced a huge number of civilian casualties and as many as 100,000 refugees. In its aftermath the bodies of 2,800 South Vietnamese who had been executed by NLF and North Vietnamese forces were discovered in mass graves in and around Hue, suggesting the communist insurgency was as capable as the United States and the South Vietnamese of using terror as an instrument of war. Popular uprisings did take place in the rural south, often with considerable enthusiasm from local populations, but NLF forces had to abandon many of their victories in the villages to meet continuing demands by Tet's planners in Hanoi to push back militarily in cities and towns.

The offensive was a major military defeat for the North and the NLF. Much of the Front's civilian infrastructure and military forces was destroyed in the fierce fighting during and after the offensive. The NLF lost 80 per cent of its fighting force, suffering as many as 50,000 casualties. Political cadres, particularly those in urban areas, came out from under cover to lead the failed general uprising, and many were subsequently arrested. Hanoi's insistence on high-level confrontation throughout 1968 further increased NL[...] rural support for the general uprising was initially wides[...] many cadres returned to their villages and refused to fight when[...] became clear that Tet-induced hopes of the fall of the South Vietnamese regime had not materialized. In the remaining years of the American war, the NLF was less able than in the past to mobilize effectively the local population in the South, who were even more dispirited by the war after Tet. Recruitment efforts faltered as the Front was no longer seen as a desirable route of advancement for rural youth, reflected in the shrinkage in the numbers of NLF cadres from as many as 250,000 in 1968 to some 197,000 in 1971. In the aftermath of the offensive, General Tran Van Tra, who commanded PLAF forces in the B2 theatre north and north-west of Saigon during Tet, wrote: 'we suffered large sacrifices and losses with regard to manpower and *matériel*, did not correctly evaluate the specific balance of forces between ourselves and the enemy, [and] did not fully realize that the enemy still had considerable capabilities and that our capabilities were limited. . . . [We] set requirements that were beyond our strength.'[6]

But if Tet fell short of its most ambitious goals, it did fundamentally alter the nature of the American war. The psychological shock of the Tet attacks throughout southern Vietnam undermined the frequent promises of General William Westmoreland, the American commander in Vietnam, that he could see 'the light at the end of the tunnel'. The gap between rhetoric and reality in the early days of the offensive astounded and outraged many Americans, so much so that President Johnson felt compelled to quit his re-election campaign in the aftermath of Tet. Even after American and South Vietnamese forces rallied to defeat the offensive, Tet proved to be a turning point in US perceptions and policy towards the war. Support for the war and the American relationship with the South Vietnamese government began to unravel. As the former secretary of state Dean Acheson told President Johnson in a meeting in late March 1968, 'We can no longer do the job we set out to do in the time we have left and we must begin to take steps to disengage.'[7] Public opinion polls in the wake of Tet

...rity of Americans believed the United
...gress in the war in Vietnam. In the tumul-
...1968, which eventually brought Richard
...y, US policy moved from visions of possible
...etnam to a far more ambiguous sense of the
...he might take. Tet also shifted the subsequent
...f the war on the communist side. Only a limited
number o... Vietnamese troops were engaged in the offensive,
with many units held in reserve pending a favourable outcome on
the ground. As such, NLF forces bore the brunt of the casualties
during the offensive and in its aftermath. The severe reduction in
the numbers of NLF troops and faltering efforts at rural mobilization meant that North Vietnamese troops took over the fighting for
much of the rest of the American war, and conventional rather than
guerrilla warfare became the norm.

A Shifting War

Richard Nixon came to the White House in 1969 with what he had
promised during the 1968 election campaign was a secret plan to
win the war. That such a plan actually existed during the campaign
itself appears unlikely, but once in office Nixon and his national
security adviser Henry Kissinger quickly introduced a series of
policies to build up the South Vietnamese state and widen the
geographical parameters of the conflict aimed at challenging
North Vietnam's increasing dominance on the ground in the
South. Recognizing American war-weariness and the growing
power of the anti-war movement, Nixon embraced a policy of
Vietnamization that reflected a persisting American belief that it was
the United States who would make South Vietnam Vietnamese. In
June 1969 he announced the withdrawal of 25,000 US ground
troops; American troop levels fell to 475,000 at the end of 1969
and 140,000 by the end of 1971. As the administration shifted
responsibility for fighting the war to the South Vietnamese, it
significantly increased military and economic assistance to the
Saigon government. The level of ARVN forces, about 850,000

when Nixon took office, increased rapidly to over 1 million. The US turned over huge quantities of weapons to South Vietnam, including more than a million M16 rifles as well as machine guns, grenade launchers, and heavy mortars and howitzers. The South Vietnamese were also given large numbers of ships, planes, helicopters, and military vehicles. Military schools were expanded to a capacity of more than 100,000 students per year, and efforts were made to improve ARVN morale by raising pay scales, expanding veterans' benefits, and improving conditions in military camps.

The impact of Vietnamization in Vietnam was ambiguous. By 1970 it was in full swing and most observers agreed that some gains had been made. Almost overnight ARVN had become one of the largest and best-equipped armies in the world. When properly led, ARVN units could fight well, and some American advisers noted that perhaps out of necessity ARVN performance began to improve as US support units were withdrawn. But if on paper ARVN was a formidable force, many of its fundamental weaknesses persisted. The process of 'ghosting', by which the names of dead and deserted soldiers were kept on pay rosters so that the officer in charge could pocket the pay, ran as high as 20 per cent. Desertion remained a chronic problem, as was the severe shortage of qualified, competent, and honest officers at all levels. Even the stronger ARVN units sometimes manifested an unwillingness to engage the enemy in sustained combat, prompting American military advisers to question if the South Vietnamese army would ever become aggressive enough to counter the highly motivated troops of the PLAF and PAVN. Many in the ARVN feared that Vietnamization was the prelude to the full withdrawal of US support for South Vietnam. As one ARVN officer recalled, 'Many of us believe the U.S. was simply giving up, that Washington had set us on this course and was now abandoning us in our hour of greatest need.'[8] The commitment of American ground troops to the war effort also weakened after Vietnamization. With the purposes of the war increasingly murky, US forces were less willing to put their lives on the line than they had earlier in the American war. Unit discipline broke down, attempts to assassinate officers, or what was termed 'fragging', rose sharply (more than 200 incidents were reported in 1970), drug abuse became more common, and outbreaks of racial incidents between African American and white soldiers grew more numerous.[9]

Along with Vietnamization, Nixon's policy towards South Vietnam also sought to accelerate the battle for 'hearts and minds', or pacification, of the rural population. Pacification was not a new strategy; it had been central to the Diem era policies of agrovilles and strategic hamlets and his Denounce the Communists campaign. American critics of the big-unit warfare that formed the core of US military strategy in Vietnam since 1965 had long argued that what was really needed was a sustained effort to break the hold of the NLF in the countryside. Pacification efforts expanded under the Johnson administration in the wake of the Tet Offensive, but they further accelerated with the coming of Vietnamization. ARVN forces assigned to improving village security were expanded to half a million men, whose efforts were supplemented by enlarged village militias. Projects to clear roads, repair bridges, and establish schools and hospitals were launched, as were new programmes to expand agricultural production, including the distribution of new, higher-yield 'miracle rice' and technology that improved planting, threshing, and irrigation. Americans also pushed the South Vietnamese government to undertake rural reforms, including the restoration of village elections in 1969 and an ambitious Land to the Tiller land reform programme in 1970.[10]

Critical to the Nixon pacification campaign were efforts to identity and destroy the NLF infrastructure in the South through the Phoenix programme. In theory, this American-directed pro- gramme sought to gather intelligence on Front cadres which would then be given to the South Vietnamese military, who, in the language of the day, could 'neutralize' the cadre. In practice this meant getting him or her to rally to the side of the South Vietnamese government, or face imprisonment and sometimes death. In its implementation, the programme was plagued by many of the problems that had impeded US and South Vietnamese efforts to force a collapse of the NLF. For instance, the intelligence that Phoenix uncovered on the Front was not always accurate. To have any hope of success, the programme needed to identify high-level cadres that controlled the NLF's organizational structure. Several factors made that difficult: the most important cadres were heavily protected and increasingly lived in sanctuaries on the Cambodian side of the Vietnamese border; widespread popular fear of NLF retribution on informants; and the prevalence of intra-villages rivalries and feuds that some-times prompted people to put forward names of people who had little if nothing to do with the Front. There were also problems on the American side. Six-month rotations and one-year tours of duty for American military personnel meant there was little time to accumulate the knowledge of local conditions necessary for effective intelligence-gathering. Because few US soldiers spoke Vietnamese, they had to rely on ARVN interpreters, who generally came from provinces far from where their units were operating and had little first-hand knowledge of local conditions. The uses to which this limited and sometimes faulty intelligence was put also hindered efforts to break the NLF. Rivalries between the ARVN, the national police, and local forces limited success, as did the workings on the ground of a quota system set up as an incentive to kill or capture NLF cadres. Low-level cadres were easier to locate and filled most of the quotas, whereas high-level cadres whose capture was more significant continued to go free. Still, NLF cadres acknowledged that in some areas the Phoenix programme was 'dangerously effective'.[11]

Without question the NLF was weaker in the southern coun-tryside by 1972 than it had been in 1968, though less because of Vietnamization and American-led pacification than because of the decimation of the Front's military forces in the Tet Offensive and the capture of the many formerly underground NLF cadres who had surfaced to lead the failed general uprising. The rural south was quieter and safer for peasants as the shift to more conventional warfare after 1968 left them increasingly alone and freer to engage in the rhythms of the household agricultural cycle. But if the American war began to feel different for rural Vietnamese, these new sensibilities did not necessarily translate into support for the

South Vietnamese Nguyen Van Thieu government. Thieu's land reform in 1969, though more far-reaching than efforts in the Diem period, did little more than recognize land titles the NLF had given out in the 1950s and 1960s. Many Vietnamese peasants remained exhausted by the war, retreating into their family lives and seeking to avoid the political realm altogether.[12]

If the situation in South Vietnam was somewhat calmer, under the Nixon administration the American war expanded with ferocity into neighbouring Cambodia and Laos. In March 1969 Nixon ordered the secret bombing of Cambodia. Over the next fifteen months some 3,000 B-52 raids were flown, dropping more than 100,000 tons of bombs on Cambodia. The operation was dubbed, with singular inappropriateness, Menu, and its individual components Breakfast, Lunch, Supper, Dinner, Dessert, and Snack. The bombing also took place in Laos, with the Lunch strikes directed at the Lao-Cambodian border. A separate campaign from 1969 to 1973 pushed deeper into Laos, with almost 1.5 million tons of bombs dropped. In bombing Cambodia and Laos, Nixon was intent upon destroying the supply lines North Vietnam used to infiltrate troops and supplies to southern Vietnam through the Ho Chi Minh Trail. The trail, which crossed into both Cambodia and Laos along the Vietnamese border, had been transformed by the late 1960s from a relatively primitive set of jungle trails to a dense network of carefully maintained roads and bridges that could accommodate bicycles and military vehicles carrying as many as 5,000 soldiers each month and 400 tons of supplies each week into South Vietnam. The Nixon administration believed the most important target was the Central Office for Southern Vietnam (COSVN), located just inside Cambodia's border with South Vietnam, which directed the communist war effort in the South. Two other dimensions of Nixon war strategy shaped its planning for these unprecedented bombing campaigns. At a time of Vietnamization, extending the war into Cambodia and Laos was seen as demonstrating a continuing seriousness on the part of the United States in the American war. The bombing was also the first example of what Nixon termed his 'madman theory', a willingness to use savage force to keep North Vietnam guessing about American intentions that Nixon believed marked a sharp departure from Johnson's more gradualist approach to the war.[13]

Despite the massive bombing, COSVN proved an elusive target, and in April 1970 Nixon ordered the invasion of Cambodia, sending in 90,000 US ground troops and 40,000 ARVN forces in what was a major geographical expansion of the American war. The invasion set off a firestorm of controversy in the United States, pushing the fervour of the anti-war movement to new heights and prompting increasingly vocal Congressional opposition to Nixon's policy in Vietnam. The bombing and invasion did disrupt northern supply lines, though not enough to change the direction of the war. COSVN itself was never decisively hit, in large measure because the Nixon administration's perception of COSVN as a jungle version of the US Pentagon obscured the reality of it as a series of impermanent makeshift huts that was more about the people who inhabited them than about the place itself. When US intelligence did pinpoint COSVN's position, Soviet intelligence was often able to get warnings to the North and the NLF about American intentions. One NLF official who experienced the fierce bombings described their impact in this way:

We were awakened by the familiar thunder—nearer now than it had been in recent days. . . . as the cataclysm walked in on us, everybody hugged the earth—some screaming quietly, others struggling to suppress attacks of violent, involuntary trembling. Around us the ground began to heave spasmodically, and we were engulfed in a monstrous roar. Then, abruptly, it stopped. . . . The last of the bomb craters had opened up less than a kilometer away. Again, miraculously, no one had been hurt. . . . spirits began to revive. COSVN's Pham Hung and General Trung joked that 'Even though we ran like hell, still we'll win,' sentiments that Henry Kissinger anticipated in his 1968 *Foreign Affairs* article: 'Guerillas win if they don't lose. A standard army loses if it does not win.'[14]

If the American bombing and invasion left the NLF command and the Ho Chi Minh Trail largely intact, it did set in motion a destabilizing set of developments within Cambodia itself. Cambodia had preserved a precarious decade-long neutrality in the American war. Norodom Sihanouk, the neutralist leader of Cambodia, turned a blind eye to the North Vietnamese and NLF use of Cambodian territory in the 1960s, and the Johnson administration, worried about the dangers of an escalating war, largely prohibited attacks on Vietnamese sanctuaries in Cambodia. Nixon's attitudes towards Cambodia marked a clear shift in policy, and Sihanouk vehemently protested Nixon's secret bombing. In March 1970, a month before the American invasion of Cambodia, Sihanouk was overthrown in a military coup, whose pro-American leaders demanded the withdrawal of North Vietnamese troops from Cambodian soil. Although the extent of US involvement in the coup remains a matter of debate, the hopelessly inept and extremely weak regime received strong American backing and drew an ever more chaotic Cambodia directly into the American war. North Vietnamese and NLF troops drove deeper into the Cambodian countryside in the wake of the US bombing and invasion. There they began to work in an often acrimonious partnership with the Cambodian Communist Party, better known as the Khmer Rouge, who under Pol Pot would establish a genocidal regime in the country after 1975. Scholars of modern Cambodian history contend that popular support for the Khmer Rouge before the American intervention in Cambodia was very limited. They argue that the American bombing campaign, which killed as many as 150,000 Cambodian civilians, was critical in drawing ordinary Cambodians into the arms of the revolutionary movement.[15]

The American war also spread to neighbouring Laos. Between 1960 and 1974 the US Central Intelligence Agency (CIA) had maintained a secret army of 30,000 Hmong tribesmen in mountainous northern Laos to fight against a Lao communist insurgency. An upland people whose economy was dominated by subsistence agriculture, the Hmong had become involved in the cultivation of opium during the period of French colonial rule. To encourage the Hmong leadership to provide a mercenary army for the CIA, the Agency used its clandestine air network to transport Hmong opium for sale on the world drug market.[16] As the war escalated in Cambodia, this low-level insurgency and the beginnings of massive US bombing in Laos were augmented by the use of ARVN troops in direct fighting near the Lao border. In the Lam Son 719 campaign of February 1971, one of the first major tests of Vietnamization, US military planners sought to thwart an expected North Vietnamese drive into the South using the portion of the Ho Chi Minh Trail that ran through the Lao panhandle. A Congressional amendment passed after the Cambodian invasion barred US ground troops from entering either Cambodia or Laos, so the Lam Son campaign had to be run using ARVN troops backed by US air support. Plans for the campaign, however, were leaked to Hanoi well before the attack and what was intended to be a surprise turned out to be a major ARVN defeat. At the beginning of February, South Vietnam sent 17,000 of the ARVN's best troops into southern Laos. Almost immediately, President Thieu issued secret instructions to halt the offensive if 3,000 men became incapacitated. When ARVN losses mounted, Thieu ordered a retreat without informing US military commanders. At this point only massive American air support prevented a complete disaster for the badly coordinated and frightened elite ARVN units. Even so, more than 9,000 ARVN troops were killed or wounded with many US Army helicopters and planes destroyed or damaged. Nixon administration assertions that the ARVN had conducted an 'orderly retreat' were belied by the haste and confusion which marked the withdrawal from Laos and revealed the very limited gains that the policies of an expanded war and Vietnamization had brought for the Americans and the South Vietnamese.[17]

The War for Peace

Prior to the Tet Offensive neither Washington nor Hanoi had been especially keen on a negotiated settlement to the American war in Vietnam. The United States rejected European efforts to promote the neutralization of South Vietnam before the massive American escalation in 1965, as they did attempts by the United Nations and France to bring North Vietnam and the US into diplomatic contact when war broke out. Hanoi was pressed by its Soviet and Chinese allies in very different directions on negotiations. The Soviets, who saw the American war as an impediment to a desired relaxation of tensions with the United States, increasingly favoured negotiations, while the Chinese, then in the most radical phase of the Cultural Revolution and opposed to any accommodation with the West, strongly opposed them. Given Hanoi's reliance on military and economic support from both parties, these very differing Soviet and Chinese views weighed heavily on the North Vietnamese leadership. Somewhat to American surprise, they responded favourably to the Johnson administration's offer to open negotiations in Paris in March 1968.

Formal talks opened in Paris in May. Though they quickly reached stalemate, the very decision to engage in negotiations prompted renewed strains in the Sino-Vietnamese relationship. In a heated meeting in Beijing in October between Chen Yi, China's vice-premier and foreign minister, and Le Duc Tho, the North's chief negotiator with the US in Paris, both sides accused the other of making basic errors in handling negotiations with the Americans, highlighting persisting Vietnamese bitterness over Chinese pressures to accept the Geneva settlement that had brought an end to the French war. Chen Yi told Le Duc Tho, 'you have accepted the compromising and capitulationist proposals put forward by the Soviet revisionists. . . . now the cause is more difficult and the price for victory more expensive', prompting an acrimonious exchange, in which Le Duc Tho replied:

we will wait and see. And the reality will give us the answer. We have gained experience over fifteen years. Let reality justify . . . We signed the Geneva accords in 1954 when the US did not agree to do so. We withdrew our armed forces from the South to the North, thus letting people in the South be killed . . . Because we listened to your advice.

Chen Yi countered:

You just mentioned that in the Geneva conference, you made a mistake because you followed our advice. But this time, you will make another mistake if you do not take our words into account.[18]

In fact the northern leadership was closer to the Chinese view than these tense exchanges suggest. They had agreed to the Paris talks with little interest in substantive negotiation, viewing the meetings as the diplomatic dimension of the broader political and military struggle, or what the North termed 'negotiating while fighting, fighting while negotiating'.

President Thieu of South Vietnam also sought to stall the negotiations before the US presidential election in November, believing if Richard Nixon won he would be a more reliable negotiating partner. He recognized the dangers negotiation posed to the viability of the South Vietnamese state, telling Johnson in October: 'You are powerful. You can say to a small nation what you want . . . but you cannot force us to do anything against our interests. This negotiation is not a life and death matter for the U.S., but it is for Vietnam.'[19] Thieu only agreed to send representatives to Paris after Nixon's election victory. In what became known as the battle of the tables, Thieu signalled his intransigence by refusing to agree to the shape of the negotiating table. After considerable back and forth, the Americans, who preferred two rectangular tables, and the North Vietnamese, who advocated a square table, acquiesced to a round table, which would privilege none of the four parties to the talks, which, along with the US and North Vietnam, included South Vietnam and the NLF's Provisional Revolutionary Government (PRG). Thieu had opposed seating the PRG at all, fearful it would accord greater legitimacy to the Front. But after agreeing to their presence in Paris, he refused to have South Vietnam's representative sit next to or across the table from the PRG or Hanoi. The round table was out. Throughout most of December 1968 American negotiators floated a creative series of geometric shapes. With reluctance, both Thieu and Hanoi ultimately agreed to a round table placed between two rectangular tables. The peace talks were not going well.

More substantively, there was a yawning gap between the North Vietnamese and US negotiating positions. Hanoi wanted the US to withdraw fully from South Vietnam and to have the Thieu government replaced by a coalition that included the NLF. For its part Washington sought an agreement that provided for the mutual withdrawal of forces, both US and North Vietnamese, and refused to talk of replacing the South Vietnamese government. None of the efforts of the Nixon administration in 1969 to break the diplomatic stalemate—opening a secret negotiating track with the North Vietnamese, escalating the war through the savage bombing of Cambodia, and threatening even more massive American bombing in northern Vietnam—forced North Vietnam's hand. Perceptions of the persisting weakness of the South Vietnamese state, their own fears about the waning post-Tet fortunes of the NLF, and China's continuing pressure to resist settlement combined to shape the resolve of North Vietnam to avoid compromise.[20] Short of a decisive shift on the battlefield in Vietnam or a fundamental change in the international environment, prospects for a negotiated peace remained dim.

Such a diplomatic revolution did come in late 1971. Since the beginning of his term in office, Nixon had hoped to persuade the Soviet Union and China to press the North Vietnamese to end the war. Recognizing growing Soviet interest in détente, he sought to induce its cooperation with promises of arms control and trade agreements. At the same time Nixon believed the Sino-Soviet split could be exploited to American advantage, and that perhaps Mao would be receptive to a rapprochement with the United States as a counterweight to the Soviets. This kind of triangular diplomacy, Nixon believed, could give the US and the Chinese additional leverage in their dealings with the Soviets. In turn, the Chinese might be willing to persuade their Vietnamese allies to agree to a negotiated settlement on American terms. Nixon's efforts initially centred on trying to link talks with the Soviets over nuclear arms limitation with progress in the Paris peace negotiations. Serious overtures to China began in the fall of 1970 and the Chinese proved increasingly receptive to them. Nixon's announcement of Henry Kissinger's secret trip to China in July 1971 and his own visit there in February 1972 promised a dramatic shift in Sino-American relations.[21]

Both South and North Vietnam viewed these developments with alarm, despite efforts by the Americans and the Chinese to ease suspicions of betrayal among their allies. Thieu feared that the Americans would sell out South Vietnam in its desire to build a strategic partnership with China, telling his advisers, 'America has been looking for a better mistress and now Nixon has discovered China. He does not want to have his old mistress hanging around. Vietnam has become old and ugly.'[22] Thieu sent a number of envoys to Washington in the fall of 1971 in an effort to dissuade the administration from linking the war in Vietnam to the improvement of Sino-American relations. But increasingly certain that the Nixon administration would compromise on the terms of a peace settlement, he also pushed for ever greater amounts of aid and equipment for the South Vietnamese army. As the North Vietnamese became aware of the possibility of Sino-American rapprochement, they immediately noted a change in Chinese attitudes towards negotiation. At a meeting in September 1970 between Mao and the Vietnamese prime minister, Pham Van Dong, in Beijing, one quite different in tone from the earlier Sino-Vietnamese encounter in fall 1968, Mao said, 'I see that you can conduct the diplomatic struggle and you do it well. Negotiations have been going on for two years. At first we were a little worried that you were trapped. We are no longer worried.'[23] Suspicious that geostrategic interests would again trump ideological fraternity as they had at Geneva in 1954, Hanoi unsuccessfully urged both the Soviets and the Chinese to disavow closer relations with the United States throughout 1971. When the Chinese began to urge North Vietnam to withdraw their demand for Thieu's removal from office to jump-start the Paris negotiations, Hanoi officials, like their counterparts in Saigon, began to extract as much economic and military support as they could from both Moscow and Beijing in case the flow of aid was later turned off. The pay-off for these efforts was substantial. Although Soviet and Chinese support for the North never reached the levels it was at in 1967, Soviet air missile systems, arms, petroleum, and other military supplies sent to Vietnam jumped from an estimated $70 million in 1970 to $100 million in 1971. Chinese supplies of ammunition, radio transmitters, tanks, and military trucks also doubled in this same period.[24]

Under increasing diplomatic pressure from their allies, the North Vietnamese wanted to come to the bargaining table in Paris in the strongest possible position on the battlefield. To do so Hanoi launched the Easter Offensive in late March 1972. Military planners did not anticipate a full-scale rout of the American and South Vietnamese forces, but they sought to demonstrate the continuing weakness of the ARVN and to stabilize and deepen the territory under NLF control. The timing of the offensive between Mao and Nixon's February meeting and the Soviet–American summit in May, along with the fact that the North provided little information about its military planning to the Soviets and Chinese, also suggested that Hanoi was as determined to use the offensive to show its resolve to Beijing and Moscow as it was to the United States.[25] The offensive struck in three directions: across the demilitarized zone that separated North and South Vietnam, along the Cambodian border, and in the central highlands. Unlike Tet, it was North Vietnamese rather than NLF forces that did the bulk of the fighting through relatively conventional battles. With strong support from American airpower, the ARVN was able to blunt the offensive's reach, suggesting that some progress had been made through Vietnamization. Casualties were high on both sides, but northern losses of some 100,000 would set back the North's offensive capacity for several years. By the end of the offensive, however, the northern leadership held more southern territory than they did before it began, including control of half of the four northernmost provinces of South Vietnam as well as territory along the Cambodian and Lao borders and the central coast. The Easter Offensive also allowed the NLF to make renewed inroads into the countryside and further destabilized southern Vietnamese society. As many as 25,000 civilians were killed, and 1 million displaced persons further crowded already burgeoning refugee camps and urban centres, where conditions remained difficult. An ARVN soldier recalled that his unit felt 'impending doom' after the Easter Offensive: 'We all believed we had fought heroically . . . but that our best was not good enough. The Communists simply replaced their losses and continued to march on.'[26]

Nixon was enraged by the Easter Offensive and in May 1972 ordered the most drastic escalation of the war since the introduction of American ground forces in 1965. To signal continuing American resolve to the North Vietnamese and support for its allies in the South, he began one of the war's most sustained and expansive bombing campaigns of the North, placed mines in the harbour of northern port city of Haiphong, and initiated a naval blockade in a combined effort known as Linebacker I. 'The bastards have never been bombed like they're going to be bombed this time,' Nixon told his advisers.[27] He also hoped to send a message to the Soviets and the Chinese that they needed to put additional pressure on Hanoi to compromise in the Paris peace negotiations. Soviet and Chinese responses to Linebacker, despite the fact that several of their ships were bombed and Premier Kosygin was in Hanoi at the height of the bombing, were relatively muted. Both Soviet and Chinese representatives urged the Vietnamese to return to the negotiating table, suggesting to the North Vietnamese that their overriding interest in détente and rapprochement continued to take prominence over ideological solidarities.[28]

The fall of 1972 did bring a diplomatic breakthrough in the stalled negotiations. North Vietnamese demands for a ceasefire in place, meaning northern troops could remain in the South after the settlement, and US insistence that the Thieu government remain in power had been the major obstacles to an agreement. In secret negotiations between the US and North Vietnam conducted outside the formal Paris negotiating framework, the Americans agreed to the complete withdrawal of US forces, accepted a ceasefire in place for all Vietnamese forces, and endorsed the creation of a tripartite electoral commission in which the Thieu government would have equal representation along with the NLF's Provisional Revolutionary Government and a neutralist grouping. For its part, North Vietnam withdrew opposition to allowing the Thieu government to remain in power until the elections provided for in the peace accord had taken place.

Nguyen Van Thieu was outraged by the agreement, convinced that it provided the means for the North to overthrow his government, and he refused to lend his support to it. He also feared that American agreement to the tripartite electoral commission represented a substantial weakening of US support for his government. Thieu told the Americans, 'If we accept the document as it stands, we will commit suicide—and I will be committing suicide,' and demanded major changes including the withdrawal of all North Vietnamese forces from the South.[29] To placate Thieu, the Nixon administration returned to the negotiating table and asked for a series of sixty-nine concessions, most of them minor but some designed to provide for at least a token withdrawal of northern forces from the South and to weaken the NLF's political status in the post-settlement period. North Vietnamese officials, furious at the US effort to reopen negotiations, rejected the American proposal out of hand and raised their own series of demands, including a return to their earlier insistence that the Thieu government could not remain in power in the transition to elections. Hanoi was in part under significant pressure from the NLF, who were as unhappy as Thieu was with the provisions of the accords (and had as little voice as Thieu did in their negotiation) as they believed it gave South Vietnam power of veto over the democratic transition and did not adequately provide for the release of NLF cadres in South Vietnamese jails.[30]

With the Paris negotiations at stalemate, Nixon again launched a fierce bombing campaign against North Vietnam to demonstrate continuing support for Thieu and his resolve against Hanoi. Linebacker II, better known as the Christmas bombings of 1972, was a twelve-day assault in which the Americans dropped 36,000 tons of bombs, an amount that exceeded in tonnage all the bombs the US had used in the American war from 1969 to 1971. Typical of these savage attacks, seventy-two US bombers hit Hanoi on the night of 29 December from four different directions, while eighteen bombers dropped their loads on the rail centre north of the city and an additional thirty bombers struck Haiphong. Nixon indicated he would stop the bombing if the North Vietnamese agreed to return to the negotiating table. Although the Soviets and Chinese strongly condemned the bombing, they again pressured Hanoi towards a settlement.[31] Having exhausted the stock of Soviet surface-to-air missiles critical for their defence against the American bombing at the end of December, North Vietnam acquiesced.

The North Vietnamese and the United States did agree to a peace settlement in January 1973. Nixon later insisted that Hanoi signed the agreement only because of the Christmas bombing. But in truth the final agreement signed in Paris was little different from the text of the accords both sides had agreed to the previous fall, suggesting that the massive bombings had no substantive impact on the actual terms of the agreement. The accords did bring the end of direct American military intervention in Vietnam, with the last US troops departing from South Vietnam in March 1973. But not only did the peace agreement outline a very fuzzy mechanism for political transition in South Vietnam, its recognition of a ceasefire in place for northern troops already in the South, what contemporary observers called the 'leopard-spot peace', was an inherently unstable arrangement. Under strong American pressure Thieu let it be known he would not oppose the settlement, but his private commitment to what throughout the peace negotiations he had very publicly termed the 'Four Noes'—no neutrality, no coalition government, no concession of southern territory to North Vietnam, and no communist activity in South Vietnam—did not bode well for its implementation.

Scholars have long debated Nixon's larger motivations for supporting the Paris peace accords, with some contending that he looked for no more than a 'decent interval' between the withdrawal of American forces and a likely northern victory over South Vietnam, while others argued that Nixon knew he had negotiated a faulty peace but aimed for an indefinite stalemate in which American airpower would underlie a 'permanent war' to protect the South from a decisive northern attack.[32] In fact, the peace quickly unravelled, with both sides blaming each other for the renewed outbreaks of fighting in the South and the inability to move towards a political settlement. Events on the ground in

Vietnam, both the continuing instabilities of the Thieu government and North Vietnamese resolution to launch a final decisive offensive, along with Nixon's own ignominious departure from the American political stage, soon made US intentions about the peace beside the point.

The End of the Line

Along with the leopard-spot peace, the withdrawal of US forces severely weakened the already fragile South Vietnamese state. Its effect on the urban southern economy was immediate. Not only were US troops gone by the end of March 1973, but most of the military support personnel and the large American construction firms that had built much of the infrastructure of South Vietnam soon departed as well. US military aid dropped from $2.3 billion in 1973 to $1 billion in 1974, and the $400 million the US had annually spent in South Vietnam ceased altogether. At the same time, the impact of the international oil crisis began to throw the world economy in disarray when Arab oil-producing states in the Middle East significantly increased the price of crude oil. The economic effects of the oil crisis were global, but along with the substantial reductions in US aid they further weakened the southern Vietnamese economy, with inflation reaching 90 per cent and 3–4 million people unemployed. Corruption, which had been endemic in South Vietnam since the beginning of the American war, reached new levels as the economy soured and it prompted renewed political instability. For the first time, Thieu began to lose the support of some of the South's most vocal anti-communists, including Catholic political parties, which launched a big anti-corruption campaign against the Thieu government in 1974. Buddhist groups, which had been relatively quiet politically since the late 1960s, viewed Thieu's regime with increasing disdain and renewed their agitation for peace and reconciliation. As in the past, political protesters were quickly jailed. A war-weary South Vietnamese population became ever more uncertain about the future.[33]

Thieu believed he could weather these domestic storms because he assumed South Vietnam retained the support of the Nixon administration. After the Easter Offensive, Nixon had sent Thieu a series of secret letters promising the full support of the United States against any substantial renewed North Vietnamese military effort in the South. In pushing Thieu to drop his objections to the Paris accords in January 1973, Nixon renewed his pledge, telling him in one top-secret letter: 'You have my assurance of continued assistance in the post-settlement period and that we will respond with full force should the settlement be violated by the North Vietnamese.'[34] Thieu viewed these repeated assurances as a kind of security blanket. But political events in the US in 1973 and 1974 called into question Nixon's commitment in a way that Thieu apparently did not fully understand. In July 1973 the extent of the secret bombing of Cambodia emerged in US Senate hearings. It shocked and outraged members of Congress and much of the general public. The details of the Watergate scandal and other Nixon era abuses of power were becoming better known that summer as well. By late 1973 Nixon's public approval ratings were at an all-time low and left him fighting a desperate rearguard action to save his political life. The US Congress passed the War Powers Act in November 1973 in a direct response to what it saw as the improper use of presidential authority by Nixon in Cambodia. Strengthening the role of Congress in overseeing the war-making capacity of the president, the new law made it less likely that Thieu would be able to count on the kind of American support Nixon had promised him. And in August 1974 the Watergate scandal forced President Nixon to resign.

With Nixon gone, the dissidence and misperceptions only increased for Nguyen Van Thieu. When Nixon's vice-president, Gerald R. Ford, assumed the presidency, Ford continued to make pledges of support to South Vietnam, although he was unaware of the scope of the secret promises Nixon had made earlier. But Thieu apparently believed that Nixon and Ford were making the same expansive guarantees of US assistance. Moreover, his perceptual blinders meant Thieu did not fully understand the impact of resurgent Congressional authority in US foreign policy-making and the reticence of Congressional leaders to undertake further involvement in Vietnam. He assumed the American legislature worked like that of South Vietnam, where the executive had little if any need for legislative approval.[35] As a result, Thieu made few sustained contingency plans, believing that in the eleventh hour the United States would come to his aid if necessary. As it happened, the eleventh hour was fast approaching.

That a major northern military offensive would eventually come, given the persisting armed skirmishes between Hanoi and Saigon and the determination of North Vietnam, was no surprise. But the losses the North had incurred during the Easter Offensive and its uncertainties about the kinds of military support South Vietnam might continue to receive from the United States prompted the North Vietnamese to move cautiously. The Hanoi leadership believed it would take two years of planning and preparation to launch a successful final offensive in 1976. Throughout 1974 over 10,000 North Vietnamese troops were detailed to build more than 16,000 miles of roads that could deliver equipment for a future offensive. At the same time North Vietnamese and NLF troops in the South began making substantial inroads against South Vietnamese forces in the central highlands and the Mekong delta far more quickly than many in the northern leadership had anticipated. When PAVN and PLAF troops gained control of two provincial capitals near the Cambodian border in late 1974, and the United States did not intervene in substantial ways to support the South Vietnamese, Hanoi approved an offensive to take Ban Me Tuot, the largest city in the central highlands, with its regular main-force units.[36]

Largely using PAVN main-force units, the attack on Ban Me Tuot began on 10 March. Two days later the city fell to northern forces. Within another week, six provinces in the central highlands were under northern control, and Hanoi ordered PAVN to turn its attention to the central coast with the aim of taking Hue and Danang. In mid-March the United States decided to evacuate its consular personnel from Danang, setting off a panic among southern civilians, many of whom were now convinced the United States intended to abandon South Vietnam and that a North Vietnamese victory might be imminent. As many as a million civilians made a chaotic and panicky trek south, increasing the already substantial logistical difficulties for ARVN officers, who had been ordered to get reinforcements up to Danang from Saigon to confront the communist advances. Hue and Danang were captured by PAVN forces in late March.

The speed of the South Vietnamese government's collapse in central Vietnam surprised Hanoi officials, but they quickly readjusted their calendar for victory. On the final day of March the leadership ordered its southern military commanders to begin a general offensive against Saigon, dubbed the Ho Chi Minh Campaign: 'Strategically, militarily and politically, we now possess overwhelmingly superior strength and the enemy is on the verge of disintegration. The United States appears virtually powerless, and even reinforcements cannot reverse the enemy's situation.... From this moment, the final strategic decisive battle of our army and people has begun.'[37] In this final hour, Thieu continued to hope that the United States would come to the rescue of South Vietnam. Just before the fall of Ban Me Tuot, the US Congress had rejected President Ford's request for additional military aid for South Vietnam. Thieu made a last-minute appeal to the Americans in early April. The Ford administration, many of whom believed the cause was lost and opposed the further use of American airpower in Vietnam, agreed to seek $700 million in emergency aid. Congress again rejected the measure.[38]

On 21 April, Thieu resigned as the president of South Vietnam. Chaos ensued in Saigon as the United States ordered the evacuation of all US personnel. Many southern Vietnamese with connections to the Americans, fearful of their treatment after the northern victory, desperately sought exit visas and a berth on US ships and helicopters. Images of US Marines using rifle butts to keep the Vietnamese from grabbing the skids of helicopters or of angry South Vietnamese soldiers firing on departing Americans formed the final tableau of the American war and the US–South

Vietnamese relationship. Meanwhile, North Vietnamese and NLF forces drew ever closer to Saigon. They reached the city, now quiet, on 30 April 1975. About noon, a North Vietnamese tank crashed through the presidential palace to take the final surrender of the South Vietnamese state.

After War

Three decades of war against the French and the Americans were at an end. Like the French before them, the massive American military intervention ended in defeat. The North had won. The South Vietnamese state was quickly no more than a memory. From the perspective of the North, however, the wars for Vietnam had always been about more than national liberation. Its twin goal was the socialist transformation of state and society. As one war came to an end, another began. But in this one the North Vietnamese leadership was unable to replicate battlefield successes: its ability to impose a socialist vision on a reunified southern and northern Vietnam proved to be elusive.

Surprised by the speed of the northern victory, Hanoi did not initially have a fully formed conception of how it would integrate the southern economy and society with that of the North. A go-slow policy that delayed formal reunification and permitted some free-market economic activity shaped initial post-war policy. But in July 1976 the country formally became the Socialist Republic of Vietnam, with many of the most prominent members of the National Liberation Front pushed aside in favour of a government headed by the Hanoi leadership, who had crafted the final victory in the American war. In part because of shortages of experienced southern-born NLF cadres, northerners were sent down to oversee the regional and local government in the South and their presence was often resented by the southern population. Several hundred thousand southerners were sent to re-education camps, largely those associated with the former South Vietnamese state and military whom the regime believed to be politically unreliable. Many others were under continual surveillance and denied employment because of their backgrounds. More surprisingly some members of the NLF whose ideological and class identities were seen as a danger to the establishment of the new regime were also put into camps. Conditions in the re-education camps were primitive and sometimes brutal, though the southern 'bloodbath' in the wake of the communist victory that American and South Vietnamese officials had predicted never occurred.[39]

In a broader sense, the new regime was keen to root out what it termed 'bourgeois' attitudes and quickly transformed the southern education system and curriculum along northern socialist models. Concerned about southern religious institutions, especially Vietnamese Catholics, who had been among the most loyal supporters of the South Vietnamese regime, the new regime sought to control Catholic, Buddhist, Cao Dai, Hoa Hao, and other organized expressions of religious faith. Officials also began to attack 'the civilization of the dollar' (*van minh cua dong do la*), which they believed had corroded wartime social values in South Vietnam. One campaign banned the playing of 'yellow music' (*nhac vang*), especially love songs like those of Trinh Công Son (who himself was briefly sent to a post-war re-education camp) so popular in the South during the American war, because they evoked 'in hapless listeners a gloomy, embittered, impotent and cynical mood towards life, an attitude negating youth's desire to be cheerful, a sensation of being drowned in loneliness in a withered and desolate world'.[40]

These political changes were soon accompanied by a dramatic shift in economic policy. The war-ravaged Vietnamese economy suffered from low agricultural and industrial output, high unemployment, and, in the South, rampant inflation. Faced with an extremely harsh post-war economic embargo by the United States that was honoured by most of the developed world and by limited economic assistance from the socialist world, Vietnam was largely on its own to deal with these serious economic problems. In the immediate aftermath of the war, a few major industries and utilities were taken over by the state and the property of some wealthy business people confiscated, but middle-class southerners were encouraged to continue their economic activities. Household agricultural production was also initially left largely alone. But in mid-1977 the Vietnamese state began to collectivize southern agricultural production, building upon efforts that had begun as early as 1974 in the North to reorganize and improve declining agricultural cooperatives. Along with collectivization, the state targeted the massive refugee population in southern cities, who represented the bulk of the unemployed, and northerners in overpopulated provinces for resettlement in New Economic Zones in the under-cultivated and underpopulated central highlands. And in March 1978 all private trade was quite suddenly outlawed in Vietnam in the 'campaign to eliminate the comprador capitalists' (*chien dich bai tru tu san mai ban*).

The results of these policies were disastrous. The ban on private trade heavily affected ethnic Chinese, who had traditionally dominated major sectors of the southern economy; many of them, along with middle-class ethnic Vietnamese, fled on foot or by boat in the first of several major exoduses that involved more than a million people, who took with them much of the human capital that might have made the post-war Vietnamese economy work. Those sent to the New Economic Zones frequently found a harsh climate and little real governmental support for the development of agriculture. Many secretly returned to their home villages in the North and South despite limited economic prospects there, and those who remained eked out no more than a subsistence existence. By late 1979 the effort to collectivize agriculture in the South and improve it in the North had also failed. In the South there was open resistance, with some villagers lying down in front of the state tractors that ploughed collectivized fields. Others subverted the spirit of cooperatives by working in slipshod ways. Among those most resistant were rural southerners who had become middle peasants through the NLF's land reforms of the 1960s and jealously guarded the economic self-sufficiency this position had brought to their households. Vietnam's efforts at creating a socialist economy, along with its American-enforced isolation from the world economy, catapulted the country into dire poverty. Grain shortages forced the government to institute food rationing amid reports of spot famines. High unemployment persisted and grew larger.

International development indicators placed Vietnam as the third poorest country on earth in the early 1980s.[41]

These economic problems were intensified by the Vietnamese state's post-war foreign policy towards Cambodia and China. April 1975 not only marked the end of the American war in Vietnam, it also brought to power in Cambodia Pol Pot's Khmer Rouge, who quickly launched a genocidal terror that claimed the lives of as many as 1.7 million of its people. Tensions between the Vietnamese and Khmer Rouge centred less on the genocide, whose scope was not yet fully apparent, than on Khmer Rouge purges of Vietnamese-trained communists, massacres of ethnic Vietnamese living in Cambodia, and border raids into Vietnam. Tensions were heightened by the deterioration of Sino-Vietnamese relations. The Chinese were strong supporters of the Khmer Rouge and had been angered by Vietnam's decision to align with the Soviet Union in the post-war period. In the summer and fall of 1978 Pol Pot, fearing a Vietnamese attack, made a series of pre-emptive strikes into southern Vietnam. The Vietnamese responded with a full-scale invasion in 1979, taking control of Phnom Penh on 7 January 1979. They put in place a puppet government and began what would become a ten-year military occupation of Cambodia. To punish the Vietnamese for attacking its Khmer Rouge clients, China invaded the northernmost provinces of Vietnam in February 1979. After seizing several provincial capitals and encountering heavy Vietnamese resistance, the Chinese withdrew their forces in late March.[42] Both the war with China and the long occupation of Cambodia deepened Vietnam's economic crisis. The Chinese invasion seriously damaged northern Vietnam's industrial base, while the Cambodian occupation kept the military from undertaking economic reconstruction at home and diverted limited government revenues away from investments in infrastructure development, education, and public health. Moreover, many demobilized veterans of the Cambodian war and occupation returned home to face under- or unemployment, further increasing dissatisfaction with the policies of the regime, which during the American war had been so attentive to veteran concerns.[43]

To arrest the stagnation and poverty that was engulfing the nation, Vietnam undertook a radical economic transformation in 1986 by adopting the policy of *doi moi*, or renovation. Abandoning socialist economics, but not the one-party Leninist state, *doi moi* marked the introduction of market reforms into the Vietnamese economy. Failing agricultural collective and state industrial enterprises were replaced by household agricultural farms and an opening up to foreign investment to build the industrial and service economies. *Doi moi* also brought a generational shift in Hanoi's leadership. The northern-born stalwart leaders of the party and state during the French and Americans wars—including Le Duan, Truong Chinh, Le Duc Tho, and Pham Van Dong—left the political stage. This transformation was exemplified at the Sixth Party Congress, which adopted the *doi moi* reforms in the election of a new head for the party, Nguyen Van Vinh, who had been a leader of the resistance war in the South and oversaw some of the early reform efforts in Ho Chi Minh City.[44]

The aggregate changes in the Vietnamese economy in the twenty years since the policies of *doi moi* were adopted have been dramatic. Vietnam has reduced the numbers of people living in abject poverty—those earning less than one dollar per day—from 51 per cent in 1990 to 9 per cent in 2006. Its economic growth rate in 2007 was a remarkable 8.5 per cent. Among other things, Vietnam now produces and uses more cement than its former colonial master, France. With its new-found economic prowess, however, have also come problems: a growing gap between the wealthy and the poor, rampant corruption within the state and party over the spoils of the economic reforms, gender differentials in employment and political participation, and a significant deterioration in providing health care and educational access for all its citizens, what the Vietnamese socialist regime for all its peacetime problems did best. And while the party and state maintain their monopoly on political power without significant challenge, their ability to set the agenda for how individuals and families view their social and cultural well-being is fast waning.

Some observers have argued that the history of post-war Vietnam demonstrates that North Vietnam may have won the war but lost the peace. Revisionist historians in the United States go even further, arguing that the embrace of the market and the rise of a liberal capitalist economic order in Vietnam reveal that the United States in fact won the American war in Vietnam. After all, they ask, isn't that ultimately what the US was fighting for?[45] Leaving aside, as these revisionists do, the uncomfortable fact that the North did militarily defeat the United States and its South Vietnamese ally, there are considerable ironies in the post-war turn to the market economy. Not only did the southern middle peasantry in part created by the NLF resist the post-war collectivization of agriculture, their insistence on maintaining household production and selling surplus on the market presaged the contract system that underlay the collapse of agricultural collectives and the rise of family farms under the *doi moi* reforms. Diasporic Vietnamese, many of whose families had been closely associated with the South Vietnamese government after 1954 and were driven out of the country by the regime after the war, have become among the most important 'foreign' investors in the Vietnamese economy under *doi moi*. In 2004 the estimated 2.5 million overseas Vietnamese (Viet kieu) sent $3.8 billion to Vietnam through official channels, even more unofficially; total direct foreign investment in 2004 was just over $4 billion, making overseas Vietnamese remittances as important to the economy as top investors like Singapore, Taiwan, Hong Kong, South Korea, and the United States.[46]

The ideological guardians of the regime's history have had to turn rhetorical somersaults to offer their own revisionist accounts of the Vietnam's post-war economic transformations. For many of them, *doi moi* posed not so much a conversion to capitalism as a recognition of the errors of the past in interpreting the still-central canon of Marxist-Leninism and Ho Chi Minh thought:

We are backward in many ways, especially in our understanding of socialist industrialization, of socialist transformation in production relations, of the mechanism of management and of distribution and circulation. We were prejudiced against laws of goods production and actually did not recognize their existence. We failed to correctly apply the objective laws that govern the process of transition to socialism. We acted with subjectivism and voluntarism.[47]

Their reinterpretation of the correct path to socialism has also necessitated a substantial revision in portrayals of southern Vietnam, which has been the driving engine of the market reforms. No longer were southern peasants 'ensnared in the American way of life, namely the prostitutes, hooligans, ruffians, drug-addicts' and victims of the 'civilization of the dollar', as the North had argued during and immediately after the war. Now the regime draws attention to the 'spirit of close mutual affection and assistance' in the South and to the presence there of a 'thriving commerce', a 'commodity economy', and 'extensive market relations' as early as the seventeenth century to offer an almost timeless imaginary genealogy for southern economic success after 1986, one that carefully glosses over any role the French and American presence might have played in the region's recent embrace of the market.[48]

Notwithstanding these ironies, the certainty that the end of history in either its liberal capitalist or socialist internationalist variants is close at hand in Vietnam is far from most contemporary Vietnamese sensibilities. Rather than closing down a sense of the ways in which the past informs the present, *doi moi* has opened up a space through which the Vietnamese at home and in the diaspora have advanced their own complex reassessments of meanings of the wars for Vietnam—and through it once again offered multiple and contested visions of what a new, post-war future might bring.

Pham Thi Ky burns incense at her veteran husband's grave on the fiftieth anniversary of the battle of Dien Bien Phu

CODA

'The future lied to us, there long ago in the past,' claims the narrator of Bao Ninh's *Sorrows of War* (*Noi buon chien tranh*). 'There is no new life, no new era nor hope for a beautiful future.'[1] In this 1991 novel the northern Vietnamese author, a veteran of the American war, tells the story of his anti-heroic protagonist Kien's transformational experiences of war from an eager young recruit as a *boi doi*, or ordinary soldier in the North Vietnamese army, to a hardened warrior and veteran deeply critical of the self-delusions of the military leadership, scornful of widespread corruption among party officials, and bitter that the sacrifices of war and revolution go unrewarded in the post-war period.

The sense of disillusionment and betrayal that hovers over Bao Ninh's novel, which emerged during a period of more relaxed state control of the cultural realm after the adoption of the *doi moi* reforms in 1986, was part of a broader challenge to the official narrative of sacred war and heroic self-sacrifice so carefully constructed by the North Vietnamese state throughout the wars against the French and the Americans. These state efforts persisted in the post-war period. Almost as soon as the American war was over, the state began to construct monuments to the war dead (*dai liet si*) throughout Vietnam. The monuments are visible across the Vietnamese landscape, usually tall cenotaphs with gold or red stars at their top and the words 'The Fatherland Remembers Your Sacrifice' etched upon them. The celebration of Liberation Day (Ngay Giai Phong) every April to commemorate the end of the American war has joined War Invalids and Martyrs' Day in the official calendar of war memory, with both holidays providing the opportunity for speeches, parades, and gifts to the families of the war dead. The Vietnamese state created a new honorific of the 'heroic mother' (*me anh hung*) in 1995, venerating with medals women who had lost at least three children in war and including them in ceremonies marking the sacrifices of war.

But however popular official commemorative practices remain for families of the war dead, the state under *doi moi* has increasingly lost the ability to control the memory of war. As it has, popular apprehensions of the Vietnamese past and future—expressed through contemporary fiction, film, and the visual arts as well as in a remarkable resurgence of religiosity and the modernist imaginings of the colonial era—have taken war memory as a starting point to offer not only sharp critiques of the state but alternative ways of being in the world in the post-war and post-socialist present.

The emerging contestations between local and state war memory as families and village communities began to stake their own claims to the war dead are at the centre of Dang Nhat Minh's 1984 film *When the Tenth Month Comes* (Bao gio cho den thang muoi). Set during the Vietnamese invasion of Pol Pot's Cambodia in 1979, the film reflected the sceptical response of a war-weary population to the state's efforts to render the Vietnamese invasion and subsequent occupation of Cambodia within the official narrative of war as patriotic self-sacrifice, particularly when the state appeared unable to find employment in the civilian sector for demobilized veterans returning from the Cambodian campaigns. It is likely that the Cambodian setting of the film, released two years before the rise of the *doi moi* agenda began to ease official control on artistic production, also provided the director with a thinly disguised parable to advance his critique of state memorializing practices in a manner that implicated but did not directly challenge the more sacrosanct claims of state narratives about the French and American wars.

When the Tenth Month Comes tells the story of the decision of a young woman named Duyen to keep the news that her husband has been killed in battle hidden from her husband's family and village. By the end of the film Duyen comes to know that her behaviour is improper. Kneeling by her father-in-law's deathbed, she cries out:

'I haven't told the truth.... I've done wrong.' From the state's perspective, the nature of Duyen's error would have been obvious: she prevented her husband's memory from fulfilling its officially sanctioned commemorative purposes. At points the film does acknowledge the legitimacy of state claims on the fallen soldier's memory. Early in the film Duyen's father-in-law calls the death of his elder son during the American war a 'patriotic sacrifice for the advancement of the national liberation movement and the socialist revolution'. Similarly, the final scene of the film, after the dead soldier's family and village have come to know of his wife's deception, appears to suggest that official order has been restored. As martial music swells, Duyen and her son, surrounded by children carrying party banners, gaze admiringly upward at the yellow star and red background of the Vietnamese flag snapping purposefully in the wind. But these rather perfunctory scenes are oddly disconnected from the larger narrative of the film, reflecting a nod to the real concerns of continuing state censorship rather than a full embrace of official commemorative practices.

Tenth Month concentrates on the impact of the war on the interior lives of Duyen and her husband's family in a manner that subtly undermines the state's monopolizing claims on the memory of her dead husband, particularly in its focus on Duyen's failure to fulfil her filial duties to her husband's family and his lineage and her moral obligations to his village. The film articulates its disapproval of Duyen's actions in a crucial scene in which her husband's family observe the anniversary of her mother-in-law's death. At the culminating feast one family member reads a letter full of filial devotion purportedly written by the heroine's husband. The letter, however, is actually fabricated, written at Duyen's request by a village schoolteacher as a way of convincing the family that her husband remains alive. In using a death anniversary at which the soul of the departed ancestor is believed to be present to advance her deception, Duyen's actions emerge as a particularly egregious violation of the traditional Vietnamese practices of remembering and propitiating the dead. The rites of the death anniversary, one leading scholar of these practices argues, are essential to affirming the primary familial obligations of filial piety (*hieu*), 'symbolically joining the living, dead and yet to be born members of the family . . . in an intimate relationship of mutual dependency'.[2]

In highlighting the feasting component of the death anniversary, *Tenth Month* also reinforces its focus on the claims of family and village, rather than the state, to the memory of Duyen's husband. The feast marking the anniversary, in which a family traditionally invited its neighbours to share, was among the central targets of the sustained campaign by North Vietnam in the 1950s against superstitious practices. For the state, the elaborate network of social exchange promoted through the feast incurred wasted expenditure better used for collective economic purposes, and represented undesirable feudal customs that reflected social inequality and competition for status. In its place, the state urged a simple didactic ceremony among the immediate family of the deceased that focused on the departed ancestor's contribution to the rise of a new revolutionary society. The inclusions of the feast in *Tenth Month*'s depiction of the rites of the anniversary, which reflects the return of such traditional ritual practices in northern Vietnamese society in the 1980s, pointedly places the memory of the dead within the village community and suggests that Duyen's deceptions violate familial and village more than state norms.[3] In the end, the film suggests, at the very least the state must share the memory of the fallen soldier with his widow, his family, and his village.

Tenth Month anticipated a revival of ritual and religiosity in Vietnam in the 1990s, one that continues to the present, which eroded not only state claims to own the memories of the war dead but its broader efforts since the 1950s to control belief and practice. The explosion of local ritual and religious practice is evident almost everywhere in present-day Vietnam. It can be seen in overflowing Buddhist temples and Catholic churches, the enormous crowds attending religious festivals, fairs, ceremonies, and feasts, the profusion of religious display and altars in homes, the resurgence of family and local rituals, the lavish refurbishing of pagodas, churches, and shrines, and the pilgrimage of millions to shrines of gods and goddesses like that of Ba Chua Xu, the Lady of the Realm, in southern Vietnam. The intensification of religious sensibilities and ritual in part rests on the new wealth generated through the market reforms. At the same time, it addresses the cultural anxieties unleashed by them in some of the same ways that Buddhist modernism and expressions of popular religion in the 1930s sought to mediate the spiritual challenges posed by French colonial rule.[4]

But this regeneration of religion and ritual is also bound up in efforts to make sense of the sorrows of war. Along with the return of more elaborate ceremonies and feasting for death anniversaries, the souls of war dead are increasingly installed in local Buddhist temples, themselves the object of renewed local attention and devotion after years of neglect under the state's wartime religious prohibitions, where they are believed to 'eat of the Buddha's good fortune' (*an may cua Phat*). Stories of wandering ghosts (*bach linh*), those who died in war but whose bodies have never been recovered, and their power to do harm to the living are again prevalent as a means through which many Vietnamese make sense of the complex aftermath of war, as is a renewed reliance on spirit mediums (*nhap xac*) to locate the missing remains of fallen soldiers.[5] Shifts in ritual kinship practices have become an especially important means through which families who lost sons on both sides of the American war have reclaimed their memories. Although having family members involved in multiple sides of the war was not uncommon, the post-war Vietnamese state offered no consolation for war dead who served in the former South Vietnam. Indeed, families often concealed these traces of their past. In recent years, however, they have been less willing to do so. The household family altar, a space once policed by the dictates of high socialism, can now display for veneration and propitiation the photographs of dead sons who served in the ARVN as well as in the northern army or the military forces of the NLF. In a language that reinforces the importance of the spiritual world and filial piety for Vietnamese apprehensions of the war, an older woman in Danang described to her grandchildren her decision in 1996 to return a long-hidden photograph of her younger son Kan, who was an ARVN soldier, to the family altar next to that her older son Tan, who served in the northern army:

Uncle Kan admired Uncle Tan. Uncle Tan adored little Kan. And the two were sick at the thought that they might meet in a battle. I prayed to the Fairies of the Marble Mountains that my two boys should never meet. The Fairy listened. The boys never met. The Fairy carried them away to different directions so they could not meet. The gracious Fairy carried them too far. She took my prayer and was worried. To be absolutely sure that the boys didn't meet in this world, the Fairy took them to her world, both of them. We can't blame the Fairy. So here we are. My two children met finally. I won't be around, breathing, for much longer. You, my children, should look after your uncles. They don't have children, but they have many nephews and nieces. Remember this, my children. Respect your uncles.[6]

This widespread religious revival is not the only challenge to the state's ability to control the meanings of the contemporary moment in Vietnam. The re-examination of the French and American wars among some writers and artists also produced a critique of what they saw as the wider post-war selfishness and immorality of the *doi moi* era and a deeply felt sense that wartime promises of socialist revolution had gone unfulfilled. A damning portrait of society under the market economic reforms shaped Tran Van Thuy's 1987 documentary film *How to Behave* (*Chuyen tu te*). To set up its themes, the film-maker profiles several veterans of the French and American wars who barely eke out a subsistence living as cyclo drivers and bicycle repairmen and whose decorated service is now ignored by the state. It then asks if kindness (*tu te*), a term the film tellingly defines as 'acting in the public rather than individual interest', can still be found in Vietnamese society. Ultimately the film finds kindness not among party cadres or state bureaucrats— one of whom interviewed says, 'No one has time for such out-moded notions these days'—but in a leper colony run by Catholic nuns, a particularly charged choice given the intense hostility of the socialist state in Vietnam towards the Catholic Church. If the devotion of the nuns to the lepers, as the film claims, rests on 'faith', *How to Behave* suggests that the callousness of society at large represents a loss of faith in the state's socialist ideals. Pointedly noting that 'the people' (*nhan dan*) are 'sacred words' in the state's vocabulary as the objects of 'sacrifice, devotion and generosity', the film sets the difficult lives of ordinary people against the indifference of powerful party officials whose lives are marked by material ease to suggest that 'the gap between words and deeds has become too wide'. The mixture of sorrow and anger through which *How to Behave* advances its sense of the post-war betrayal of wartime ideals emerges most sharply in the closing frames of the film. A quotation appears on screen, 'Only animals can turn from the suffering of men and busy themselves preening their furs and feathers,' to which the film's narrator adds, 'This quotation is not by my friend but by the venerated Karl Marx.'

In other films and novels, a gendered construction of war memory serves as the vehicle for a blistering critique of contemporary Vietnamese society. They pit a series of grasping younger women against the probity of war veterans whose virtuous behaviour stands in sharp contrast to the dominant ethos of corruption and selfishness at the heart of the market economy. This metaphorical dichotomy builds in part upon the traditional Vietnamese division of gender roles that contrasts women as 'generals of the interior' (*noi tuong*), who dominate the domestic sphere and oversee the family's budget, with men who properly inhabit the public realm, where they conduct the more contemplative official business of family life and governance. By rendering the contours of *doi moi* society as a feminine landscape forgetful of the self-sacrifices of war, the symbolic vocabularies of these works suggest that the power of the market economy has dangerously extended the private domain of women into the masculine, public sphere and dislodged more traditional forces of moral order and authority in society.[7]

Tran Vu and Nguyen Huu Luyen's 1987 film *Brothers and Relations* (*Anh va em*) uses the lens of gender to explore the conflict within a northern family over locating the remains of a son killed in the American war. The problem was a common one in post-war Vietnam. The bodies of hundreds of thousands of soldiers who died in the war have never been recovered, and northern families regularly organize trips to central and southern Vietnam to search for the remains of the missing. In a scene at the beginning of the film, the elderly mother says goodbye to the guests attending the anniversary of the death of her son. After the last guests depart, she collapses onto the floor crying and calls out for her family to assemble around her. Reminding them that their brother's bones are still lying in a military cemetery in the South, she implores them to bring his remains home so that she can lie next to him when she dies. Her son agrees, adding, 'Thank heaven my sister has so many connections.' His observation prompts an increasingly acrimonious exchange between his sister and his wife:

Sister: Shouldn't we all help? I'm busy with my husband's business trip to Singapore. You both have never seen Saigon. You could combine business with a little sightseeing.

Wife: My husband is busy with the shop and I'm taking care of mother. You have more time.

Sister: I'll talk straight. You joined this family. Help take care of it. You got my brother's room because he died.

Wife: And you got some of mother's gold. We don't get paid for taking care of her.

Sister: I had to borrow that gold to grease a few wheels.

Wife: Our family has special status because our brother got killed. That's why they let you pass your exam and get a job in Hanoi.

Sister: You're wrong. I got that another way. But it is through family status that they don't close your store!

Wife: Look at my husband. He can't go. I don't know my way around the South. How could we exhume the bones?

Sister: You think I'm good at it? It is hard enough to take care of my husband and his family. It's expensive to transport bones. Where would I get the money?

Offering a solution to this impasse, the sister suggests that her husband's brother, an unemployed veteran, could use the money and go on behalf of the family. The veteran agrees but refuses the money. The sister tells him, 'Stop living in the clouds. No one is like you now—doing something for nothing.' To which the veteran replies, 'Your brother died asking for nothing.' As the narrative of the film unfolds, *Brothers and Relations* juxtaposes the selfless virtue of the veteran, who collects and buries the remains of the fallen soldier, with the sister's single-minded pursuit of material advantage in planning the potentially lucrative business trip to Singapore for her husband that blinds her to her familial obligations.

In *The General Retires* (*Tuong ve huu*, 1988), a short story by Nguyen Huy Tiep, who is perhaps the leading writer in contemporary Vietnam, a decorated general and his daughter-in-law serve as the central protagonists in a narrative that disturbingly links societal amnesia about the war and the perils of the marketplace to gender. The general, a figure of quiet authority and simple tastes who is clearly devoted to serving the ideals of the state, comes to live with his son's family after he retires from military service. But he quickly feels out of place as he experiences the market-generated rhythms of life in the household. One day he discovers that his son's wife, a doctor at a maternity clinic, brings home aborted fetuses from the clinic to feed a pack of Alsatian dogs she is raising to sell as guard dogs to supplement the family's income. Appalled by her behaviour and devastated to realize that the spiritual emptiness he finds in the household pervades contemporary society, the general leaves the house to rejoin his elderly military comrades, among whom he dies. *The General Retires* uses the emasculation of husbands by their wives to foreground the corrupting seductiveness of the marketplace and its corrosive penetration into all realms of human relations. It depicts the son of the general as an impotent figure powerless to resist the moral transgressions of the market that his wife has introduced into the household. When the general points out to his son what his wife has been doing, implicitly calling upon him to reassert his authority and end the practice, he somewhat stiffly replies, as if to hide his embarrassment, 'I had known about this but dismissed it as something of no importance.'[8]

These critiques of wartime legacies and the market economy are not ubiquitous in present-day Vietnam. For those born after 1975 the war and its meanings are increasingly remote from their consciousness. Over two-thirds of Vietnam's population is under 21 and many have fully embraced the market. Students are preoccupied with studying business, computers, English, accounting, and tourism in preparation for what they hope will be positions in the upper tier of the new Vietnamese economy, and are more concerned with the newest music, fashion, and consumer goods coming into Vietnam from Asia, Europe, and the United States than they are with their elders' stories about the war. The differences in generational sensibilities starkly emerged in Le Hung's play *Fable for the Year 2000* (*Huyen thai nam 2000*). In one critical scene, an old man and a young student are involved in a stand-off on a bridge. The old man insists he should go first because his generation produced everything of value in Vietnamese society: houses, roads, the contested bridge, even the young student. The student, angry and impatient that old men 'occupy all the most important positions except in homes for the ageing', proclaims, with a notable absence of Confucian filial piety, that he cannot wait until the old man 'has walked his last step', and criticizes the 'pathetic' legacy the older generation has left for him and his friends.[9] Similarly, the slyly satirical paintings by the young Hanoi-based surrealist artist Nguyen Manh Hung such as *A Group of SU 22* (see Plate 18) picture the Soviet-made fighter planes that Hung's father had piloted during the American war; but any notion of gloriousness is undercut by the fat bright-orange carrots that serve in the place of the planes' wheels.

For many diasporic Vietnamese, especially the millions who settled in the United States after 1975, the war remains a palpable presence. The traces of their own war dead and the former South Vietnamese state have been effaced in Vietnam itself. ARVN soldiers who died in the American war are not buried or commemorated in the war cemeteries constructed by the Vietnamese state. The monuments built to celebrate them by the South Vietnamese government have long been dismantled, and the ARVN cemeteries, many of them razed after 1975, lie in ruins. But the streets of 'little Saigons' in southern California, where the majority of Vietnamese-Americans live, remain decorated with the yellow flag crossed by three red stripes that flew over South Vietnam. Among an older generation, anti-communist sentiments remain high and 30 April 1975 is commemorated as a National Day of Shame (Ngay Quoc Han), rather than Liberation Day as it is in Vietnam. In the diasporic community too, however, generational divides about the war and its legacies have emerged. If some first-generation Vietnamese-Americans continue to yearn for a restoration of the South Vietnamese regime, the 1.5 generation (born in Vietnam but who settled in the United States at a young age) and the second generation (born in the United States) see Vietnam and the war quite differently. In 2003 a Vietnamese-American television network in southern California started to produce a lifestyle show for younger Vietnamese-Americans, largely concerned with social and cultural rather than political issues. One show, however, did a short feature on a soon-to-be-released documentary entitled *Saigon, USA*. The feature simply talked about the making of the film, but within hours the network was deluged with calls to say the documentary itself was filled with a pro-communist bias that the feature story had done nothing to criticize. Something, these callers said, needed to done. In reaction the network cancelled the programme altogether, suggesting how charged memories of the war remain among the Vietnamese-American community.[10]

And yet the sensibilities of the diasporic Vietnamese community in the United States and elsewhere are increasingly in flux, as are the attitudes of the Vietnamese state to them. Not only are overseas Vietnamese across the generations putting ever larger amounts of money into the contemporary *doi moi* economy, a phenomenon increasingly welcomed and facilitated by the Vietnamese state, but more and more families, especially their youngest members, are returning to Vietnam. Some go for shorter visits, often around the Tet holidays. Others aim to settle permanently, or move back and forth between Vietnam and the West. For those younger generations who grew up outside Vietnam, coming to terms with the war and what it means to go home is far less about communism and anti-communism than it has been for their parents and grandparents. Their own complex sentiments about the Vietnamese past and future emerge in the work of several young diasporic visual artists. The Vietnamese-American photographer An-My Lê explored the war in part through photographs of re-enactments of the American war, an increasingly popular if somewhat strange summer pastime in the United States. The re-enactors, who sometimes had difficulty finding people to play the 'enemy', asked Lê to play along: 'they would often concoct elaborate scenarios around my character,' Lê said in an interview. 'I have played the sniper girl . . . the lone guerrilla left over in a booby-trapped village . . . the captured prisoner.' Despite the odd disjunctures—Lê was born in 1960 of Vietnamese parents in a Francophile home in Saigon and went to the United States in 1975—she saw herself and the re-enactors in a similar way: 'many of them had complicated personal issues they were trying to resolve, but I was also trying to resolve mine. In a way, we were all artists trying to make sense of our own personal baggage.'[11]

The war emerges in more elliptical ways in the works of Liza Nguyen and Dinh Q. Lê. Nguyen, born in 1979 to parents who immigrated to France in the mid-1960s, is a French- and German-trained photographer who travelled to Vietnam for the first time in 2000 to collect sacks of earth from well-known battlefields and sites of massacres from the French and Americans wars like Dien Bien Phu and My Lai. She photographed them in almost clinical fashion back in her Düsseldorf studio, spreading each into oval mounds and producing final images that were magnified to 5 feet high. The resulting collection of photographs, *Surfaces* (see Plate 19), does not so much speak directly to the war and its aftermath as raise more elliptical questions about the quotidian meanings of the simultaneously ordinary and extraordinary ground that forms the basis of her work. Dinh Q. Lê was born in South Vietnam in 1968, and moved with his parents to the United States ten years later. He returned to Vietnam in the early 1990s after completing his artistic training in California and New York City, and now lives in Ho Chi Minh City. Some of his work has engaged displaced memories of family and home for the overseas Vietnamese. For his *Spending One's Life Trying to Find One's Way Home* (*Mot Coi Di Ve*), Lê sought out family photographs in Vietnamese second-hand stores (his own family photographs were left behind and lost when his family went to the United States). He juxtaposed them with texts from interviews with Vietnamese-Americans about their past lives in

Vietnam and present ones in America to form a massive collage that aims to recover and evoke the texture of life in the 1950s and 1960s in southern Vietnam. More recently his work has shifted from an elegiac to a political register. In the series *Vietnam: Destination for the New Millennium* (see Plate 20), Lê sharply critiques the Vietnamese state for its efforts to reinvent Vietnam as an international tourist destination known for beaches and natural beauty in ways that efface the lingering traces of the war.[12]

In Vietnam itself, the generational differences over the meanings of the French and American wars and apprehensions of the present moment have sometimes recalled the rich legacies of Vietnamese modernist thought from the 1920s and the 1930s. Along with the re-emergence and reworking of spiritual belief and practices, the recent period has brought a rediscovery of 1930s reportage, long suppressed by the Vietnamese state because of its individualistic rather than collectivist inclinations, with classic works republished for a wide and appreciative urban readership. The editor of one of these collections pointedly noted, 'People who write genuine *reportage* are always people who defend reason and justice.' At the same time a new wave of contemporary investigative journalism that explored corruption and poverty, consciously modelled on Vietnamese reportage of the 1930s, filled the columns of the Hanôi and Hô Chi Minh City press.[13] As it had in the 1930s, reportage and what it signalled about the need for individual freedom and moral autonomy provided an alternative space outside prevailing orthodoxies for working out new relations between self and society. The resurgence of these sensibilities, the growing range of new local social organizations—from family lineage groups and mutual credit associations to spirit medium groups, Buddhist associations, pilgrimage fraternities, and ritual associations—and the more inchoate yearnings in the diaspora to engage in what it means to be Vietnamese have together introduced a 'creeping pluralism' into Vietnamese society that now shapes the texture of everyday life.[14]

'I am looking for this,' the young man Hinh, in the short story 'The Prophecy', with which I opened the Prelude to this book, asserts to the crowd gathered around him. As the story concludes,

The crowd continued on after Hinh departed, like a torrent in a stream that never runs dry. They had no idea what 'this' was they were looking for, but still they hoped. A full stomach, a warm bed . . . no matter that it was a nebulous future possibility, it was still alluring enough that they poured after it like a stream of water . . .
  Noon.
  Then evening.
  And still the multitude pushed and jostled in the midst of a flower garden called Spring.[15]

In a very real sense the crowd's search persists. After three decades of post-war peace, the multiple worlds that the Vietnamese articulated and imagined over more than a century of colonialism, revolution, and war remain in the process of becoming.

FURTHER READING

PRELUDE

There is at present no satisfactory single-volume history of twentieth-century Vietnam, although Hue-Tam Ho Tai's *History of Modern Vietnam* (Cambridge: Cambridge University Press, forthcoming) promises to redress that imbalance in definitive ways. In the meantime, Duong Van Mai Elliott beautifully explores the history of Vietnam through lives of four generations of her own family in *The Sacred Willow* (New York: Oxford University Press, 1999) as does Andrew Pham's family memoir *The Eaves of Heaven* (New York: Harmony, 2008). The history of high policy-making within the Vietnamese Communist Party and state over the course of the twentieth century emerges in William J. Duiker's *The Communist Road to Power*, 2nd edn (Boulder, Colo.: Westview Press, 1996), and his shorter *Sacred War: Nationalism and Revolution in a Divided Vietnam* (New York: McGraw-Hill, 1995). David W. P. Elliott traces the history of the war in a single Vietnamese province in his magisterial two-volume *The Vietnam War: Revolution and Social Change* (Armonk, NY: M. E. Sharpe, 2003); an abridged version appeared under the same title in 2006. Vietnamese visual images provide another introduction to the history of the war and its meanings. A remarkable collection of rare North Vietnamese photographs of Vietnamese society at war between 1945 and 1975, some of which are used in this book, can be found in *Another War: Pictures of the War from the Other Side* (Washington, DC: National Geographic Society, 2002), and at <http://www.anothervietnam. com>. The cultural politics of Vietnamese painting is discussed in compelling ways in Nora Taylor's *Painters in Hanoi: An Ethnography of Vietnamese Art* (Honolulu: University of Hawaii Press, 2004); an online collection of twentieth-century Vietnamese art is maintained by the Indochina Arts Partnership at <http://www.iapone.org>. Among the most important one-volume histories of the American war in Vietnam are George C. Herring's *America's Longest War: The United States and Vietnam, 1950–1975*, 4th edn (New York: McGraw-Hill, 2002), and Marilyn B. Young's *The Vietnam Wars, 1945–1990* (New York: Harper Perennial, 1995). An introduction to the newer scholarship on the American and Vietnamese dimensions of the wars in Vietnam emerges in contributions to Mark Philip Bradley and Marilyn B. Young (eds), *Making Sense of the Vietnam Wars: Local, National and Transnational Perspectives* (New York: Oxford University Press, 2008). The newly launched

Journal of Vietnamese Studies promises to be an important venue for future scholarship on the war.

CHAPTER 1

The seminal work of David G. Marr is the starting point for understanding Vietnamese anticolonialism and the coming the August Revolution. See his *Vietnamese Anticolonialism, 1885–1925* (Berkeley: University of California Press, 1971); *Vietnamese Tradition on Trial, 1920–45* (Berkeley: University of California Press, 1981); and *Vietnam 1945: The Quest for Power* (Berkeley: University of California Press, 1995). On the rise of radicalism and Vietnamese communism, see Hue-Tam Ho Tai, *Radicalism and the Origins of the Vietnamese Revolution* (Cambridge, Mass.: Harvard University Press, 1992); Huynh Kim Khanh, *Vietnamese Communism, 1925–1945* (Ithaca, NY: Cornell University Press, 1982); Peter Zinoman, *The Colonial Bastille: A History of Imprisonment in Vietnam, 1862–1940* (Berkeley: University of California Press, 2001); and Shawn McHale, *Print and Power* (Honolulu: University of Hawaii Press, 2004). On the relationship between Vietnamese revolutionaries and the United States in the colonial and early post-colonial periods, see Mark Philip Bradley, *Imagining Vietnam and America: The Making of Postcolonial Vietnam, 1919–1950* (Chapel Hill: University of North Carolina Press, 2000). For accounts of the life of Ho Chi Minh, see the biographies by William J. Duiker, *Ho Chi Minh* (New York: Hyperion, 2000), and Pierre Brochuex, *Ho Chi Minh* (Cambridge: Cambridge University Press, 2007). Three classic examples of Vietnamese reportage from the 1930s, including Tam Lang's *I Pulled a Rickshaw*, are nicely translated by Greg Lockhart in *Light of the Capital* (Kuala Lumpur: Oxford University Press, 1996). Vu Trong Phung's 1936 novel *Dumb Luck*, a wicked satire of the craze for modernity among colonial urban Vietnamese, is available in a marvellous translation by Peter Zinoman and Nguyen Nguyet Cam (Ann Arbor: University of Michigan Press, 2002). The intensification of religiosity in late colonial Vietnam is explored in Hue-Tam Ho Tai, *Millenarianism and Peasant Politics in Vietnam* (Cambridge, Mass.: Harvard University Press, 1983); Jayne S. Werner, *Peasant Politics and Religious Sectarianism*, Yale University Southeast Asia Studies, Monograph Series, No. 23 (New Haven, 1981); and McHale, *Print and Power*.

CHAPTER 2

The literature on the French war, especially its international history, is large but much of it is dated. For an introduction to the newer scholarship, see Mark Atwood Lawrence and Fredric Logevall (eds), *The First Vietnam*

War: Colonial Conflict and Cold War Crisis (Cambridge, Mass.: Harvard University Press, 2007). Along with Duiker's account in his *Communist Road to Power*, the complexities of DRV political and military strategy emerge in Stein Tønnesson, *1946: Déclenchement de la guerre d'Indochine* (Paris: Harmattan, 1987); Greg Lockhart, *Nation in Arms: The Origins of the People's Army of Vietnam* (Sydney: Allen & Unwin, 1986); and Christopher Goscha, *Thailand and the Southeast Asian Networks of the Vietnamese Revolution, 1885–1954* (London: Curzon, 1999). American, French, and British policy towards the war is best understood through Mark Atwood Lawrence, *Assuming the Burden* (Berkeley: University of California Press, 2005). Soviet and Chinese policy towards the French war emerge in Qiang Zhai, *China and the Vietnam Wars, 1950–1975* (Chapel Hill: University of North Carolina Press, 2000); and Ilya Gaiduk, *Confronting Vietnam: Soviet Policy toward the Indochina Conflict, 1954–1963* (Stanford, Calif.: Stanford University Press, 2003). The most engrossing depiction of the battle of Dien Bien Phu remains Bernard Fall, *Hell Is a Very Small Place: The Siege of Dien Bien Phu* (1966; repr. New York: De Capo Press, 2002). On the uneasy relationship between Vietnamese state policies during the French war and intellectuals, see Kim N. B. Ninh, *A World Transformed: The Politics of Culture in Revolutionary Vietnam, 1945–1965* (Ann Arbor: University of Michigan Press, 2002); and Georges Boudarel, *Cent Fleurs éclosés dans la nuit Vietnam: Communisme et dissidence, 1954–1956* (Paris: Jacques Bertoin, 1991). On the problems of building socialism in the North after the war, see Benedict J. Tria Kerkvliet, *The Power of Everyday Politics: How Vietnamese Peasants Transformed National Policy* (Ithaca, NY: Cornell University Press, 2005); and Duong Thu Huong's account of the failed land reform in her novel *Paradise of the Blind* (New York: Harper Perennial, 2002).

CHAPTER 3

A voluminous literature on the history of American involvement in Vietnam during the period from 1954 to 1965 is not matched in size and scope by histories of the Ngo Dinh Diem regime, the rise of the National Liberation Front, the Buddhist protest movements, or North Vietnamese policy towards the war, though Elliott's *The Vietnamese War* and Jeffrey Race's *War Comes to Long An* (Berkeley: University of California Press, 1972) are critical in getting a sense of many of these developments at the local level. George M. Kahin's *Intervention: How American Became Involved in Vietnam* (New York: Anchor, 1987) is especially good on the politics of the South Vietnamese state and the Buddhist protests. On Diem, much of the literature has been either hagiography or denouncement, but a more three-dimensional portrait of Diem drawing on Vietnamese-language sources has recently emerged in Edward Miller, 'Vision, Power and Agency: The Ascent of Ngo Dinh Diem, 1945–54', in Bradley and Young (eds), *Making Sense of the Vietnam Wars*; and Philip Catton, *Diem's Final Failure: Prelude to America's War in Vietnam* (Lawrence: University Press of Kansas, 2002). On the rise of the NLF, Nguyen Thi Dinh's *No Other Road to Take* (Ithaca: Cornell University Press, 1976) and Truong Nhu Tang, *A Viet Cong Memoir* (New York: Vintage, 1986), offer very different first-person accounts. The best accounts of American policy in this period are Seth Jacobs, *America's Miracle Man in Southeast Asia* (Durham, NC: Duke University Press, 2004); and Frederic Logevall, *Choosing War* (Berkeley: University of California Press, 1999). The increasing tensions between Hanoi and its allies in Moscow and Beijing are chronicled in Zhai, *China and the Vietnam Wars*; and Gaiduk, *Confronting Vietnam*.

CHAPTER 4

The social history of wartime Vietnam in the 1960s is only now beginning to be written. Dang Thuy Tram's diary, which created a sensation when it was first published in Vietnam in 2004, is available in a lovely English translation by Andrew X. Pham as *Last Night I Dreamed of Peace* (New York: Harmony Books, 2007). The experience of southern Vietnamese soldiers is captured in part through oral history interviews in Robert K. Brigham, *ARVN: Life and Death in the Vietnamese Army* (Lawrence: University Press of Kansas, 2006). The starting point for North Vietnam's experiences of the American war remains William S. Turley, 'Urbanization in War: Hanoi, 1946–73', *Pacific Affairs*, 48/3 (Autumn 1975), 370–97, but also see Shaun K. Malarney's discussion of local ritual and state war commemoration in his *Culture, Ritual and Revolution in Vietnam* (London: Routledge, 2002). Though written after the war came to a close, the novels of veteran authors evoke a sense of time and place as well as a more critical perspective on the northern experiences of war; those readily available in English translations include Bao Ninh, *The Sorrow of War* (New York: Riverhead, 1996); Duong Thu Huong, *Novel without a Name* (New York: Penguin, 1996); and Le Luu, *A Time Far Past* (Amherst: University of Massachusetts Press, 1997). David Hunt's *Vietnam's Southern Revolution: From Peasant Insurrection to Total War, 1958–1968* (Amherst: University of Massachusetts Press, 2009) is a wonderfully evocative account of interior worlds of the NLF; critical too is Elliott's *The Vietnam Wars*.

CHAPTER 5

The best introduction to Vietnamese decision-making on the Tet Offensive and its impact are Lien-Hang T. Nguyen, 'The War Politburo: North Vietnam's Diplomatic and Political Road to the Tet Offensive', *Journal of Vietnamese Studies*, 1/1–2 (Feb.–Aug. 2006), 19–25; and Elliott, *The Vietnamese War*. Vietnamese perspectives on the Paris peace negotiations emerge in Luu Van Loi and Nguyen Anh Vu, *Le Duc Tho–Kissinger Negotiations* (Hanoi: Gioi Publishers, 1996); Nguyen Tien Hung and Jerrold L. Schecter, *The Palace File* (New York: Harper & Row, 1986); and Robert K. Brigham, *Guerilla Diplomacy: The NLF's Foreign Relations and the Vietnam War* (Ithaca, NY: Cornell University Press, 1999). On the expansion of the war into Cambodia and Laos, see Ben Kiernan, *How Pol Pot Came to Power*, 2nd edn (New Haven: Yale University Press, 2004), and James Hamilton-Merritt, *Tragic Mountains: The Hmong, Americans and the Secret Wars in Laos, 1942–1992* (Bloomington: Indiana University Press, 1993). Nixon's controversial policies towards Vietnam are best discussed in Jeffrey Kimball, *Nixon's Vietnam War* (Lawrence: University Press of Kansas, 1988); Stephen P. Randolph, *Brutal and Powerful Weapons: Nixon, Kissinger and the Easter Offensive* (Cambridge, Mass.: Harvard University Press, 2007), and Larry Berman, *No Peace, No Honor: Nixon, Kissinger and Betrayal in Vietnam* (New York: Simon & Schuster, 2002). On the internal and external crises facing Vietnam in the immediate post-war period, see William J. Duiker, *Vietnam since the Fall of Saigon* (Athens: Ohio University Press, 1989); Kerkvliet, *The Power of Everyday Politics*; Philip Taylor, *Fragments of the Present: Searching for Modernity in Vietnam's South* (Honolulu: University of Hawaii Press, 2001); and Nayan Chanda, *Brother Enemy: The War after the War* (New York: Free Press, 1988). For useful introductions to the coming of *doi moi* and its varied impact, see Börje Ljunggren (ed.), *The Challenge of Reform in Indochina* (Cambridge, Mass.: Harvard Institute for International Development, 1993); and Jayne Werner and Danièle Bélanger (eds), *Gender, Household, State: Doi Moi in Viet Nam* (Ithaca, NY: Cornell University Southeast Asian Publications, 2002).

CODA

The complexities of war memory in contemporary Vietnam are explored in Hue-Tam Ho Tai (ed.), *The Country of Memory: Remaking the Past in Late Socialist Vietnam* (Berkeley: University of California Press, 2001). Also important are Heonik Kwon's *After the Massacre: Commemoration and*

Consolation in Ha My and My Lai (Berkeley: University of California Press, 2006) and *Ghosts of War* (Cambridge: Cambridge University Press, 2008). Along with the post-war novels about the war mentioned above, the non-profit Curbstone Press's Voices from Vietnam series provides excellent translations of some of the most important works of contemporary Vietnamese fiction; *Crossing the River* (2004) presents the short fiction of Nguyen Huy Thiep, including the short story 'The General Retires'. Recent Vietnamese films dealing with the wartime and post-war periods are difficult to locate in the West, but the Asian Film Archive in Singapore (<http://www.asianfilmarchive.org>) is one source for DVD editions with English-language subtitles. The resurgence of religiosity in contemporary Vietnam is explored in Malarny, *Culture, Ritual and Revolution in Vietnam*, and Philip Taylor, *Goddess on the Rise: Pilgrimage and Popular Religion in Vietnam* (Honolulu: University of Hawaii Press, 2004). For the work of Vietnamese artists in the diaspora, see An–My Lê, *Small Wars* (New York: Aperture, 2005), *Vietnam: Destination for the New Millenium: The Art of Dinh Q. Lê* (New York: Asia Society, 2005), and <http://www.liza-nguyen.com>. Important works of fiction of the diaspora that reflect upon the displacements of the war include Tran Vu, *The Dragon Hunt* (New York: Hyperion, 1999), Dao Strom, *Grass Roof, Tin Roof* (New York: Houghton Mifflin, 2003), and Nam Le, *The Boat* (New York: Alfred A. Knopf, 2008).

NOTES

PRELUDE

1. Tran Huy Quang, 'Linh Nghiem' [The Prophecy], *Van Nghe*, 27 (1992), trans. Sherée Carey, *Viet Nam Forum*, 14 (1993), 55–60.
2. 'Cau Hu Lau Van' [Indictment of Corrupt Customs] (*c.*1907), trans. in David G. Marr, *Vietnamese Anticolonialism, 1885–1925* (Berkeley: University of California Press, 1971), 176.
3. Frances Fitzgerald, *Fire in the Lake: The Vietnamese and the Americans in Vietnam* (Boston: Little, Brown, 1972). Fitzgerald drew her analysis of traditional Vietnamese society from the work of orientalist French scholars, most notably Paul Mus, *Viêt-Nam: Sociologie d'une guerre* (Paris: Seuil, 1952).
4. Among them are Keith Weller Taylor, *The Birth of Vietnam* (Berkeley: University of California Press, 1983); John K. Whitmore, *Vietnam, Ho Quy Ly and the Ming, 1371–1421*, Yale University Southeast Asia Studies (New Haven, 1985); Alexander Woodside, *Community and Revolution in Modern Vietnam* (Boston: Houghton Mifflin, 1976); Jayne Werner, *Peasant Politics and Religious Sectarianism: Peasant and Priest in Cao Dai Vietnam*, Yale University Southeast Asia Studies (New Haven, 1981); Hue-Tam Ho Tai, *Millenarianism and Peasant Politics in Vietnam* (Cambridge, Mass.: Harvard University Press, 1983); David G. Marr, *Vietnamese Tradition on Trial, 1920–1945* (Berkeley: University of California Press, 1981). Although published somewhat earlier, Woodside's *Vietnam and the Chinese Model: A Comparative Study of Nguyen and Ch'ing Civil Government in the First Half of the Nineteenth Century* (Cambridge, Mass.: Harvard University Press, 1971) and Marr's *Vietnamese Anticolonialism* are also among these foundational works.
5. Nhung Tuyet Tran and Anthony Reid, 'Introduction: The Construction of Vietnamese Historical Identities', in Tran and Reid (eds), *Viet Nam: Borderless Histories* (Madison: University of Wisconsin Press, 2006), 3.
6. Marr, *Vietnamese Tradition on Trial*, p. x.

CHAPTER 1

1. Ho Chi Minh, 'Tuyen Ngon Doc Lap' [Declaration of Independence], in *Ho Chi Minh Toan Tap* [Ho Chi Minh's Collected Works], iii: *1930–1945* (Hanoi: Nha Xuat Ban Su That, 1983), 383, 387.
2. The most important study of this early history remains Keith Taylor, *The Birth of Vietnam* (Berkeley: University of California Press, 1983).
3. On the Nguyen state, see Alexander Woodside, *Vietnam and the Chinese Model: A Comparative Study of Vietnamese and Chinese Government in the First Half of the Nineteenth Century* (Cambridge, Mass.: Harvard University Press, 1971).
4. The complexities and heterogeneity of southern Vietnam emerge in Li Tana, *Nguyễn Cochinchina: Southern Vietnam in the Seventeenth and Eighteenth Centuries*, Southeast Asia Program (Ithaca, NY: Cornell University, 1998); George Dutton, *The Tây Son Uprising: Society and Rebellion in Eighteenth Century Vietnam* (Honolulu: University of Hawaii Press, 2006).
5. On pre-colonial Vietnamese village economies and social life, see Charles F. Keyes, *The Golden Peninsula* (Honolulu: University of Hawaii Press, 1995), 188–92; Pierre Gourou, *Les Paysans du delta tonkinois* (Paris: Éditions d'art et d'histoire, 1936).
6. Quoted in James W. Trullinger, Jr., *Village at War: An Account of Revolution in Vietnam* (New York: Longman, 1980), 22.
7. See, for instance, Tu Binh Tran, *The Red Earth: A Vietnamese Memoir of Life on a Colonial Rubber Plantation*, trans. John Spragens, Jr. (Athens: Ohio University Center for Southeast Asian Studies, 1985).
8. For a useful village-level account of these transformations and their impact, see Hy Van Luong, *Revolution in the Village: Tradition and Transformation in North Vietnam, 1925–1988* (Honolulu: University of Hawaii Press, 1992).
9. The following discussion of the reform movement is based in part on David G. Marr, *Vietnamese Anticolonialism, 1885–1925* (Berkeley: University of California Press, 1971); Vuong Tri Nham (ed.), *Phan Boi Chau and the Dong-Du Movement*, Yale University Southeast Asia Studies (New Haven, 1988).
10. *Van Minh Tan Hoc Sach* [The Civilization of New Learning], in Dang Thai Mai, *Van Tho Cach Mang Viet-Nam Dau The Ky XX* [Vietnamese Revolutionary Poetry and Prose in the Early Twentieth Century] (Hanoi: Nha Xuat Ban Van Hoc, 1974), 208–28.

11. On Vietnamese interpretations of social Darwinism, see Hue-Tam Ho Tai, *Radicalism and the Origins of the Vietnamese Revolution* (Cambridge, Mass.: Harvard University Press, 1992), 20–2.

12. *Van Minh Tan Hoc Sach*, 210.

13. Dong Kinh Free School text, *c.*1907, cited in Dang Thai Mai, *Van Tho Cach Mang Viet-Nam*, 76.

14. *Van Minh Tan Hoc Sach*, 210.

15. My discussion of Vietnamese radicalism in the 1920s is in part informed by Tai, *Radicalism*; David G. Marr, *Vietnamese Tradition on Trial, 1920–45* (Berkeley: University of California Press, 1981).

16. Aware of the potentially subversive uses to which the Vietnamese could put Western thought, French colonial censors often banned or censored portions of books and articles that presented Western ideas, a practice that eventually prompted a measure of indigenous self-censorship.

17. For a discussion of the place of Vietnamese, Chinese, and European figures in the radical biographical literature of the 1920s, see Marr, *Vietnamese Tradition on Trial*, 258–65.

18. *Dong Tay Vi Nham: Lam-Khang* [Great Men of Asia and Europe: Lincoln] (Saigon, 1929). An illustration of French fears that these books could serve purposes inimical to the colonial regime, this biography was among the works banned by French colonial censors in the late 1920s.

19. *Dong Tay Vi Nhan: Lam-Khang*, 35.

20. My discussion of the rise of Vietnamese communism relies on Huynh Kim Khanh, *Vietnamese Communism, 1925–1945* (Ithaca, NY: Cornell University Press, 1982).

21. William J. Duiker, *Ho Chi Minh* (New York: Hyperion, 2000).

22. The full text of Ho Chi Minh's 1927 *Road to Revolution* is reprinted in *Ho Chi Minh Toan Tap* [Ho Chi Minh's Collected Works], ii: *1930–1945* (Hanoi: Nha Xuat Ban Su That, 1981), 173–254. My reading of the text is shaped in part by Greg Lockhardt, *Nation in Arms* (Sydney: Allen & Unwin, 1989), 53–9.

23. On the Nghe-Tinh Soviets, see Ngo Vinh Long, 'The Indochinese Communist Party and Peasant Rebellion in Central Vietnam, 1930–31', *Bulletin of Concerned Asian Scholars*, 10/4 (Oct.–Dec. 1978), 15–34.

24. On the VNQDD, see Khanh, *Vietnamese Communism*, 91–9.

25. The Constitutionalists and other Francophile nationalist politics in the South are discussed in Hue-Tam Ho Tai, 'The Politics of Compromise: The Constitutionalist Party and the Electoral Reforms of 1922 in French Cochinchina', *Modern Asian Studies*, 18/4 (1984), 371–91;

Meagan Cook, *The Constitutionalist Party in Cochinchina: The Years of Decline, 1930–1942* (Victoria: Monash University Center for Southeast Asian Studies, 1977).

26. Tai, *Radicalism and the Vietnamese Revolution*, 246.

27. Tam Lang, *Toi keo xe* [I Pulled a Rickshaw], repr. in Vuong Tri Nhan (ed.), *Tam Lang, Trong Lang, Hoang Dao: Phong su chon loc* [Tam Long, Trong Lang, Hoang Dao: Selected Reportage] (Hanoi: Hoi nha van, 1995), 13–14, trans. in Greg Lockhart, *Light of the Capital* (Kuala Lumpur: Oxford University Press, 1996), 52–3.

28. Tam Lang, *Toi keo xe*, 97, trans. in Lockhart, *Light of the Capital*, 113.

29. Nhat Linh, *Doan Tuyet* [Breaking the Ties] (1935), trans. in Neil L. Jamieson, *Understanding Vietnam* (Berkeley: University of California Press, 1993), 144, 145.

30. My discussion of, and the quoted translations from, Tran Trong Kim's *Confucianism* rely on Shawn McHale, *Print and Power* (Honolulu: University of Hawaii Press, 2004), 77–83.

31. On the Buddhist revival of the 1930s, see McHale, *Print and Power*, ch. 5.

32. For studies of the Hoa Hao and Cao Dai, see Hue-Tam Ho Tai, *Millenarianism and Peasant Politics in Vietnam* (Cambridge, Mass.: Harvard University Press, 1983); Jayne S. Werner, *Peasant Politics and Religious Sectarianism*, Yale University Southeast Asia Studies, Monograph Series (New Haven, 1981).

33. My discussion of the August Revolution draws upon Huynh Kim Khanh, *Vietnamese Communism*, chs 5–6; David G. Marr, *Vietnam 1945: The Quest for Power* (Berkeley: University of California Press, 1995); and my *Imagining Vietnam and America: The Making of Postcolonial Vietnam, 1919–1950* (Chapel Hill: University of North Carolina Press, 2000), ch. 4.

34. For a harrowing first-person account of the famine, see Tran Van Mai, 'Who Committed this Crime?', trans. in Ngo Vinh Long, *Before the Revolution: The Vietnamese Peasants under the French* (New York: Columbia University Press, 1991), 219–76.

35. These arguments emerge in Nguyen Khac Vien, 'Confucianism and Marxism', in David G. Marr and Jayne S. Werner (eds), *Tradition and Revolution in Vietnam* (Berkeley: Indochina Resource Center, 1974).

36. *Ho Chi Minh: Selected Writings* (Hanoi: Foreign Language Publishing House, 1977), 50.

37. *Dan Moi* (Hanoi), no. 10 (5 Sept. 1945), quoted in Marr, *Vietnam 1945*, 538.

38. Marr, *Vietnam 1945*, 2.

39. McHale, *Print and Power*, 137–8.
40. Duong Van Mai Elliott, *The Sacred Willow: Four Generations in the Life of a Vietnamese Family* (New York: Oxford University Press, 1999), 115.

CHAPTER 2

1. Nguyen Dinh Thi, 'Nhan duong' [Recognizing the Way], 31 Dec. 1947, repr. in Vien Van Hoc, *Cach mang, khuang chien va doi song van hoc, 1945–54* [Revolution, Resistance, and the Literary Life, 1945–1954] (Hanoi: Nha Xuat Ban Tac Pham Moi, 1985), i. 9, 18, trans. in Kim N. B. Ninh, *A World Transformed: The Politics of Culture in Revolutionary Vietnam, 1945–1965* (Ann Arbor: University of Michigan Press, 2002), 69, 70.
2. Andrew Vickerman, *The Fate of the Peasantry: Premature 'Transition to Socialism' in the Democratic Republic of Vietnam* (New Haven: Yale University Center for Southeast Asian Studies, 1986), 49–72.
3. William J. Duiker, *The Communist Road to Power*, 2nd edn (Boulder, Colo.: Westview Press, 1996), 115–16.
4. David G. Marr, 'Creating Defense Capability in Vietnam, 1945–1947', in Mark Atwood Lawrence and Fredrik Logevall (eds), *The First Vietnam War: Colonial Conflict and Cold War Crisis* (Cambridge, Mass.: Harvard University Press, 2007), 77–8.
5. Stein Tønnesson, *1946: Déclenchement de la guerre d'Indochine* (Paris: Harmattan, 1987); Philippe Devillers, *Paris, Saigon, Hanoi: Les Archives de la guerre 1944–1947* (Paris: Gallimard/Julliard, 1988).
6. Greg Lockhart, *Nation in Arms: The Origins of the People's Army of Vietnam* (Sydney: Allen & Unwin, 1986), 139–40, 170; Duiker, *Communist Road to Power*, 119, 127, 138–9; Shawn McHale, 'Liberation, Terror and the Frontiers of Belief: The Mekong Delta during the First Indochina War (1945–54)', unpub. paper; Sophie Quinn-Judge, 'Through a Glass Darkly: Reading the History of the Vietnamese Communist Party, 1945–1975', in Mark Philip Bradley and Marilyn B. Young (eds), *Making Sense of the Vietnam Wars: Local, National and Transnational Perspectives* (New York: Oxford University Press, 2008).
7. Tønnesson, *1946*; Devillers, *Paris, Saigon, Hanoi*; Duiker, *Ho Chi Minh* (New York: Hyperion, 2000), 353–83.
8. Vu Ky, 'Nhung chang duong truong ky khang chien nhat dinh thang loi' [Stages in the Protracted Resistance Certain of Victory], *Tap Chi Lich Su Quan Su* [Journal of Military History], no. 36 (Dec. 1988), 81, cited and trans. in Marr, 'Creating Defense Capability', 102; my discussion of the immediate outbreak of war in this and the following paragraph relies on Marr, ibid. 101–3.

9. Truong Chinh's 1946 tract 'The Resistance Will Win' is translated in *Truong Chinh: Selected Writings* (Hanoi: Foreign Languages Publishing House, 1977).

10. Mark Philip Bradley, *Imagining Vietnam and America: The Making of Postcolonial Vietnam, 1919–1950* (Chapel Hill: University of North Carolina Press, 2000), 41–3.

11. Vo Nguyen Giap, *Chien dau trong vong vay* [Fighting while Encircled] (Hanoi: Quan Doi Nhan Dan and Thnah Nien, 1995), 91, trans. in Marr, 'Creating Defense Capacity', 103. On the problems facing the Vietnamese in the early years of the war more generally, see Lockhart, *Nation in Arms*, ch. 6.

12. *Cuoc Khang Chien Than Thanh cua Nhan Dan Viet Nam* [The Sacred Resistance War of the Vietnamese People], ii (Hanoi: Nha Xuat Ban Su That, 1958), 40–1, trans. in Lockhart, *Nation in Arms*, 185.

13. Bradley, *Imaging Vietnam and America*, 148–9. On DRV diplomacy with the international communist world in this period, see Christopher A. Goscha, 'Courting Diplomatic Disaster? The Difficult Integration of Vietnam into the International Communist Movement (1945–1950)', *Journal of Vietnamese Studies*, 1/1–2 (Feb.–Aug. 2006), 59–103.

14. Lockhart, *Nation in Arms*, 188–221; Hy Van Luong, *Revolution in the Village: Tradition and Transformation in North Vietnam, 1925–1988* (Honolulu: University of Hawaii Press, 1992), 147–58.

15. Christopher Goscha, *Thailand and the Southeast Asian Networks of the Vietnamese Revolution, 1885–1954* (London: Curzon, 1999), ch. 6; Bradley, *Imagining Vietnam and America*, 151–8.

16. Goscha, *Thailand and the Southeast Asian Networks*, ch. 5; Bradley, *Imagining Vietnam and America*, 158–60.

17. Yves Gras, *Histoire de la guerre d'Indochine* (Paris: Plon, 1979), 159–77.

18. Mark Atwood Lawrence, *Assuming the Burden: Europe and the American Commitment to War in Vietnam* (Berkeley: University of California Press, 2005), 115–44; *Sondages*, 16/4 (1954), 10.

19. Lawrence, *Assuming the Burden*, 106–15.

20. Gary R. Hess, *The United States' Emergence as a Southeast Asian Power, 1940–1950* (New York: Columbia University Press, 2000), ch. 6; Lawrence, *Assuming the Burden*, 45–74.

21. Virginia Thompson, *French Indo-China* (New York: Macmillan, 1937), 43–4.

22. Minutes of the Pacific War Council, 21 July 1943, Franklin D. Roosevelt Library, Hyde Park, New York, Naval Aide's Files, Pacific War #2, box 168, Map Room file, 1941–45.

23. Bradley, *Imagining Vietnam and America*, ch. 3.

24. Andrew Rotter, *The Path to Vietnam: The Origins of the American Commitment to Southeast Asia* (Ithaca, NY: Cornell University Press, 1989), chs 6 and 7; Michael Schaller, 'Securing the Great Crescent: Occupied Japan and the Origins of Containment in Southeast Asia', *Journal of American History*, 69/2 (Sept. 1982), 392–414.

25. Memorandum of Conversation between Bullitt and Ogden, 29 May 1947, National Archives of the United States, Washington, box 4, Confidential Records of the Saigon Consulate, Record Group 84.

26. Secretary of State to Embassy in Paris, 3 Feb. 1947, in US Department of State, *Foreign Relations of the United States 1947*, vi: *The Far East* (Washington: US Government Printing Office, 1972), 67–8. Official US attitudes towards Vietnam in the period emerge in Lawrence, *Assuming the Burden*, 171–9; Hess, *United States' Emergence*, ch. 10; Bradley, *Imagining Vietnam and America*, ch. 5.

27. Lawrence, *Assuming the Burden*, 247–77.

28. Heath (Saigon) to Secretary of State, 27 Nov. 1950, US Department of State, *Foreign Relations of the United States 1950*, vi: *The Far East* (Washington: US Government Printing Office, 1975), 939.

29. On the persistent problems dividing the French and Americans, see Bradley, *Imagining Vietnam and America*, 177–86; Hugues Tertrais, *La Piastre et le fusil: Le Coût de la guerre d'Indochine, 1945–1954* (Paris: Comité pour l'histoire économique et financière de la France, 2002); Kathryn C. Statler, *Replacing France: The Origins of American Intervention in Vietnam* (Lexington: University of Kentucky Press, 2007).

30. David W. P. Elliott, *The Vietnamese War: Revolution and Social Change in the Mekong Delta, 1930–1975*, i (Armonk, NY: M. E. Sharpe, 2003), 120–44.

31. Ibid. 144–57.

32. Sophie Quinn-Judge, *Ho Chi Minh: The Missing Years* (Berkeley: University of California Press, 2002), 200–33.

33. Mari Olsen, *Solidarity and National Revolution: The Soviet Union and the Vietnamese Communists, 1954–1960* (Oslo: Institutt for forsvarsstudier, 1997); Ilya Gaiduk, *Confronting Vietnam: Soviet Policy toward the Indochina Conflict, 1954–1963* (Stanford, Calif.: Stanford University Press, 2003); id., *The Soviet Union and the Vietnam War* (Chicago: Ivan R. Dee, 1996).

34. Qiang Zhai, *China and the Vietnam Wars, 1950–1975* (Chapel Hill: University of North Carolina Press, 2000), chs 1–3; Chen Jian, 'China and the First Indochina War, 1950–1954', *China Quarterly*, 133 (Mar. 1993), 85–110; Lockhart, *Nation in Arms*.

35. Duiker, *Communist Road to Power*, 156–8.

36. Trans. from Chen Geng's diary in Zhai, *China and the Vietnam Wars*, 64.

37. Zhai, *China and the Vietnam Wars*; Chen Jian, 'China and the First Indochina War'.

38. Duiker, *Communist Road to Power*, 148–9, 160–2; Quinn-Judge, 'Through a Glass Darkly'.

39. Cited in Elliott, *Vietnamese War*, 119.

40. Duong Van Mai Elliott, *Sacred Willow*, 203.

41. To Ngoc Van, 'Hoc hay khong hoc?' [Study or Not?], *Van Nghe*, no. 10 (Mar. 1949), 54–8, in Ninh, *A World Transformed*, 82.

42. Truong Chinh, 'Chu nghia Mac va van hoa Viet Nam' [Marxism and Vietnamese Culture] (1948), in Truong Chinh, *Ve van hoa va nghe thuat* [Culture and Thought], i (Hanoi: Van Hoc, 1985).

43. Bernard Fall, *The Two Vietnams* (New York: Praeger, 1964), 122–5; Michel Bodin, *Soldats d'Indochine, 1945–1954* (Paris: Harmattan, 1997).

44. John Prados, 'Assessing Dien Bien Phu', in Mark Atwood Lawrence and Fredrik Logevall (eds), *First Indochina War* (Cambridge, Mass.: Harvard University Press, 2007), 217–18.

45. Bodin, *Soldats d'Indochine*; Henri Navarre, *Agonie de l'Indochine* (Paris: Plon, 1956), 103–10; Vo Nguyen Giap, *Dien Bien Phu*, 5th edn (Hanoi: Foreign Languages Publishing House, 1994).

46. The literature on the Geneva conference that I draw on here includes: Robert F. Randle, *Geneva 1954: The Settlement of the Indochina War* (Princeton: Princeton University Press, 1969); James Cable, *The Geneva Conference of 1954 on Indochina* (New York: St Martin's Press, 1986); Chen Jian, 'China and the Indochina Settlement at the Geneva Conference of 1954', in Lawrence and Logevall (eds), *First Indochina War*, 241–9.

47. On the battle of Dien Bien Phu itself, see Bernard Fall, *Hell Is a Very Small Place: The Siege of Dien Bien Phu* (New York: J. B. Lippincott, 1967); Jules Roy, *The Battle of Dien Bien Phu* (New York: Carroll & Graf, 1984); Georges Boudarel, 'Comment Giap a failli perdre la bataille Dien Bien Phu', *Nouvel Observateur*, 8 Apr. 1983, 97.

48. Melanie Billings-Yun, *Decision against War: Eisenhower and Dien Bien Phu, 1954* (New York: Columbia University Press, 1988); Richard Immerman, 'Between the Unattainable and the Unacceptable: Eisenhower and Dienbienphu', in Richard A. Melanson and David Mayers (eds), *Reevaluating Eisenhower: American Foreign Policy in the 1950s* (Urbana: University of Illinois Press, 1987), 120–54.

49. Zhou Enlai to Chinese Communist Party Central Committee, 4 July 1954, cited in Chen Jian, 'China and the Indochina Settlement', 255.

On Chinese pressures at Geneva and Vietnamese responses more generally, see Chen Jian, ibid., *passim*; Zhai, *China and the Vietnam Wars*, ch. 2.

50. Benedict J. Tria Kerkvliet, *The Power of Everyday Politics: How Vietnamese Peasants Transformed National Policy* (Ithaca, NY: Cornell University Press, 2005), 37–8; Balazs Szalontai, 'Political and Economic Crisis in North Vietnam, 1954–56', *Cold War History*, 5 (Nov. 2005), 404–9.

51. Edwin E. Moise, *Land Reform in China and North Vietnam: Consolidating the Revolution at the Village Level* (Chapel Hill: University of North Carolina Press, 1983), chs 10–12; Szalontai, 'Political and Economic Crisis', 401–4.

52. Cited in Kerkvliet, *Power of Everyday Politics*, 52.

53. Cited in Ninh, *A World Transformed*, 184.

54. On the Nhan Van Giai Pham movement, see Georges Boudarel, *Cent Fleurs écloses dans la nuit Vietnam: Communisme et dissidence, 1954–1956* (Paris: Jacques Bertoin, 1991); Hirohide Kurihara, 'Changes in the Literary Policy of the Vietnamese Workers' Party, 1956–1958', in Takashi Shiraishi and Motoo Furuta (eds), *Indochina in the 1940s and 1950s* (Ithaca, NY: Cornell University Southeast Asia Program, 1992), 165–96. My discussion of Tran Dan follows Ninh, *A World Transformed*, 126–41.

55. Ninh, *A World Transformed*, 139.

56. Boudarel, *Cent Fleurs*, ch. 1; my discussion of these concepts is also indebted to Ninh, *A World Transformed*, 122–3.

CHAPTER 3

1. David Halberstam, *The Making of a Quagmire* (New York: Random House, 1965), 211.

2. Bao Dai, *Dragon d'Annam* (Paris: Plon, 1980), 329. On Diem's early history, see Edward Miller, 'Vision, Power and Agency: The Ascent of Ngo Dinh Diem, 1945–54', *Journal of Southeast Asian Studies*, 35/3 (Oct. 2004), 433–58.

3. Dulles to U.S. Embassy in France, 18 Aug. 1954, cited in Kathryn C. Statler, *Replacing France: The Origins of American Intervention in Vietnam* (Lexington: University of Kentucky Press, 2007), 120.

4. Statler, *Replacing France*, 128.

5. David Anderson, *Trapped by Success: The Eisenhower Administration and Vietnam, 1953–1961* (New York: Columbia University Press, 1991), ch. 5.

6. For the text of the ballots, see Jessica Chapman, 'Staging Democracy: South Vietnam's 1955 Referendum to Depose Bao Dai', *Diplomatic History*, 30/4 (Sept. 2006), 696.

7. Seth Jacobs, *Cold War Mandarin: Ngo Dinh Diem and the Origins of America's War in Vietnam, 1950–1963* (Lanham, Md.: Rowman & Littlefield, 2006), ch. 4.

8. Miller, 'Vision, Power and Agency', 337–52.

9. Jeffrey Race, *War Comes to Long An* (Berkeley: University of California Press, 1972), 26–7, 37–9; William J. Duiker, *Sacred War* (New York: McGraw-Hill, 1995), 109–10.

10. David W. P. Elliott, *The Vietnamese War: Revolution and Social Change in the Mekong Delta, 1930–1975*, i (Armonk, NY: M. E. Sharpe, 2003), 194.

11. Race, *War Comes to Long An*, 53–4, 55, 69; Elliott, *Vietnamese War*, 203–8; Joseph J. Zasloff, *Rural Resettlement in Vietnam: An Agroville in Development* (Saigon: Michigan State University Vietnam Advisory Group, 1961).

12. Robert Brigham, *ARVN: Life and Death in the South Vietnamese Army* (Lawrence: University Press of Kansas, 2006), 4–7.

13. Elliott, *Vietnamese War*, 195–203; William J. Duiker, *The Communist Road to Power in Vietnam*, 2nd edn (Boulder, Colo.: Westview Press, 1996), 203.

14. 'Manifesto of the Eighteen, 26 April 1960', in *Pentagon Papers: The Gravel Edition*, i (Boston: Beacon Press, 1971), 316–21; 'Dictatorial Rule in Saigon Claimed', *New York Times*, 1 May 1960, A1.

15. George M. Kahin, *Intervention: How America Became Involved in Vietnam* (New York: Alfred A. Knopf, 1986), 124.

16. 'A Party Account of the Situation in the Nam Bo Region of Vietnam, 1954–1960', cited in Duiker, *Sacred War*, 102.

17. Ralph B. Smith, 'Appendix: The Vietnam Workers' Party and its Leaders', in Smith, *An International History of the Vietnam War*, i: *Revolution versus Containment, 1955–61* (London: Macmillan, 1983).

18. Elliott, *Vietnamese War*, ch. 6.

19. Mari Olsen, 'Forging a New Relationship: The Soviet Union and Vietnam, 1955', in Priscilla Roberts (ed.), *Behind the Bamboo Curtain: China, Vietnam, and the World Beyond Asia* (Stanford, Calif.: Stanford University Press, 2006); Qiang Zhai, *China and the Vietnam Wars, 1950–1975* (Chapel Hill: University of North Carolina Press, 2000), 77–81; Duiker, *Communist Road to Power*, 189–91.

20. *Cuoc Khang Chien Chong My Cuu Nuoc, 1954–1975* (Hanoi: Quan Doi Nhan Dan, 1980), 49, 50, cited in Duiker, *Sacred War*, 120, 121.

21. Ibid. 122, 124–7.

22. Nguyen Thi Dinh, *No Other Road to Take: Memoir of Mrs. Nguyen Thi Dinh*, trans. Mai Elliott (Ithaca, NY: Cornell University Southeast Asia Program, 1976), 69–70.

23. Carlyle A. Thayer, *War by Other Means: National Liberation and Revolution in Vietnam 1954–60* (Sydney: Allen & Unwin, 1989); Duiker, *Communist Road to Power*, 228–30; Brigham, *ARVN*, 9.

24. On the founding of the NLF, see Thayer, *War by Other Means*, 122. On its structure and organization, see Elliott, *Vietnamese War*, ch. 11; Douglas Pike, *Viet Cong: The Organization and Techniques of the National Liberation Front of South Vietnam* (Cambridge, Mass.: MIT Press, 1966), chs 4 and 5.

25. Elliot, *Vietnamese War*, ch. 10; Race, *War Comes to Long An*, chs 3 and 4.

26. James W. Trullinger, Jr., *Village at War: An Account of Revolution in Vietnam* (New York: Longman, 1980), 99.

27. Philip Catton, *Diem's Final Failure: Prelude to America's War in Vietnam* (Lawrence: University Press of Kansas, 2002), chs 4–5, 7; Race, *War Comes to Long An*, 190–6; Bernard B. Fall, *Vietnam Witness, 1953–66* (New York: Praeger, 1966), 197–8.

28. Race, *War Comes to Long An*, ch. 4.

29. Nguyen Thi Dinh, *No Other Road to Take*.

30. Truong Nhu Tang, *A Viet Cong Memoir* (New York: Vintage, 1986), chs 1–4.

31. David Hunt, 'Noticing the Everyday', in Mark Philip Bradley and Marilyn B. Young (eds), *Making Sense of the Vietnam Wars* (New York: Oxford University Press, 2008), 182.

32. The classic account of the battle of Ap Bac is Neil Sheehan's *A Bright Shining Lie: John Paul Van and America in Vietnam* (New York: Random House, 1988), 201–66. See also Catton, *Diem's Final Failure*, 180–2.

33. Kahin, *Intervention*, 148–9; Stanley Karnow, *Vietnam: A History* (New York: Penguin, 1997), 294–7.

34. Nguyen The Anh, 'L'Engagement politique du Bouddhisme au Sud Viet-Nam dans les années 1960', in Alain Forest, Eiichi Kato, and Léon Vandermeersch (eds), *Bouddhismes et sociétés et asiatiques* (Paris: Harmattan, 1990), 112–24; Edward Miller, 'Puppet, Despot, Sage: Reassessing Ngo Dinh Diem and the First Republic of Vietnam (1954–1963)', unpub. paper in the author's possession.

35. Kahin, *Intervention*, 150–2; Karnow, *Vietnam*, 301–2.

36. Ellen J. Hammer, *A Death in November: America in Vietnam 1963* (New York: Oxford University Press, 1988).

37. Duiker, *Communist Road to Power*, 239; Elliott, *Vietnamese War*, 610–16.

38. Odd Arne Westad, *The Global Cold War* (Cambridge: Cambridge University Press, 2006), 160–9; Ilya Y. Gaiduk, *Confronting Vietnam: Soviet Policy toward the Indochina Conflict, 1954–63* (Stanford, Calif.: Stanford University Press, 2003), ch. 6.

39. Qiang Zhai, *China and the Vietnam Wars, 1950–1975* (Chapel Hill: University of North Carolina Press, 2000), chs 3 and 5; Chen Jian, 'China's Involvement in the Vietnam War, 1964–69', *China Quarterly*, no. 142 (June 1995), 356–66, cited in Zhai, *China and the Vietnam Wars*, 119.

40. Duiker, *Communist Road to Power*, 239–43.

41. Sophie Quinn-Judge, 'Through a Glass Darkly: Reading the History of the Vietnamese Communist Party, 1945–1975', in Mark Philip Bradley and Marilyn B. Young (eds), *Making Sense of the Vietnam Wars: Local, National and Transnational Perspectives* (New York: Oxford University Press, 2008), 126.

42. Elliott, *Vietnamese War*, ch. 12; Duiker, *Communist Road to Power*, 245–7.

43. Kahin, *Intervention*, 203–14, 227–35.

44. The authoritative study of the Gulf of Tonkin incident is Edwin E. Moise, *Tonkin Gulf and the Escalation the Vietnam War* (Chapel Hill: University of North Carolina Press, 1996).

45. Ang Cheng Guan, 'The Vietnam War, 1962–1964: The Vietnamese Community Perspective', *Journal of Contemporary History*, 35 (Oct. 2000), 617; Duiker, *Sacred War*, 166–72.

46. Ilya V. Gaiduk, *The Soviet Union and the Vietnam War* (Chicago: Ivan R. Dee, 1999), chs 1 and 3; Zhai, *China and the Vietnam Wars*, 132–3.

47. The most important analysis of these critical American decisions for war is Fredrik Logevall, *Choosing War: The Lost Chance for Peace and the Escalation of War in Vietnam* (Berkeley: University of California Press, 1999).

48. George McGovern, *Grassroots: The Autobiography of George McGovern* (New York: Random House, 1977), 104–5.

49. Yuen Foong Khong, *Analogies at War: Korea, Munich, Dien Bien Phu and the Vietnam Decisions of 1965* (Princeton: Princeton University Press, 1992), 47–147.

50. Zhai, *China and the Vietnam Wars*, 133–9; James G. Hershberg and Chen Jian, 'Informing the Enemy: Sino-American "Signaling" and the Vietnam War, 1965', in Roberts (ed.), *Behind the Bamboo Curtain*, 193–258.

51. Le Duan to Southern Central Department, Nov. 1965, in *Thu Vao Nam* [Letters to the South] (Hanoi: Nha Xuat Ban Su That, 1965), 119.

CHAPTER 4

1. For a recent English language translation of the diary, see *Last Night I Dreamed of Peace: The Diary of Dang Thuy Tram*, trans. Andrew X. Pham (New York: Harmony Books, 2007).

2. George M. Kahin, *Intervention: How America Became Involved in Vietnam* (New York: Alfred A. Knopf, 1986), 414–15; Robert Topmiller, *The Lotus Unleashed: The Buddhist Peace Movement in South Vietnam, 1964–1966* (Lexington: University of Kentucky Press, 2002), ch. 1.

3. Topmiller, *Lotus Unleashed*, chs 3 and 5.

4. Kahin, *Intervention*, 429–32; Stanley Karnow, *Vietnam: A History* (New York: Penguin Books, 1977), 466.

5. Kahin, *Intervention*, 409–10.

6. Jonathan Schell, *The Village of Ben Suc* (New York: Alfred A. Knopf, 1967).

7. Michael Sallah and Mitch Weiss, *Tiger Force* (New York: Little, Brown, 2006); Heonik Kwon, *After the Massacre: Commemoration and Consolation in Ha My and My Lai* (Berkeley: University of California Press, 2006), ch. 2.

8. John Laurence, *The Cat from Hue* (New York: Public Affairs, 2002), 349.

9. Robert Brigham, *ARVN: Life and Death in the Vietnamese Army* (Lawrence: University Press of Kansas, 2006), 16.

10. This paragraph and the preceding one draw upon Brigham, *ARVN*, chs 1, 3, 5.

11. Gabriel Kolko, *Anatomy of a War: Vietnam, the United States, and the Modern Historical Experience* (New York: Pantheon Books, 1985), 224–5.

12. Ibid. 227–8; 'Corruption is Taking Up to 40% of U.S. Assistance in Vietnam', *New York Times*, 13 Nov. 1966, 1; George C. Herring, *America's Longest War: The United States and Vietnam, 1945–1975*, 4th edn (Boston: McGraw-Hill, 2002), 198.

13. Phuoc Tin, 'Phu nu phai can kiem' [Women Must Become Thrifty], *Quyet Tien*, 6 Nov. 1968, trans. and cited in Alec Woodside, 'Some Southern Vietnamese Writers Look at the War', *Bulletin of Concerned Asian Scholars*, 2/1 (Oct. 1966), 56.

14. Vo Phien, 'Loi Yeu Hom Nay' [The Way of Loving Today], in Vo Phien, *Tap but 3* [Essays on Literary Topics 3] (Saigon: Thoi Moi, 1966), 279–80, trans. and cited in John C. Schafer, *Vo Phien and the Sadness of Exile* (DeKalb: Northern Illinois University Southeast Asian Studies Program, 2006), 199.

15. Kil J. Yi, 'The U.S.–Korean Alliance in the Vietnam War: Years of Escalation, 1964–68', in Lloyd C. Gardner and Ted Gittinger (eds), *International Perspectives on Vietnam* (College Station: Texas A & M University Press, 2000), 164–5. On the perspectives of South Korean soldiers and civil society, see Anh Junghyo, *White Badge* (New York:

Soho Press, 1989); Hyun Sook Kim, 'Korea's "Vietnam Question":
War Atrocities, National Identity and Reconciliation in Asia', *Positions: East Asia Cultures Critique*, 9/3 (2001), 622–35.

16. Nguyen Thi Thuy Vu, *Lao vao lua: Truyen* [Embrace of Fire: A Novel]
(Saigon: Kim Anh, 1967); Vo Phien, *Literature in South Vietnam, 1954–1975*,
trans. Vo Dinh Mai (Melbourne: Vietnamese Language and Culture
Publications, 1972).

17. Woodside, 'Southern Vietnamese Writers', 53, 54.

18. John C. Schafer, 'The Trinh Công Son Phenomenon', *Journal of Asian
Studies*, 66/3 (Aug. 2007), 597–643; trans. of 'Lullaby of Cannons for
the Night', ibid. 637.

19. The Uyen, *Nghi trong mot xa hoi tan ra* [Thoughts from within a
Disintegrating Society] (Saigon: Thai Do, 1967), 81–2, trans. and
cited in Woodside, 'Southern Vietnamese Writers', 55.

20. This paragraph and the next one closely follow the social anthropolo-
gist Heonik Kwon's meticulous reconstruction of this network in his
'Co So Cach Mang and the Social Network of War', in Mark Philip
Bradley and Marilyn B. Young (eds), *Making Sense of the Vietnam Wars:
Local, National and Transnational Perspectives* (New York: Oxford
University Press, 2008), 201–2.

21. My discussion of Rolling Thunder and its impact draws upon Mark
Clodfelter, *The Limits of Air Power: The American Bombing of North
Vietnam* (New York: Free Press, 1989), ch. 4; William S. Turley,
'Urbanization in War: Hanoi, 1946–73', *Pacific Affairs*, 8/3 (Autumn
1975), 380–2; William S. Logan, *Hanoi: Biography of a City* (Sydney:
University of New South Wales Press, 2000), 149–61.

22. Bao Ninh, *The Sorrow of War* (London: Secker & Warburg, 1993), 62.

23. Clodfelter, *Limits of Air Power*, ch. 6; Turley, 'Urbanization in War',
383–8; Logan, *Hanoi*, 168–76.

24. Martha Hess, *Then the Americans Came: Voices from Vietnam* (New
Brunswick, NJ: Rutgers University Press, 1994), 37.

25. Benedict J. Tria Kerkvliet, *The Power of Everyday Politics: How Vietnamese Peasants Transform National Policy* (Ithaca, NY: Cornell University Press, 2005), 84, 108, 81–2; quotations from 15 Jan. 1967 report
from the DRV's General Statistic Office and Phan Khanh, *So Thai
Lich Su Thuy Loi Viet Nam, 1945–1995* [History of Irrigation in Viet-
nam] (Hanoi: Nha Xuat Ban Chinh Tri Quoc Gia, 1997), 104, trans.
and cited in Kerkvliet, *Power of Everyday Politics*, 135, 136.

26. Military History Institute of Vietnam, *Victory in Vietnam: The Official
History of the People's Army of Vietnam, 1954–1975*, trans. Merle Pribbenow

(Lawrence: University Press of Kansas, 2002), 4–5; Douglas Pike, *PAVN: People's Army of Vietnam* (Novato, Calif.: Presidio, 1986), 102–3, 281–3, 285–96; Duiker, *Sacred War*, 196, 202.

27. Vietnam Institute of Philosophy, *Dang ta ban ve dao duc* [Our Party Discusses Ethics] (Hanoi: Uy Ban Khoa Hoc Xa Hoi Viet Nam, 1973), 286, trans. and cited in Shaun Kingsley Malarney, ' "The Fatherland Remembers your Sacrifice": Commemorating War Dead in North Vietnam', in Hue-Tam Ho Tai (ed.), *The Country of Memory: Remaking the Past in Late Socialist Vietnam* (Berkeley: University of California Press, 2001), 48.

28. Pike, *PAVN*, 150–61.

29. Mark Philip Bradley, 'Contests of Memory: Remembering and Forgetting War in the Contemporary Vietnamese Cinema', in Tai (ed.), *Country of Memory*, 208.

30. Malarney, 'The Fatherland Remembers your Sacrifice', 49–50, 52–5.

31. Trans. and cited in Kerkvliet, *Power of Everyday Politics*, 111.

32. Sandra C. Taylor, *Vietnamese Women at War: Fighting for Ho Chi Minh and Revolution* (Lawrence: University Press of Kansas, 1999), ch. 6.

33. Dang Thuy Tram, *Last Night I Dreamed of Peace*, 32, 25.

34. Bao Ninh, *Sorrow of War*, 75.

35. Nora Taylor, 'Framing the National Spirit: Viewing and Reviewing Painting under the Revolution', in Tai (ed.), *Country of Memory*, 123–4; Bui Xuan Phai, *Viet duoi anh den dau* [Under the Light of an Oil Lamp] (Hanoi: Nha Xuat Ban My Thuat, 2000).

36. Viet Phuong, 'Cua Mo' [Open Door] (1969), trans. in Georges Boudarel and Nguyen Van Ky, *Hanoi: City of the Rising Dragon* (Lanham, Md.: Rowman & Littlefield, 2002), 147.

37. Sophie Quinn-Judge, 'Through a Glass Darkly: Reading the History of the Vietnamese Communist Party, 1945–1975', in Mark Philip Bradley and Marilyn B. Young (eds), *Making Sense of the Vietnam Wars: Local, National and Transnational Perspectives* (New York: Oxford University Press, 2008), 127–30.

38. Malarney, 'The Fatherland Remembers your Sacrifice', 55–8.

39. Ibid. 59–67. See also Heonik Kwon, *Ghosts of War in Vietnam* (Cambridge: Cambridge University Press, 2008), ch. 3.

40. Malarney, 'The Fatherland Remembers your Sacrifice', 72.

41. Quoted in David Hunt, *Vietnam's Southern Revolution: From Peasant Insurrection to Total War, 1959–1968* (Amherst: University of Massachusetts Press, 2009), ch. 11; my discussion of time and the policies of the NLF is indebted to Hunt's arguments in this chapter.

42. Cited in David W. P. Elliott, *The Vietnamese War: Revolution and Social Change in the Mekong Delta, 1930–1975*, ii (Armonk, NY: M. E. Sharpe, 2003), 1007–8.

43. On the relationship between land distribution and political attitudes, I closely follow the argument of Elliott, *Vietnamese War*, 497–502, 517–19, 971–1035, 1222–4. For a different view of the class dimensions of the rural south and their impact on NLF support, see David Hunt, 'Revolution in the Delta', *Critical Asian Studies*, 35/4 (Dec. 2003), 599–620.

44. Hunt, *Vietnam's Southern Revolution*, ch. 6.

45. Truong Nhu Tang, *A Viet Cong Memoir* (New York: Vintage, 1986), 186–9; Quinn-Judge, 'Through a Glass Darkly', 129; Elliott, *Vietnamese Wars*: 785–86.

46. Cited in Elliott, *Vietnamese War*, 990.

47. Casualty figures are drawn from 'Hanoi Puts War Dead at 1.1 Million Fighters', *Boston Globe*, 4 Apr. 1995, 2; Harry G. Summers, *The Vietnam War Almanac* (Novato, Calif.: Presidio Press, 1999), 111–13. For comparisons to the American civil war, see Drew Gilpin Faust, *This Republic of Suffering: Death and the American Civil War* (New York: Alfred A. Knopf, 2008).

48. 'Nhat Ky Dang Thuy Tram' [Dang Thuy Tram Diary Manuscript], 20 June 1970, Vietnam Center at Texas Tech University.

CHAPTER 5

1. Vien Lich Su Quan Su Viet Nam [Military History Institute of Vietnam], *Huong tien cong va noi day: Tet Mau Than o Tri-Thien-Hue (Nam 1968)* [Direction of the General Offensive and General Uprising: The Lunar New Year in Tri-Thien-Hue] (Hanoi, 1988), 5, trans. in Robert J. Destatte and Merle L. Pribbenow, *The 1968 Tet Offensive and Uprising in the Tri-Thien-Hue Theatre* (Washington: US Army Center for Military History, 2001), p. i.

2. Truong Son, *Five Lessons of a Great Victory* (Hanoi: Foreign Languages Publishing House, 1967), 35; see also Nguyen Chi Thanh, 'Cong tac tu tuong trong quan va dan mien Nam ta voi chien thang mua kho 1965–1966' [Ideological Tasks of the Army and the People of the South and the Victories of the 1965–1966 DRV Season], *Hoc Tap*, 126/7 (1966), 1–10.

3. 'General Vo Nguyen Giap on the Strategic Role of the Self-Defense Militia' (Jan. 1967), in Patrick J. McGarvey (ed.), *Visions of Victory: Selected Vietnamese Communist Military Writings, 1964–1968* (Stanford, Calif.: Hoover Institution on War, Revolution and Peace, 1969), 168–98; Vo

Nguyen Giap, 'Ca nuoc mot long day manh cuoc chien tranh yeu nuoc vi dai kien quyet danh thang giac My xam luoc' [The Will of the Entire Country Strongly Pushes the Great Liberation Struggle to Defeat the Invading Americans], *Hoc Tap*, 120/1 (1966), 1–30. My discussion of the debates between Thanh and Giap follows Lien-Hang T. Nguyen, 'The War Politburo: North Vietnam's Diplomatic and Political Road to the Tet Offensive', *Journal of Vietnamese Studies*, 1/1–2 (Feb.–Aug. 2006), 19–25.

4. Mao Zedong and Pham Van Dong, Vo Nguyen Giap, Beijing, 11 Apr. 1967, in Odd Arne Westad et al. (eds), *77 Conversations between Chinese and Foreign Leaders on the Wars in Indochina, 1964–1977* (Washington: Woodrow Wilson Center Cold War International History Project, 1998), 105.

5. My discussion of the planning, execution, and impact of the Tet Offensive relies upon David W. P. Elliott, *The Vietnamese War: Revolution and Social Change in the Mekong Delta 1930–1975*, ii (Armonk, NY: M. E. Sharpe, 2003), 1036–119; William J. Duiker, *The Communist Road to Power*, 2nd edn (Boulder, Colo.: Westview Press, 1996), 255–99; Military History Institute of Vietnam, *Victory in Vietnam: The Official History of the People's Army of Vietnam, 1954–75*, trans. Merle Prebbenow (Lawrence: University Press of Kansas, 2002), 206–33; James H. Willbanks, *The Tet Offensive: A Concise History* (New York: Columbia University Press, 2006).

6. Tran Van Tra, *Nhung chang duong lich su cu B2 thanh dong*, v: *(Ket thuc cuoc chien tranh 30 nam)* (Ho Chi Minh City: Van Nghe, 1982), trans. as *Vietnam: History of the Bulwark B2 Theatre*, v: *(Concluding the 30-Years War)* (Washington: Joint Publications Research Service, 1983), 35. See also Tran Van Tra, 'Tet: The 1968 General Offensive and General Uprising', in Jayne S. Werner and Luu Doan Huynh (eds), *The Vietnam War: Vietnamese and American Perspectives* (Armonk, NY: M. E. Sharpe, 1993).

7. Walter Issacson and Evan Thomas, *The Wise Men: Six Friends and the World They Made* (New York: Simon & Schuster, 1986), 705–6. On Johnson's decision-making in this period, see Lloyd C. Gardner, *Pay Any Price: Lyndon Johnson and the Wars for Vietnam* (Chicago: Ivan R. Dee, 1995), 409–58.

8. Cited in Robert Brigham, *ARVN: Life and Death in the South Vietnamese Army* (Lawrence: University Press of Kansas, 2006), 99.

9. My discussion of Vietnamization is informed by Jeffrey Kimball, *Nixon's Vietnam War* (Lawrence: University Press of Kansas, 1998),

137–9, 180–2; Jeffrey J. Clarke, *Advice and Support: The Final Years* (Washington: US Center for Military History, 1988), 341–90, 443–5.

10. My discussion of Nixon era pacification efforts and their impact relies upon Eric H. Bergerud, *Dynamics of Defeat: The Vietnam War in Hau Nghia Province* (Boulder, Colo.: Westview Press, 1991), 255–81, 293–308; Neil Sheehan, *A Bright Shining Lie: John Paul Van and America in Vietnam* (New York: Vintage, 1989), chs 6 and 7.

11. Truong Nhu Tang, *A Vietcong Memoir* (New York: Harcourt Brace Jovanovich, 1985), 201–2. Historiographical controversy over the Phoenix program has been particularly sharp, and its definitive history drawing on Vietnamese sources remains to be written. See Douglas Valentine's severely critical and sometimes sensationalist *The Phoenix Program* (New York: Morrow, 1990); Mark Moyar's more exculpatory *Phoenix and the Bird of Prey* (Annapolis, Md.: Naval Institute Press, 1997); and Dale Andradé's focus on official US policy in *Ashes to Ashes: The Phoenix Program and the Vietnam War* (Lexington, Mass.: Lexington Books, 1990).

12. On the ambiguous impact of Thieu's land reforms, see Elliott, *Vietnamese War*, ii. 1235–44. For an alternative view of Thieu era reforms, see C. Stuart Callison, *The Land-to-the-Tiller Program and Rural Resource Mobilization in the Mekong Delta of South Vietnam* (Athens: Ohio University Center for International Studies, 1974).

13. H. R. Haldeman, *The Ends of Power* (New York: Times Books, 1978), 87–98. On the Nixon decisions to expand the war into Cambodia and Laos and their impact, I rely in part upon Kimball's *Nixon's Vietnam War*, 124–49, 194–6, 202–13.

14. Tang, *Vietcong Memoir*, 177, 182.

15. On the impact of the bombings on Cambodia, see William Shawcross, *Sideshow: Kissinger, Nixon and the Destruction of Cambodia*, 2nd edn (New York: Simon & Schuster, 1987), 112–27, 220–35, 280–99; Ben Kiernan, *How Pol Pot Came to Power*, 2nd edn (New Haven: Yale University Press, 2004), 269–393. Henry Kissinger has vehemently, if unpersuasively, challenged the analysis offered by Shawcross; see his *Ending the Vietnam War: A History of America's Involvement in and Extraction from the Vietnam War* (New York: Simon & Schuster, 2003), 500–17, 567–91, and the exchange between Shawcross and Peter Rodman in *Sideshow*, 430–51.

16. On the CIA's secret war with Laos, see Jane Hamilton-Merritt, *Tragic Mountains: The Hmong, Americans and the Secret Wars in Laos, 1942–1992* (Bloomington: Indiana University Press, 1993); Alfred W. McCoy,

The Politics of Heroin, 2nd edn (Chicago: Lawrence Hill Books, 2003), 284–349.

17. On Lam Son 719, see Clarke, *Advice and Support*, 472–6.

18. Chen Yi and Le Duc Tho, Beijing, 17 Oct. 1968, in Westad et al. (eds), *77 Conversations*, 136–7. While the translated text of this document ascribes the sentences 'We signed the Geneva accords in 1954 when the US did not agree to do so. We withdrew our armed forces from the South to the North, thus letting people in the South be killed' to Chen Yi, the context of the conversation suggest these statements more likely came from Le Duc Tho and I cite them in that way here.

19. Secretary of State to Embassy in Saigon, 30 Oct. 1968, cited in George C. Herring, *America's Longest War: The United States and Vietnam, 1945–1975*, 4th edn (Boston: McGraw-Hill, 2002), 264.

20. On American and North Vietnamese attitudes towards the Paris negotiations in 1969, see Kimball, *Nixon's Vietnam War*, 103–24, 158–70; Luu Van Loi and Nguyen Anh Vu, *Le Duc Tho–Kissinger Negotiations in Paris* (Hanoi: Gioi Publishers, 1996), 75, 85, 104.

21. On US–Soviet relations in this period, see Raymond L. Garthoff, *Detente and Confrontation: American–Soviet Relations from Nixon to Reagan* (Washington: Brookings Institution, 1994); on US rapprochement with China, see Margaret Macmillan, *Nixon and China: The Week that Changed the World* (New York: Random House, 2007).

22. Nguyen Tien Hung and Jerrold L. Schecter, *The Palace File* (New York: Harper & Row, 1986), 10.

23. Mao Zedong and Pham Van Dong, 23 Sept. 1970, in Westad et al. (eds), *77 Conversations*, 180.

24. On the responses of Hanoi and Saigon to changing Soviet–Chinese–American relations, see Lien Hang T. Nguyen, 'Cold War Contradictions: Toward an International History of the Second Indochina War, 1969–1973', in Mark Philip Bradley and Marilyn B. Young (eds), *Making Sense of the Vietnam Wars: Local, National and Transnational Perspectives* (New York: Oxford University Press, 2008), 229–35; Stephen P. Randolph, *Powerful and Brutal Weapons: Nixon, Kissinger and the Easter Offensive* (Cambridge, Mass.: Harvard University Press, 2007), 33–4; Qiang Zhai, *China and the Vietnam Wars, 1950–1975* (Chapel Hill: University of North Carolina Press, 2000), 137.

25. On the role of North Vietnam's relations with the Soviet Union and China in the planning of the offensive, see David Elliott, *NLF–DRV Strategy and the 1972 Offensive* (Ithaca, NY: Cornell University Press, 1974).

26. Quoted in Brigham, *ARVN*, 101.

27. Quoted from Raymond Price, *With Nixon* (New York: Viking Press, 1977), 112. On Nixon's response to the Easter Offensive, see Randolph, *Powerful and Brutal Weapons*.

28. Kimball, *Nixon's Vietnam War*, 312–27; Loi and Vu, *Le Duc Tho–Kissinger Negotiations*, 239–72; Nguyen, 'Cold War Contradictions', 236.

29. Hung and Schecter, *Palace File*, 98–106.

30. Robert K. Brigham, *Guerilla Diplomacy: The NLF's Foreign Relations and the Vietnam War* (Ithaca, NY: Cornell University Press, 1999), 104–10.

31. Zhai, *China and the Vietnam Wars*, 206; Ilya V. Gaiduk, *The Soviet Union and the Vietnam War* (Chicago: Ivan R. Dee, 1996), 244.

32. On the 'decent interval', see Kimball, *Nixon's War*, and William Bundy, *A Tangled Web: The Making of a Foreign Policy in the Nixon Presidency* (New York: Hill & Wang, 1998); on 'permanent war', see Larry Berman, *No Peace, No Honor: Nixon, Kissinger, and Betrayal in Vietnam* (New York: Simon & Schuster, 2002).

33. Ngo Vinh Long, 'Post-Paris Struggles and the Fall of Saigon', in Jayne S. Werner and Luu Doan Huynh (eds), *The Vietnam War: Vietnamese and American Perspectives* (Armonk, NY: M. E. Sharpe, 1993), 206–12.

34. Nixon to Thieu, 5 Jan. 1973, in Hung and Schecter, *Palace File*, 392.

35. Thieu's thinking in this period emerges in Hung and Schecter, *Palace File*, 238–62, 276–89.

36. On preparations for the offensive, see Military History Institute of Vietnam, *Victory in Vietnam*, 333–77; Duiker, *Communist Road to Power*, 329–44.

37. *Thu Vao Nam* [Letters to the South] (Hanoi: Su That, 1986), 401, trans. in Duiker, *Communist Road to Power*, 345. For a triumphalist account of the North Vietnamese victory by the commander of the northern forces, General Van Tien Dung, see his *Our Great Spring Victory* (New York: Monthly Review Press, 1977).

38. Hung and Schecter, *Palace File*, 302–3.

39. William J. Duiker, *Vietnam since the Fall of Saigon*, Ohio University Monographs in International Studies/Southeast Asia (Athens, 1989), 3–39, 47. For first-person accounts of life in post-war re-education camps, see Huynh Sanh Thong (ed. and trans.), *To Be Made Over: Tales of Socialist Reeducation in Vietnam* (New Haven: Yale Council on Southeast Asian Studies, 1988).

40. To Vu, 'Nhac vang la gi?' [What Is Yellow Music?], *Van Hoa Nghe Thuat*, 5 (1976), 46, trans. in Philip Taylor, *Fragments of the Present:*

Searching for Modernity in Vietnam's South (Honolulu: University of Hawaii Press, 2001), 43.

41. On post-war economic policies and crisis, see Duiker, *Vietnam since the Fall*, 41–70; Andrew Hardy, *Red Hills: Migrants and the State in the Highlands of Vietnam* (Honolulu: University of Hawaii Press, 2003); Benedict J. Tria Kerkvliet, *The Power of Everyday Politics: How Vietnamese Peasants Transformed National Policy* (Ithaca, NY: Cornell University Press, 2005), 143–89; Elliott, *The Vietnam War*, ii. 1222–3, 1380, 1394–8.

42. Nayan Chanda, *Brother Enemy: The War after the War* (New York: Free Press, 1988).

43. On the impact of the Cambodian and Chinese wars for the Vietnamese economy, see Tetsusaburo Kimura, *The Vietnamese Economy, 1975–1986* (Tokyo: Institute of Developing Economies, 1989); Carlyle A. Thayer, *The Vietnam People's Army under Doi Moi* (Singapore: Institute of Southeast Asian Studies, 1994).

44. For the coming of the *doi moi* reforms and their significance, see Börje Ljunggren (ed.), *The Challenge of Reform in Indochina* (Cambridge, Mass.: Harvard Institute for International Development, 1993); William S. Turley and Mark Seldon (eds), *Reinventing Vietnamese Socialism* (Boulder, Colo.: Westview Press, 1993).

45. See W. W. Rostow, 'The Case for the Vietnam War', *Times Literary Supplement*, 9 June 1995, 3–5; Timothy J. Lomperis, *The War Everyone Lost—and Won: America's Intervention in Viet Nam's Twin Struggles* (Baton Rouge: Louisiana State University Press, 1984).

46. 'Once Cursed, Vietnamese Welcomed Home', *International Herald Tribune*, 18 Mar. 2005; Vietnam Ministry of Foreign Affairs, 'Foreign Investment into Vietnam', <http://www.mofa.gov.vn/en/tt_baochi/nr041126171753/ns050223104952>, accessed 29 Mar. 2008.

47. Dao Duy Tung, 'On Renovation of Thinking', *Vietnamese Studies*, 20 (1989), 22. See the discussion in Taylor, *Fragments of the Present*, 59–65.

48. Taylor, *Fragments of the Present*, 90–118; quoted passages trans. from the original Vietnamese, ibid. 32, 95.

CODA

1. Bao Ninh, *Noi buon chien tranh* [Sorrow of War] (Hanoi: Hoi Nha Van, 1991; repr. Westminster, Calif.: Hong Linh, 1992), 67. An explosion of anti-heroic novels and short stories about the war appeared in Hanoi at about the same time; among the best known are Duong Thu Huong, *Tieu thuyet vo de* [Novel without a Name],

which was banned by the state although versions of the manuscript circulated clandestinely; and Le Luu, *Tho xa vang* [The Old Days] (1987; Hanoi: Nha Xuat Ban Thanh Nien, 1995).

2. Neil Jamieson, 'The Traditional Family in Vietnam', *Vietnam Forum*, 8 (Summer–Fall 1986), 123.

3. For a discussion of Vietnamese state reforms of the death anniversary ceremony and the resurgence of traditional ritual practices in the 1980s, see Shaun K. Malarney, *Culture, Ritual and Revolution in Vietnam* (London: Routledge, 2002), 108–47.

4. Malarney, *Culture, Ritual and Revolution in Vietnam*; Philip Taylor, *Goddess on the Rise: Pilgrimage and Popular Religion in Vietnam* (Honolulu: University of Hawaii Press, 2004), esp. ch. 3.

5. The variety of these post-war practices emerge in Shaun Malarney, ' "The Fatherland Remembers your Sacrifice": Commemorating War Dead in North Vietnam', in Hue-Tam Ho Tai (ed.), *The Country of Memory: Remaking the Past in Late Socialist Vietnam* (Berkeley: University of California Press, 2001), 69–70; Heonik Kwon, *Ghosts of War in Vietnam* (Cambridge: Cambridge University Press, 2008).

6. Kwon, *Ghosts of War*, 59–60.

7. On the place of gender in Vietnamese perceptions of war and its aftermath, see Hue-Tam Ho Tai, 'Faces of Remembrance and Forgetting', in Tai (ed.), *Country of Memory*, 167–95.

8. Nguyen Huy Thiep, 'Tuong ve huu' [The General Retires], in Thiep, *Nhung ngon gio Hua Tat* [The Breezes of Hua Tat] (Hanoi: Nha Xuat Ban Van Hoa, 1989), 23.

9. Le Hung, *Huyen thai nam 2000* [Fable for the Year 2000] (Hanoi, 1992). On youth sensibilities more generally in the first decade of the *doi moi* reforms, see David Marr and Stanley Rosen, 'Chinese and Vietnamese Youth in the 1990s', *China Journal*, 40 (July 1998), 145–72.

10. *Saigon, USA*, dir. Lindsey Jiang and Robert Winn (2003). On the controversy over the airing of *Saigon, USA*, see 'Roundtable: Political Intimidation of the Vietnamese Media—The *Saigon USA–VAX* Case Study', from the Thirty Years Beyond the War Conference, Vietnamese, Southeast Asian, and Asian/American Studies, University of California, Riverside, 20 Apr. 2005 (in author's possession).

11. An-My Lê, *Small Wars* (New York: Aperture, 2005), 121, 122.

12. *Liza Nguyen: Souvenirs of Vietnam* (Toronto: Gallery 44 Centre for Contemporary Photography, 2007); *Vietnam: Destination for the New Millennium: The Art of Dinh Q. Lê* (New York: Asia Society, 2005).

13. On the resurgence of reportage in contemporary Vietnam, see Greg Lockhart, *Light of the Capital* (Kuala Lumpur: Oxford University Press, 1996), 3, 41–2; Shawn McHale, 'Vietnam 1998: "Civilization" and "Debauchery" in the Transformation of the Public Realm', unpub. paper in the author's possession; Thu-Huong Nguyen-Vu, 'On the Way to Elsewhere: Space and Feminine Desires in Vietnamese Fictional Representations of Workers', *Gender, Place, Culture* (forthcoming).

14. On 'creeping pluralism', see Gareth Porter, *Vietnam: The Politics of Bureaucratic Socialism* (Ithaca, NY: Cornell University Press, 1993), 164. See also Shaun Malarney, 'Culture, Virtue, and Political Transformation in Contemporary Northern Viet Nam', *Journal of Asian Studies*, 56/4 (Nov. 1997), 899–920.

15. Tran Huy Quang, 'Linh Nghiem' [The Prophecy], *Van Nghe*, 27 (1992), trans. in *Viet Nam Forum*, 14 (1993), 60.

PICTURE AND TEXT
ACKNOWLEDGEMENTS

Collections Albert Kahn, Boulogne-Billancourt: plate 1; ©
Bettmann/Corbis: plates 2, 6, 10, 15; © KHAM/Reuters/Corbis:
p. 182; © Christian Simonpietri/Sygma/Corbis: plate 16; © AP
Photo/Empics: p. 8; © Eddie Adams/AP Photo/Empics: p. 146;
© Malcolm Browne/AP Photo/Empics: p. 76; © Nguyen Manh
Hung/courtesy of Art Vietnam Gallery: plate 18; Indochina Arts
Partnership: plates 4, 5; © An-My Lê: p. 3; © Dinh Dang Dinh/
Doug Niven: p. 40; © Bao Hanh/Doug Niven: plate 11; © Vo
Anh Khanh/Doug Niven: plate 8, p. 114; © Hoang Mai/Doug
Niven: plate 9; © Duong Thanh Phong/Doug Niven: plate 17;
© Dinh Thuy/Doug Niven: plate 7; unknown photographer/
Doug Niven: plates 3, 12; © Liza Nguyen: plate 19; courtesy of
the artist and P.P.O.W. Gallery, New York: plate 20; Frederic
Whitehurst Collection, the Vietnam Archive, Texas Tech
University: plates 13, 14.

We are grateful for permission to include the following extracts of
verse in this book.

Anonymous peasant verse translated by Benedict J Tria Kerkvliet
for his PhD and published in *The Power of Everyday Politics: How
Vietnamese Peasants Transformed National Policy* (Cornell University
Press, 2005), reprinted by permission of Cornell University Press.

Tran Dan: from 'We Must Win' translated by Kim N B Ninh in *A
World Transformed: The Politics of Culture in Revolutionary Vietnam
1945–1965* (University of Michigan Press, 2002), reprinted by permission of Kim N B Ninh.

Viet Phuong: 'Cua Mo' [Open Door] translated by Georges
Boudarel and Nguyen Van Ky in *Hanoi: City of the Rising Dragon*

228   PICTURE AND TEXT ACKNOWLEDGEMENTS

(Rowman & Littlefield, 2002), reprinted by permission of Editions Autrement.

Trinh Công Son: 'Lullaby of Cannons for the Night' [Dai bac ru dem] translated by John C Shafer and Cao Thu Nhu Quynh in 'The Trinh Công Son Phenomenon', *Journal of Asian Studies* 66.3 (August 2007), reprinted by permission of John C Schafer.

Young Vietnamese: 'Cau Hu Lau Van' [Indictment of Corrupt Customs] translated by David G Marr in *Vietnamese Anticolonialism 1885–1925* (University of California Press, 1971), © 1971 The Regents of the University of California, reprinted by permission of the University of California Press via Copyright Clearance Center.

INDEX